ANCIENT ROME

FROM ROMULUS AND REMUS TO THE VISIGOTH INVASION

THE BRITANNICA GUIDE TO ANCIENT CIVILIZATIONS

ANCIENT
ROME

FROM ROMULUS AND REMUS TO THE VISIGOTH INVASION

EDITED BY KATHLEEN KUIPER, MANAGER, ARTS AND CULTURE

Britannica®
Educational Publishing

IN ASSOCIATION WITH

ROSEN
EDUCATIONAL SERVICES

Published in 2011 by Britannica Educational Publishing
(a trademark of Encyclopædia Britannica, Inc.)
in association with Rosen Educational Services, LLC
29 East 21st Street, New York, NY 10010.

Distributed exclusively by Rosen Educational Services.
For a listing of additional Britannica Educational Publishing titles, call toll free (800) 237-9932.

First Edition

Britannica Educational Publishing
Michael I. Levy: Executive Editor
J.E. Luebering: Senior Manager
Marilyn L. Barton: Senior Coordinator, Production Control
Steven Bosco: Director, Editorial Technologies
Lisa S. Braucher: Senior Producer and Data Editor
Yvette Charboneau: Senior Copy Editor
Kathy Nakamura: Manager, Media Acquisition
Kathleen Kuiper: Manager, Arts and Culture

Rosen Educational Services
Jeanne Nagle: Senior Editor
Nelson Sá: Art Director
Cindy Reiman: Photography Manager
Matthew Cauli: Designer, Cover Design
Introduction by Laura Loria

Library of Congress Cataloging-in-Publication Data

Ancient Rome: from Romulus and Remus to the Visigoth invasion / edited by Kathleen Kuiper.—1st ed.
    p. cm.—(The Britannica guide to ancient civilizations)
"In association with Britannica Educational Publishing, Rosen Educational Services."
Includes bibliographical references and index.
ISBN 978-1-61530-107-2 (library binding)
1. Rome—History. I. Kuiper, Kathleen.
DG209.A55 2010
937—dc22

2009045443

Manufactured in the United States of America

On the cover: A phalanx of statues, currently housed in the Vatican Museum, stand as silent witnesses to the grandeur of ancient Rome. *Ian Shive/Aurora/Getty Images*

Photo credit pp. 17, 39, 77, 104, and 153 *Hulton Archive/Getty Images*

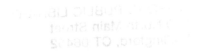

CONTENTS

INTRODUCTION 10

CHAPTER 1: ROME FROM ITS ORIGINS TO 264 BC 17
Early Italy **18**
Historical Sources on Early Rome **19**
Rome's Foundation Myth **20**
The Regal Period, 753–509 BC **21**
The Foundation of the Republic **23**
The Struggle of the Orders **24**
The Consulship **26**
The Dictatorship **26**
The Senate **27**
The Popular Assemblies **27**
The Plebeian Tribunate **28**
The Twelve Tables **30**
Military Tribunes with Consular Power **30**
Social and Economic Changes **31**
The Latin League **33**
Roman Expansion in Italy **34**
    The Samnite Wars **35**
    The Pyrrhic War, 280–275 BC **37**

CHAPTER 2: THE MIDDLE REPUBLIC (264–133 BC) 39
First Punic War (264–241 BC) **39**
Between the First and Second Punic Wars
    (241–218 BC) **41**
Second Punic War (218–201 BC) **42**
Campaigns in Sicily and Spain **45**
The War in Africa **47**
The Establishment of Roman Hegemony in the
    Mediterranean World **48**
    Roman Expansion in the Eastern
    Mediterranean **49**
    Roman Expansion in the Western
    Mediterranean **53**
    Explanations of Roman Expansion **56**
Beginnings of Provincial Administration **57**
Transformation During the Middle Republic **58**
    Citizenship and Politics in the Middle
    Republic **58**

19

48

54

Culture and Religion **61**
Economy and Society **66**
Social Changes **72**
Rome and Italy **74**

CHAPTER 3: THE LATE REPUBLIC (133–31 BC) **77**

Aftermath of Victories **77**
Changes in Provincial Administration **78**
Social and Economic Ills **78**
The Reform Movement of the Gracchi
(133–121 BC) **78**
The Program and Career of Tiberius
Sempronius Gracchus **79**
The Program and Career of Gaius Sempronius
Gracchus **81**
War Against Jugurtha **82**
The Career of Gaius Marius **83**
Events in Asia **85**
Developments in Italy **86**
Civil War and the Rule of Lucius Sulla **87**
The Early Career of Pompey **90**
Pompey and Crassus **92**
Political Suspicion and Violence **94**
The Final Collapse of the Roman Republic
(59–44 BC) **95**
Political Maneuvers **96**
Civil War **97**
The Dictatorship and Assassination of
Caesar **98**
The Triumvirate and Octavian's Achievement
of Sole Power **98**
Intellectual Life of the Late Republic **100**
Grammar and Rhetoric **101**
Law and History **102**
Philosophy and Poetry **102**

CHAPTER 4: THE EARLY ROMAN EMPIRE (31 BC–AD 193) **104**

The Consolidation of the Empire Under the
Julio-Claudians **104**

75

90

99

The Establishment of the Principate Under
Augustus **105**
The Roman Senate and the Urban
Magistracies **107**
The Equestrian Order **109**
Administration of Rome and Italy **110**
Administration of the Provinces **111**
Emperor Worship **112**
The Army **113**
Foreign Policy **115**
Economic Life **117**
Augustan Art and Literature **118**
Appraisal of Augustus **120**
The Succession **121**
Growth of the Empire Under the Flavians and
Antonines **124**
The Flavian Emperors **124**
The Early Antonine Emperors: Nerva and
Trajan **127**
Hadrian and the Other Antonine
Emperors **129**
The Empire in the Second Century **132**
Trend to Absolute Monarchy **133**
Political Life **134**
Rome and Italy **135**
Developments in the Provinces **137**
The Army **148**
Cultural Life **149**

CHAPTER 5: THE LATER ROMAN EMPIRE **153**
The Dynasty of the Severi (AD 193–235) **153**
Septimius Severus **153**
Caracalla **157**
Macrinus **157**
Elagabalus and Severus Alexander **158**
Religious and Cultural Life in the Third
Century **159**
The Rise of Christianity **161**
Cultural Life from the Antonines to
Constantine **163**

109

136

142

Military Anarchy and the Disintegration of the
    Empire (235–270) **164**
    The Barbarian Invasions **166**
    Difficulties in the East **167**
    Economic and Social Crisis **168**
The Recovery of the Empire and the Establishment
    of the Dominate (270–337) **170**
    Diocletian **172**
    Struggle for Power **177**
    The Reign of Constantine **178**
The Roman Empire Under the Fourth-Century
    Successors of Constantine **181**
    The Reign of Julian **183**
    The Reign of Valentinian and Valens **184**
    The Reign of Gratian and Theodosius I **186**
    Social and Economic Conditions **188**
    The Remnants of Pagan Culture **190**
    The Christian Church **191**
The Eclipse of the Roman Empire in the West
    (*c.* 395–500) and the German Migrations **193**
    The Beginning of Germanic Hegemony in
    the West **194**
    Barbarian Kingdoms **195**
    Analysis of the Decline and Fall **196**

**Appendix A: Table of Roman Emperors from
    27 BC through AD 476 198**
Appendix B: Ancient Italic Peoples 202

Glossary 213
Bibliography 215
Index 221

INTRODUCTION

Ancient Rome's influence cannot be overstated. The English language, government, and culture—from basics such as the alphabet and calendar to more sophisticated legal systems—are so heavily saturated with Roman traits that it is impossible to imagine what the world would be like if Rome had not flourished.

Any civilization whose influence reverberates so strongly around the globe thousands of years after its fall deserves a closer look, and that is what this book provides. *Ancient Rome: From Romulus and Remus to the Visigoth Invasion* transports readers back to a time of intrigue, conquest, invention, and empire building. Readers also will be introduced to the Caesars, warriors, senators, patricians, and plebeians who built, governed, conquered, and inhabited the ever-expanding territories under Roman rule.

From its mythical founding by Romulus on Palatine Hill, Rome had devised a political and social framework from which the empire would fall away and return and to which emerging countries and civilizations would look for centuries to come. Popular images of Rome conjure the picture of a fully formed state with vast lands and a multilayered government and social order, but its beginnings were humble. The once-small village of Rome transformed itself into an empire through organized government, an expansionist military policy, and openness to the cultures of the lands Rome had dominated throughout the ancient world.

Rome was ruled by kings until the fabled tyrant Tarquinius Superbus was, according to legend, overthrown by the populace. From then on, Rome would never again have a king, instead electing two magistrates called consuls. There were two main social classes in the early republic (509–280 BC), the patricians and the plebeians. In essence, the patricians held the power and the plebeians had the right to vote on laws. The consuls, however, were elected by the military; consequently, primarily generals who led Rome's armies were elected to consulship.

The Senate, which most likely evolved from the king's group of advisers, was composed of patrician elders. Because of their collective wealth and social status, the senators and their "advice" were taken seriously. The assembly was slightly more egalitarian, with five classes ranging from wealthy knights to the poor landless, and it passed basic legislation. A clearly defined system of law, called the Law of the Twelve Tables, was completed about 450 BC.

As leader of the Latin League, the loosely aligned individual states of Italy, Rome frequently sought to expand through what was deemed "justifiable war," though in reality Rome typically

Detail of Roman soldiers, taken from the carving Martyrdom Of St Paul, *which can be found in the Chapel Of Sisto IV in the Vatican.* Hulton Archive/Getty Images

provoked other states into war and then claimed self-defense. The Samnite Wars (343–290 BC) brought the acquisition of Campania and 13 other colonies and the establishment of the Roman navy. The Pyrrhic War (280–275 BC) brought Rome control over central Italy from coast to coast. Next came the Punic Wars, fought against Carthage in the period termed the Middle Republic (264–133 BC), which brought Sicily and some small islands under Rome's control through naval supremacy and small military movements. At the conclusion of the Second Punic War in 201 BC, the empire had gained control over Spain and the western Mediterranean. In the east, Macedonia was annexed as well.

The vastness of the empire made necessary the local rule of annexed territories, called provinces. Local administrators, who were overseen annually by senatorial magistrates, enforced Lex provincae, the rules of the conqueror. The administrators' main duties were to collect taxes through *publicani*, private debt collectors. In Rome itself, power was officially shared among the Senate, assembly, and magistrates. However, the elite of the Senate held most of the power, forcing the plebeians to pass laws without their approval, creating a power struggle.

The population was changing, too, as the influx of people from conquered lands sought Roman citizenship. Rome was generally tolerant of other cultures but was careful not to adopt too many foreign ideas, especially from Greece. Former slaves replaced farmers in the countryside, though not as landowners. Senators bought up large plots of land from fallen soldiers and rented to tenant farmers or hired slaves to work it. This relationship served both parties well for many years.

With expansion came a new emphasis on the marketplace. The landless poor flooded Rome, causing food and housing shortages. Independent of the state, manufacturing and trade were still cottage industries, but Rome provided numerous public works to facilitate growth. Infrastructure projects made good use of a recent construction material, concrete, to build arches and shore up aqueducts. The traditional family structure became less important, and child rearing fell to family slaves, who often were foreigners.

Italy was becoming homogenized in the Middle Republic (264–133 BC), as a result of several important developments. The massive construction of modern roads increased travel and relocation into and out of Rome. While Rome was reluctant to impose itself on provincial governments, the friendly relationships between the elite of Rome and other cities naturally resulted in similarities in law. The Italian peninsula was united in military campaigns at their frontiers as Roman troops helped to maintain order throughout the republic.

War was an essential part of Roman life during the Late Republic (133–31 BC), resulting in further conquests. But as the empire expanded, so did maintenance costs. The governor of each province had absolute power over the noncitizens of the city of Rome itself, which opened the door to abuse of power in the form of illegal taxation and fining. A court was established to address these issues. Though it did not punish the offenders, it was a step toward making the government accountable to the inhabitants of Rome, regardless of citizenship and social standing.

Further reform came at the hands of the Gracchus brothers, Tiberius and Gaius, known in plural as the Gracchi. Born into wealth, the brothers each had a turn as "tribune of the plebs," speaking for the common people. Tiberius Gracchus began his service in 133 BC by attempting to enforce a legal limit to how much land an individual could own, with the goal of distributing land more equally to landless citizens. Through much bargaining, eventually a compromise was reached that put control of this project into his family's hands. After a group of opposing senators killed Tiberius, his younger brother, Gaius, took up the banner. He continued to strive for more equality among the people through the redistribution of wealth, while also attempting to grant citizenship to other Latins. This tactic was to be a fatal error. Gaius was not reelected in 122, and was killed in a riot the next year. An uprising called the Social War, begun in 90 BC, resulted in citizenship for anyone who sought it, thereby resolving the issue.

Despite these advances toward egalitarianism, power struggles raged on. Pompey, who inherited his father's army and captured Spain and North Africa with it, became coconsul in 70 BC.

His term was marked by self-interest and bribery, and the nobility once again controlled the Senate and exploited the provinces. After his term as consul, he once again took up military service, gaining control over the East and its wealth. Meanwhile, Julius Caesar's star was rising. Returning from a successful and profitable governorship in Spain, Caesar became consul in 63 with the initial support of Pompey. However, that tenuous alignment was soon severed. Through Pompey's political maneuvers, Caesar was forced into exile and a civil war began. When Caesar defeated Pompey in Greece, he returned to Rome and assumed a dictatorship. His desire to please everyone, and thus his failure to end the corruption of the Republic, led to his notorious assassination in 44 BC. A triumvirate consisting of Antony, Lepidus, and Octavian, the son of Caesar, assumed power, but a struggle among them led to Octavian's victory in both the military and political arenas. Rome had one ruler now, and the republic was dead.

Octavian was technically Rome's first emperor, but he shunned titles so as not to provoke the wrath of his political enemies. By demilitarizing much of Rome and offering to refuse the consulship after one term, he gained the trust of the Senate, who named him Augustus and gave him control over much of the empire. While the people of Rome were fairly powerless, they did have access to courts of law, the protection of the army, public works such as roads, and sociopolitical mobility through the newly opened channel of the equestrian order. They were taxed heavily, but were given stability and growth in return. Augustan art and literature reflected this stability, blending Greek form with Roman values in the works of Virgil and Horace. The empire expanded in all directions under Augustus, who was beloved and deified by the people of Rome.

Augustus established a familial line of succession with mixed results. The last of his line, Nero, used brute force to control the empire. He committed suicide in the face of inevitable assassination by his many enemies. After Nero's death in 69, civil wars broke out yet again, and four military commanders claimed themselves emperor. At the end of that year, the Senate and assembly ratified Vespasian as emperor, who faced the same task Augustus had—the restoration of order. He and his sons, Titus and Domitian, the Flavian dynasty (69–96), kept control of the empire by strengthening the borders along the Rhine and Danube with auxiliary armies while creating stable posts for the legionaries.

When Vespasian's enemies assassinated Domitian, a series of foreign-born emperors ascended. The Antonine emperors, a moderate and constitutional succession, strengthened borders without expanding. Hadrian (117–138) gave members of the equestrian order the option of civil service as an alternative to the formerly required military service. Antonius Pius (138–161) had a reign of peace and prosperity and adopted son Marcus Aurelius (161–180) kept out

invaders. The Antonine dynasty ended with Commodus (180–192), who relied on provincial governors to secure borders and thus allowed another grab for power after his death.

For roughly 200 years, the Roman Empire was stable and relatively secure. The principate, or emperorship, was widely accepted by the people. The emperors kept the people's loyalty by avoiding military despotism and creating an environment that allowed prosperity and local self-government while still keeping the people subject to their total authority. The Senate's legislative power was greatly decreased during the early empire, though the emperors treated senators, who were frequently foreign-born, courteously overall.

The empire began to decline as soon as it failed to follow this format. The dynasty of the Severi (193–235) resulted in a devalued currency, military distrust of the principate, and the persecution of Christians. For the next 35 years the control of Rome alternated between military leaders and favourites of the Senate. This instability afforded the eastern provinces and barbarians to the north the opportunity to invade and recapture lost lands. An economic and social crisis caused cities to barricade themselves, including Rome.

Diocletian, who was proclaimed emperor in 284, recognized that Rome was too large to sustain itself, so he abandoned the principate and established himself as the dominant member of a tetrarchy, or four rulers. The city of Rome was no longer the sole capital, as each emperor ruled from one of four cities. Diocletian increased the size of the army and fortified the borders of Rome. He financed these maneuvers by means of heavy taxation. When he also attached divinity to his tetrarchy, he made enemies of the Christians, who now numbered 5 million of Rome's 60 million inhabitants.

The tetrarchy died with the ascension of Constantine, son of a tetrarch. Constantine, a Christian convert, was sole Caesar following the surrender of his coruler, Licinius, in 324. He established a hereditary succession plan, reformed the military to create a border patrol and an imperial guard, and christened a new capital in Constantinople for its proximity to trade routes. His sons divided the empire into eastern and western provinces, with grandson Julian left standing after a series of murders. Julian was a pagan and restored temples to Roman gods over the objections of the Christians. His successors, Valentinian and Valens, again divided the empire into eastern and western provinces, and their successors, Gratian and Theodosius, cemented the religious divide between the two.

In the 4th century Rome had a bloated government payroll of 30,000 workers, who took great entitlements as a privilege of their position. In the west, conditions for the poor were worse than in the east, most likely because of the empire's increased emphasis on eastern interests and the admittance of barbarians from the north into the Rhineland. Pagan culture was largely restricted to the universities, and Christianity was rapidly spreading through the west. Britain, Spain, France, Germany, and North Africa were being taken over by barbarians and Germanic tribes. By the end of the 5th century, Rome possessed a fraction of its former territory.

Some attribute Rome's fall to the spread of Christianity or to material excess and self-interest of the ruling class. There is also evidence that Rome simply became too large to sustain itself. Leadership was inconsistent, both in form and the conduct of individual rulers. The growth of the military did not keep pace with the physical size of the empire and could not police it effectively. Nevertheless, ancient Rome provided much that remains fundamental to modern Western thought, including a blueprint for democracy, the notion of which continues to engage people throughout the world.

CHAPTER 1

ROME FROM ITS ORIGINS TO 264 BC

Rome must be considered one of the most successful imperial powers in history. In the course of centuries Rome grew from a small town on the Tiber River in central Italy into a vast empire that ultimately embraced England, all of continental Europe west of the Rhine and south of the Danube, most of Asia west of the Euphrates, northern Africa, and the islands of the Mediterranean. Unlike the Greeks, who excelled in intellectual and artistic endeavours, the Romans achieved greatness in their military, political, and social institutions. Roman society, during the republic, was governed by a strong military ethos.

While this helps to explain the incessant warfare, it does not account for Rome's success as an imperial power. Unlike Greek city-states, which excluded foreigners and subjected peoples from political participation, Rome from its beginning incorporated conquered peoples into its social and political system. Allies and subjects who adopted Roman ways were eventually granted Roman citizenship. During the principate, the seats in the Senate and even the imperial throne were occupied by people from the Mediterranean realm outside Italy. The lasting effects of Roman rule in Europe can be seen in the geographic distribution of the Romance languages (Italian, French, Spanish, Portuguese, and Romanian), all of which evolved from Latin, the language of the Romans. The Western alphabet of 26 letters and the calendar of 12 months and 365.25 days are only two simple examples of the cultural legacy that Rome has bequeathed Western civilization.

EARLY ITALY

When Italy emerged into the light of history about 700 BC, it was already inhabited by various peoples of different cultures and languages. Most natives of the country lived in villages or small towns, supported themselves by agriculture or animal husbandry (Italia means "Calf Land"), and spoke an Italic dialect belonging to the Indo-European family of languages. Oscan and Umbrian were closely related Italic dialects spoken by the inhabitants of the Apennines. The other two Italic dialects, Latin and Venetic, were likewise closely related to each other and were spoken, respectively, by the Latins of Latium (a plain of west-central Italy) and the people of northeastern Italy (near modern Venice). Apulians (Iapyges) and Messapians inhabited the southeastern coast. Their language resembled the speech of the Illyrians on the other side of the Adriatic. During the fifth century BC the Po valley of northern Italy (Cisalpine Gaul) was occupied by Gallic tribes who spoke Celtic and who had migrated across the Alps from continental Europe. The Etruscans were the first highly civilized people of Italy and were the

only inhabitants who did not speak an Indo-European language. By 700 BC several Greek colonies were established along the southern coast. Both Greeks and Phoenicians were actively engaged in trade with the Italian natives.

Modern historical analysis is making rapid progress in showing how Rome's early development occurred in a multicultural environment and was particularly influenced by the higher civilizations of the Etruscans to the north and the Greeks to the south. Roman religion was indebted to the beliefs and practices of the Etruscans. The Romans borrowed and adapted the alphabet from the Etruscans, who in turn had borrowed and adapted it from the Greek colonies of Italy. Senior officials of the Roman Republic derived their insignia from the Etruscans: curule chair, purple-bordered toga (*toga praetexta*), and bundle of rods (*fasces*). Gladiatorial combats and the military triumph were other customs adopted from the Etruscans. Rome lay 12 miles (19.3 kg) inland from the sea on the Tiber River, the border between Latium and Etruria. Because the site commanded a convenient river crossing and lay on a land route from the Apennines to the sea, it formed the meeting point of three distinct peoples: Latins, Etruscans, and Sabines. Although Latin in speech and culture, the Roman population must have been somewhat diverse from earliest times, a circumstance that may help to account for the openness of Roman society in historical times.

HISTORICAL SOURCES ON EARLY ROME

The regal period (753–509 BC) and the early republic (509–280 BC) are the most poorly documented periods of Roman history because historical accounts of Rome were not written until much later. Greek historians did not take serious notice of Rome until the Pyrrhic War (280–275 BC), when Rome was completing its conquest of Italy and was fighting against the Greek city of Tarentum in southern Italy. Rome's first native historian, a senator named Quintus Fabius Pictor, lived and wrote even later, during the Second Punic War (218–201 BC). Thus, historical writing at Rome did not begin until after Rome had completed its conquest of Italy, had emerged as a major power of the ancient world, and was engaged in a titanic struggle with Carthage for control of the western Mediterranean. Fabius Pictor's history, which began with the city's mythical Trojan ancestry and narrated events up to his own day, established the form of subsequent histories of Rome. During the last 200 years BC, 16 other Romans wrote similarly inclusive narratives. All these works are now collectively termed "the Roman annalistic tradition" because many of them attempted to give a year-by-year (or annalistic) account of Roman affairs for the republic.

Although none of these histories are fully preserved, the first 10 books of Livy, one of Rome's greatest historians, are extant and cover Roman affairs from

Engraving of Livy (Titus Livius), the foremost historian and prose writer of the Augustan Age. The handful of his books that have survived to the present day are the best record of early Rome available. Kean Collection/Hulton Archive/Getty Images

earliest times down to the year 293 BC (extant are also Books 21 to 45 treating the events from 218 BC to 167 BC). Since Livy wrote during the reign of the emperor Augustus (27 BC–AD 14), he was separated by 200 years from Fabius Pictor, who, in turn, had lived long after many of the events his history described.

ROME'S FOUNDATION MYTH

Although Greek historians did not write seriously about Rome until the Pyrrhic War, they were aware of Rome's existence long before then. In accordance with their custom of explaining the origin of the foreign peoples they encountered by connecting them with the wanderings of one of their own mythical heroes, such as Jason and the Argonauts, Heracles (Hercules), or Odysseus, Greek writers from the fifth century BC onward invented at least 25 different myths to account for Rome's foundation. In one of the earliest accounts (Hellanicus of Lesbos), which became accepted, the Trojan hero Aeneas and some followers escaped the Greek destruction of Troy. After wandering about the Mediterranean for some years, they settled in central Italy, where they intermarried with the native population and became the Latins.

Although the connection between Rome and Troy is unhistorical, the Romans of later time were so flattered by this illustrious mythical pedigree that they readily accepted it and incorporated it into their own folklore about the beginning of their city. Roman historians knew that the republic had begun about 500 BC, because their annual list of magistrates went back that far. Before that time, they thought, Rome had been ruled by seven kings in succession. By using Greek methods of genealogical reckoning, they estimated that seven kings would have ruled about 250 years, thus making Rome's regal period begin in the middle of the eighth century BC. Ancient historians initially differed concerning the precise date of Rome's foundation, ranging from as early as 814 BC (Timaeus) to as late as 728 BC (Cincius Alimentus). By the end of the republic, it was generally accepted that Rome had been founded in 753 BC and that the republic had begun in 509 BC.

Since the generally accepted date of Troy's destruction was 1184 BC, Roman historians maintained Troy's unhistorical connection with Rome by inventing a series of fictitious kings who were supposed to have descended from the Trojan Aeneas and ruled the Latin town of Alba Longa for the intervening 431 years (1184–753 BC) until the last of the royal line, the twin brothers Romulus and Remus, founded their own city, Rome, on the Palatine Hill. According to tradition, the twins, believed to have been the children of the god Mars, were set adrift in a basket on the Tiber by the king of Alba. They survived, however, being nursed by a she-wolf, and lived to overthrow the wicked king. In the course of founding Rome the brothers quarreled, and Romulus slew Remus. This story was a Roman adaptation of a widespread ancient Mediterranean folktale told of many national leaders, such as the Akkadian king Sargon (c. 2300 BC), the biblical Moses, the Persian king Cyrus the Great, the Theban king Oedipus, and the twins Neleus and Pelias of Greek mythology.

Thus, in writing about early Rome, ancient historians were confronted with great difficulties in ascertaining the truth. They possessed a list of annual magistrates from the beginning of the republic onward (the consular *fasti*), which formed the chronological framework of their accounts. Religious records and the texts of some laws and treaties provided a bare outline of major events. Ancient historians fleshed out this meagre factual material with both native and Greek folklore. Consequently, over time, historical facts about early Rome often suffered from patriotic or face-saving reinterpretations involving exaggeration of the truth, suppression of embarrassing facts, and invention.

The evidence for the annalistic tradition shows that the Roman histories written during the 2nd century BC were relatively brief resumes of facts and stories. Yet in the course of the first century BC, Roman writers were increasingly influenced by Greek rhetorical training, with the result that their histories became greatly expanded in length. Included in them were fictitious speeches and lengthy narratives of spurious battles and political confrontations, which, however, reflect the military and political conditions and controversies of the late republic rather than accurately portraying the events of early Rome. Livy's history of early Rome, for example, is a blend of some facts and much fiction. Since it is often difficult to separate fact from fiction in his works and doing so

involves personal judgment, modern scholars have disagreed about many aspects of early Roman history and will continue to do so.

THE REGAL PERIOD, 753–509 BC

Romulus, Rome's first king according to tradition, was the invention of later ancient historians. His name, which is not even proper Latin, was designed to explain the origin of Rome's name. His fictitious reign was filled with deeds expected of an ancient city founder and the son of a war god. Thus he was described as having established Rome's early political, military, and social institutions and as having waged war against neighbouring states. Romulus was also thought to have shared his royal power for a time with a Sabine named Titus Tatius. The name may be that of an authentic ruler of early Rome, perhaps Rome's first real king. Nothing, however, was known about him in later centuries, and his reign was therefore lumped together with that of Romulus.

The names of the other six kings are authentic and were remembered by the Romans, but few reliable details were known about their reigns. However, since the later Romans wished to have explanations for their early customs and institutions, historians ascribed various innovations to these kings, often in stereotypical and erroneous ways. The three kings after Romulus are still hardly more than names, but the recorded deeds of the last three kings are more historical and can, to some extent, be checked by archaeological evidence.

According to ancient tradition, the warlike founder Romulus was succeeded by the Sabine Numa Pompilius, whose reign was characterized by complete tranquility and peace. Numa was supposed to have created virtually all of Rome's religious institutions and practices. The tradition of his religiosity probably derives from the erroneous connection by the ancients of his name with the Latin word *numen*, meaning divine power. Numa was

succeeded by Tullus Hostilius, whose reign was filled with warlike exploits, probably because the name Hostilius was later interpreted to suggest hostility and belligerence. Tullus was followed by Ancus Marcius, who was believed to have been the grandson of Numa. His reign combined the characteristics of those of his two predecessors—namely religious innovations as well as warfare.

Archaeological evidence for early Rome is scattered and limited because it has proven difficult to conduct extensive excavations at sites still occupied by later buildings. What evidence exists is often

Ruins on Palatine Hill, which archaeologists believe may have been the location of the first Roman village. On the Palatine, archaeological discoveries range from prehistoric remains to the ruins of an imperial palace. Alberto Pizzoli/AFP/Getty Images

ambiguous and cannot be correlated easily to the ancient literary tradition. It can, however, sometimes confirm or contradict aspects of the ancient historical account. For example, it confirms that the earliest settlement was a simple village of thatched huts on the Palatine Hill (one of the seven hills eventually occupied by the city of Rome), but it dates the beginning of the village to the 10th or ninth century BC, not the mid-eighth century. Rome therefore cannot have been ruled by a succession of only seven kings down to the end of the sixth century BC. Archaeology also shows that the Esquiline Hill was next inhabited, thus disproving the ancient account which maintained that the Quirinal Hill was settled after the Palatine.

Around 670–660 BC the Palatine settlement expanded down into the valley of the later Forum Romanum and became a town of artisans living in houses with stone foundations. The material culture testifies to the existence of some trade as well as to Etruscan and Greek influence. Archaeology of other Latin sites suggests that Rome at this time was a typical Latin community. In another major transition spanning the sixth century the Latin town was gradually transformed into a real city. The swampy Forum valley was drained and paved to become the city's public centre. There are clear signs of major temple construction. Pottery and architectural remains indicate vigorous trade with the Greeks and Etruscans, as well as local work done under their influence.

Rome's urban transformation was carried out by its last three kings: Lucius Tarquinius Priscus (Tarquin the Elder), Servius Tullius, and Lucius Tarquinius Superbus (Tarquin the Proud). According to ancient tradition, the two Tarquins were father and son and came from Etruria. One tradition made Servius Tullius a Latin. Another described him as an Etruscan named Mastarna. All three kings were supposed to have been great city planners and organizers (a tradition that has been confirmed by archaeology). Their Etruscan origin is rendered plausible by Rome's proximity to Etruria, Rome's growing geographic significance, and the public works that were carried out by the kings themselves. The latter were characteristic of contemporary Etruscan cities. It would thus appear that during the sixth century BC some Etruscan adventurers took over the site of Rome and transformed it into a city along Etruscan lines.

THE FOUNDATION OF THE REPUBLIC

Ancient historians depicted Rome's first six kings as benevolent and just rulers but the last one as a cruel tyrant who murdered his predecessor Servius Tullius, usurped the kingship, terrorized the Senate, and oppressed the common people with public works. The reign of Tarquinius Superbus was described in the stereotypical terms of a Greek tyranny in order to explain the major political transition from the monarchy to the republic in accordance with Greek political theory concerning constitutional evolution from monarchy to tyranny to aristocracy. This explanation provided later Romans with a satisfying patriotic story of despotism giving way to liberty. Tarquinius Superbus supposedly was overthrown by a popular uprising ignited by the rape of a virtuous noblewoman, Lucretia, by the king's son. The story is probably unhistorical, however, and merely a Roman adaptation of a well-known Greek story of a love affair in Athens that led to the murder of the tyrant's brother and the tyrant's eventual downfall.

According to ancient tradition, as soon as the Romans had expelled their last tyrannical king, the king of the Etruscan city of Clusium, Lars Porsenna, attacked and besieged Rome. The city was gallantly defended by Horatius Cocles, who sacrificed his life in defense of the bridge across the Tiber, and Mucius Scaecvola, who attempted to assassinate Porsenna in his own camp. When arrested before accomplishing the deed, he demonstrated his courage by voluntarily burning off his right hand in a nearby fire. As a result of such Roman heroism, Porsenna was supposed to have made peace with Rome and withdrawn his army.

One prevalent modern view is that the monarchy at Rome was incidentally terminated through military defeat and foreign intervention. This theory sees Rome as a site highly prized by the Etruscans of the sixth century BC, who are known to have extended their power and influence at the time across the Tiber into Latium and even farther south into Campania. Toward the end of the sixth century, Rome may have been involved in a war against King Porsenna of Clusium, who defeated the Romans, seized the city, and expelled its last king. Before Porsenna could establish himself as monarch, he was forced to withdraw, leaving Rome kingless. In fact, Porsenna is known to have suffered a serious defeat at the hands of the combined forces of the other Latins and the Greeks of Campanian Cumae. Rather than restoring Tarquin from exile to power, the Romans replaced the kingship with two annually elected magistrates called consuls.

THE STRUGGLE OF THE ORDERS

As the Roman state grew in size and power during the early republic (509–280 BC), new offices and institutions were created, and old ones were adapted to cope with the changing military, political, social, and economic needs of the state and its populace. According to the annalistic tradition, all these changes and innovations resulted from a political struggle between two social orders, the patricians and the plebeians, that is thought to have begun during the first years of the republic and lasted for more than 200 years.

In the beginning, the patricians were supposed to have enjoyed a monopoly of power (the consulship, the Senate, and all religious offices), whereas the plebeians began with nothing except the right to vote in the assemblies. During the course of the struggle the plebeians, however, were believed to have won concessions gradually from the patricians through political agitation and confrontation, and they eventually attained legal equality with them. Thus ancient historians, such as Livy, explained all aspects of early Rome's internal political development in terms of a single sustained social movement.

As tradition has it, the distinction between patricians and plebeians was as old as Rome itself and had been instituted by Romulus. The actual historical dating and explanation of this distinction still constitutes the single biggest unsolved problem of early Roman history. The distinction existed during the middle and late republic, but modern scholars do not agree on when or how it arose; they are increasingly inclined to think that it originated and evolved slowly during the early republic. By the time of the middle and late republic, it was largely meaningless. At that point only about one dozen Roman families were patrician, all others being plebeian. Both patrician and plebeian families made up the nobility, which consisted simply of all descendants of consuls. The term "patrician," therefore, was not synonymous with "noble" and should not be confused with it: the patricians formed only a part of the Roman nobility of the middle and late republic. The only difference between patricians and plebeians in later times was that each group was either entitled to or debarred from holding certain minor offices.

The discrepancies, inconsistencies, and logical fallacies in Livy's account of the early republic make it evident that the annalistic tradition's thesis of a struggle of the orders is a gross over-simplification of a highly complex series of events that had no single cause. Tensions certainly existed; no state can experience 200 years of history without some degree of social conflict and economic unrest. In fact, legal sources indicate that the law of debt in early Rome was extremely harsh and must have sometimes created much hardship. Yet it is impossible to believe that all aspects of early Rome's internal political development resulted from one cause. Early documents, if available, would have told the later annalistic historians little more than that a certain office had been created or some law passed. An explanation of causality could have been supplied only by folklore or by the imagination of the historian himself, neither of which can be relied upon. Livy's descriptions of early republican political crises evince the political rhetoric and tactics of the late republic and therefore cannot be given credence without justification. For example, early republican agrarian legislation is narrated in late republican terms. Early republican conflicts between plebeian tribunes and the Senate are likewise patterned after the politics of the Optimates and Populares of the late republic. Caution therefore must be exercised in examining early Rome's internal development. Many of the major innovations recorded in the ancient tradition can be accepted, but the ancient interpretation of these facts cannot go unchallenged.

THE CONSULSHIP

The later Romans viewed the abolition of the kingship and its replacement by the consulship as marking the beginning of the republic. The king's religious functions were henceforth performed by a priest-king (*rex sacrorum*), who held office for life. The king's military power (*imperium*) was bestowed upon two annually elected magistrates called consuls. They were always regarded as the chief magistrates of the republic, so much so that the names of each pair were given to their year of office for purposes of dating. Thus careful records were kept of these names, which later formed the chronological basis for ancient histories of the republic.

The consuls were primarily generals who led Rome's armies in war. They were therefore elected by the centuriate assembly—that is, the Roman army organized into a voting body. The two consuls possessed equal power. Such collegiality was basic to almost all Roman public offices; it served to check abuses of power because one magistrate's actions could be obstructed by his colleague.

According to the annalistic tradition, the first plebeian consul was elected for 366 BC. All consuls before that time were thought to have been patrician, and one major aspect of the struggle of the orders was supposed to have been the plebeians' persistent agitation to make the office open to them. However, if the classification of patrician and plebeian names known for the middle and late republic is applied to the consular list for the years 509–445 BC, plebeian names are well represented (30 percent). It is likely that there never was a prohibition against plebeians holding the consulship. The distinction between patrician and plebeian families may have become fixed only by the middle of the fourth century BC; and the law of that time (367 BC), which specified that one of the consuls was to be plebeian, may have done nothing more than to guarantee legally that both groups of the nobility would have an equal share in the state's highest office.

THE DICTATORSHIP

Despite the advantages of consular collegiality, in military emergencies, unity of command was sometimes necessary. Rome's solution to this problem was the appointment of a dictator in place of the consuls. According to ancient tradition, the office of dictator was created in 501 BC, and was used periodically down to the Second Punic War. The dictator held supreme military command for no longer than six months. He was also termed the master of the army (*magister populi*), and he appointed a subordinate cavalry commander, the master of horse (*magister equitum*). The office was thoroughly constitutional and should not be confused with the late republican dictatorships of Sulla and Caesar, which were simply legalizations of autocratic power obtained through military usurpation.

THE SENATE

The Senate may have existed under the monarchy and served as an advisory council for the king. Its name suggests that it was originally composed of elderly men (*senes*), whose age and knowledge of traditions must have been highly valued in a preliterate society. During the republic, the Senate was composed of members from the leading families. Its size during the early republic is unknown. Ancient sources indicate that it numbered about 300 during the middle republic. Its members were collectively termed *patres et conscripti* ("the fathers and the enrolled"), suggesting that the Senate was initially composed of two different groups. Since the term "patrician" was derived from *patres* and seems to have originally meant "a member of the *patres*," the dichotomy probably somehow involved the distinction between patricians and plebeians.

During the republic the Senate advised both magistrates and the Roman people. Although in theory the people were sovereign and the Senate only offered advice, in actual practice the Senate wielded enormous power because of the collective prestige of its members. It was by far the most important deliberative body in the Roman state, summoned into session by a magistrate

who submitted matters to it for discussion and debate. Whatever a majority voted in favour of was termed "the Senate's advice" (*senatus consultum*). These advisory decrees were directed to a magistrate or the Roman people. In most instances, they were either implemented by a magistrate or submitted by him to the people for enactment into law.

THE POPULAR ASSEMBLIES

During the republic two different assemblies elected magistrates, exercised legislative power, and made other important decisions. Only adult male Roman citizens could attend the assemblies in Rome and exercise the right to vote. The assemblies were organized according to the principle of the group vote. Although each person cast one vote, he did so within a larger voting unit. The majority vote of the unit became its vote, and a majority of unit votes was needed to decide an issue.

The centuriate assembly (*comitia centuriata*), as stated, was military in nature and composed of voting groups called centuries (military units). Because of its military character, it always met outside the sacred boundary of the city (*pomerium*) in the Field of Mars (Campus Martius). It voted on war and peace and elected all magistrates who exercised imperium (consuls, praetors, censors, and curule aediles). Before the creation of criminal courts during the late republic, it sat as a high court and exercised capital jurisdiction. Although it could legislate, this function was usually performed by the tribal assembly.

The centuriate assembly evolved through different stages during the early republic, but information exists only about its final organization. It may have begun as the citizen army meeting under arms to elect its commander and to decide on war or peace. During historical times the assembly had a complex organization. All voting citizens were placed into one of five economic classes according to wealth. Each class was allotted varying numbers of centuries, and the entire assembly consisted of 193 units.

The first (and richest) class of citizens was distributed among 80 centuries; the second, third, and fourth classes were each assigned 20 units. The fifth class, composed of the poorest people in the army, was allotted 30 centuries. In addition, there were 18 centuries of knights—men wealthy enough to afford a horse for cavalry service—and five other centuries, one of which was composed by the *proletarii*, or landless people too poor to serve in the army. The knights voted together with the first class, and voting proceeded from richest to poorest. Because the knights and the first class controlled 98 units, they were the dominant group in the assembly, though they constituted the smallest portion of the citizen body. The assembly was deliberately designed to give the greater authority to the wealthier element and was responsible for maintaining the political supremacy of the established nobility.

The tribal assembly (*comitia tributa*) was a nonmilitary civilian assembly. It accordingly met within the city inside the pomerium and elected magistrates who did not exercise imperium (plebeian tribunes, plebeian aediles, and quaestors). It did most of the legislating and sat as a court for serious public offenses involving monetary fines.

The tribal assembly was more democratic in its organization than the centuriate assembly. The territory of the Roman state was divided into geographic districts called tribes, and people voted in these units according to residence. The city was divided into four urban tribes. During the fifth century BC, the surrounding countryside formed 17 rustic tribes. With the expansion of Roman territory in central Italy (387–241 BC), 14 rustic tribes were added, thus gradually increasing the assembly to 35 units, a number never exceeded.

THE PLEBEIAN TRIBUNATE

According to the annalistic tradition, one of the most important events in the struggle of the orders was the creation of the plebeian tribunate. After being worn down by military service, bad economic conditions, and the rigours of early Rome's debt law, the plebeians in 494 BC seceded in a body from the city to the Sacred Mount, located 3 miles (4.8 km) from Rome. There they pitched camp and elected their own officials for their future protection. Because the state was threatened with an enemy attack, the Senate was forced to allow the plebeians to have their own officials, the tribunes of the plebs.

Initially there were only 2 tribunes of the plebs, but their number increased to 5 in 471 BC and to 10 in 457 BC. They had no insignia of office, like the consuls, but they were regarded as sacrosanct. Whoever physically harmed them could be killed with impunity. They had the right to intercede on a citizen's behalf against the action of a consul, but their powers were valid only within 1 mile (1.6 km) from the pomerium. They convoked the tribal assembly and submitted bills to it for legislation. Tribunes prosecuted other magistrates before the assembled people for misconduct in office. They could also veto the action of another tribune (*veto* meaning "I forbid"). Two plebeian aediles served as their assistants in managing the affairs of the city. Although they were thought of as the champions of the people, persons elected to this office came from aristocratic families and generally favoured the status quo. Nevertheless, the office could be and sometimes was used by young aspiring aristocrats to make a name for themselves by taking up populist causes in opposition to the nobility.

Plebeian tribunes were duly elected representatives of Rome's general populace in governmental matters. Though not as powerful as their Senate counterparts, tribunes could sponsor bills for legislation and punish magistrates for misconduct. Private Collection/The Stapleton Collection/The Bridgeman Art Library

Modern scholars disagree about the authenticity of the annalistic account concerning the plebs' first secession and the creation of the plebeian tribunate. The tradition presented this as the first of three secessions, the other two allegedly occurring in 449 and 287 BC. The second

THE TWELVE TABLES

The first systematic codification of Roman law followed the creation of the plebeian tribunate. The plebeians were supposed to have desired a written law code in which consular imperium would be circumscribed to guard against abuses. After years of tribunician agitation the Senate finally agreed. A special board of 10 men (decemviri) was appointed for 451 BC to draw up a law code. Since their task was not done after one year, a second board of 10 was appointed to finish the job, but they became tyrannical and stayed in office beyond their time. They were finally forced out of power when one commissioner's cruel lust for an innocent maiden named Verginia so outraged the people that they seceded for a second time.

The law code was inscribed upon 12 bronze tablets and publicly displayed in the Forum. Its provisions concerned legal procedure, debt foreclosure, paternal authority over children, property rights, inheritance, funerary regulations, and various major and minor offenses. Although many of its provisions became outmoded and were modified or replaced in later times, the Law of the Twelve Tables formed the basis of all subsequent Roman private law.

Because the law code seems not to have had any specific provisions concerning consular imperium, the annalistic explanation for the codification appears suspect. The story of the second tyrannical board of 10 is an annalistic invention patterned after the 30 tyrants of Athenian history. The tale of Verginia is likewise modeled after the story of Lucretia and the overthrow of Rome's last king. Thus the second secession, which is an integral part of the story, cannot be regarded as historical. On the basis of existing evidence, one cannot say whether the law code resulted from any social or economic causes. Rome was a growing city and may simply have been in need of a systematic body of law.

secession is clearly fictitious. Many scholars regard the first one as a later annalistic invention as well, accepting only the last one as historical. Although the first secession is explained in terms resembling the conditions of the later Gracchan agrarian crisis (see The Reform Movement of the Gracchi [133–121 BC] on page 78), given the harshness of early Roman debt laws and food shortages recorded by the sources for 492 and 488 BC (information likely to be preserved in contemporary religious records), social and economic unrest could have contributed to the creation of the office. However, the urban-civilian character of the plebeian tribunate complements the extra-urban military nature of the consulship so nicely that the two offices may have originally been designed to function cooperatively to satisfy the needs of the state rather than to be antagonistic to one another.

MILITARY TRIBUNES WITH CONSULAR POWER

The creation of the office of military tribunes with consular power in 445 BC was believed to have involved the struggle of the orders. The annalistic tradition portrayed the innovation as resulting from a political compromise between plebeian tribunes, demanding access to the consulship, and the Senate, trying to maintain the patrician monopoly of the office. Henceforth, each year the people were to decide whether to elect two patrician consuls or military tribunes with consular power who could be patricians or plebeians. The list of magistrates for 444 to 367 BC shows that the chief magistracy alternated between consuls and military tribunes. Consuls were more frequently elected down to 426 but rarely thereafter. At first there were three military tribunes, but the number increased to four in 426, and to six in 406. The consular tribunate was abolished in 367 BC and replaced by the consulship.

Livy indicates that according to some sources the consular tribunate was created because Rome was faced with three wars simultaneously. Because there is evidence that there was no prohibition against plebeians becoming consuls, scholars have suggested that the reason for the innovation was the growing military and administrative needs of the Roman state; this view is corroborated by other data. Beginning in 447 BC, two quaestors were elected as financial officials of the consuls, and the number increased to four in 421 BC. Beginning in 443 BC two censors were elected about every five years and held office for 18 months. They drew up official lists of

Roman citizens, assessed the value of their property, and assigned them to their proper tribe and century within the tribal and centuriate assemblies.

The increase in the number of military tribunes coincided with Rome's first two major wars, against Fidenae and Veii. In 366 BC six undifferentiated military tribunes were replaced with five magistrates that had specific functions: two consuls for conducting wars, an urban praetor who handled lawsuits in Rome, and two curule aediles who managed various affairs in the city. In 362 BC the Romans began to elect annually six military tribunes as subordinate officers of the consuls.

SOCIAL AND ECONOMIC CHANGES

The law reinstating the consulship was one of three tribunician bills, the so-called Licinio-Sextian Rogations of 367 BC. Another forbade citizens to rent more than 500 *iugera* (330 acres) of public land, and the third provided for the alleviation of indebtedness. The historicity of the second bill has often been questioned, but the great increase in the size of Roman territory resulting from Rome's conquest of Veii renders this law plausible. The law concerning indebtedness is probably historical as well, since other data suggest that debt was a problem in mid-fourth-century Rome. In 352 BC a five-man commission was appointed to extend public credit in order to reduce private indebtedness. A Genucian law of 342 BC (named after Genucius, tribune of that year) temporarily suspended the charging of interest on loans. In 326 or 313 BC a Poetelian law ameliorated the harsh conditions of the Twelve Tables regarding debt servitude by outlawing the use of chains to confine debt bondsmen.

Rome's economic advancement is reflected in its replacement of a cumbersome bronze currency with silver coinage adopted from the Greek states of southern Italy, the so-called Romano-Campanian didrachms. The date of this innovation is disputed. Modern estimates range from the First Samnite War to the Pyrrhic War. Rome was no longer a small town of central Italy but rather was quickly becoming the master of the Italian peninsula and was taking its place in the larger Mediterranean world.

The process of expansion is well illustrated by innovations in Roman private law about 300 BC. Since legal business could be conducted only on certain days (*dies fasti*), knowledge of the calendar was important for litigation. In early times the *rex sacrorum* at the beginning of each month orally proclaimed in Rome before the assembled people the official calendar for that month. Though suited for a small agricultural community, this parochial procedure became increasingly unsuitable as Roman territory grew and more citizens lived farther from Rome. In 304 BC a curule aedile named Gnaeus

Flavius upset conservative opinion but performed a great public service by erecting an inscription of the calendar in the Roman Forum for permanent display.

From early times, Roman private law and legal procedure had largely been controlled and developed by the priesthood of pontiffs. In 300 BC the Ogulnian law (after the tribunes Gnaeus and Quintus Ogulnius) ended the patrician monopoly of two priestly colleges by increasing the number of pontiffs from four to eight and the number of augurs from four to nine and by specifying that the new priests were to be plebeian.

In 287 BC the third (and perhaps the only historical) secession of the plebs occurred. Since Livy's account has not survived, detailed knowledge about this event is lacking. One source suggests that debt caused the secession. Many sources state that the crisis was ended by the passage of the Hortensian law (after Quintus Hortensius, dictator for 287), which was thought to have given enactments of the tribal assembly the same force as resolutions of the centuriate assembly. However, since similar measures were supposed to have been enacted in 449 and 339 BC, doubt persists about the meaning of these laws. It is possible that no difference ever existed in the degree of legal authority of the two assemblies. The three laws could be annalistic misinterpretations of a provision of the Twelve Tables specifying that what the people decided last should be binding. One source indicates that the Hortensian law

THE LATIN LEAGUE

Although the Latins dwelled in politically independent towns, their common language and culture produced cooperation in religion, law, and warfare. All Latins could participate in the cults of commonly worshiped divinities, such as the cult of the Penates of Lavinium, Juno of Lanuvium, and Diana (celebrated at both Aricia and Rome). Latins freely intermarried without legal complications. When visiting another Latin town, they could buy, sell, litigate, and even vote with equal freedom. If a Latin took up permanent residence in another Latin community, he became a full citizen of his new home.

Although the Latin states occasionally waged war among themselves, in times of common danger they banded together for mutual defense. Each state contributed military forces according to its strength. The command of all forces was entrusted by common assent to a single person from one of the Latin towns. Sometimes the Latins even founded colonies upon hostile territory as military outposts, which became new, independent Latin states, enjoying the same rights as all the other ones. Modern scholars use the term "Latin League" to describe this collection of rights and duties.

According to ancient tradition, Rome's last three kings not only transformed Rome into a real city but also made it the leader of the Latin League. There is probably exaggeration in this claim. Roman historians were eager to portray early Rome as destined for future greatness and as more powerful than it actually was. Rome certainly became one of the more important states in Latium during the sixth century, but Tibur, Praeneste, and Tusculum were equally important and long remained so. By the terms of the first treaty between Rome and Carthage (509 BC), recorded by the Greek historian Polybius (c. 150 BC), the Romans (or perhaps more accurately, the Latins generally) claimed a coastal strip 70 miles (112.6 km) south of the Tiber River as their sphere of influence not to be encroached upon by the Carthaginians.

Rome's rapid rise during the sixth century was the achievement of its Etruscan overlords, and the city quickly declined with the collapse of Etruscan power in Campania and Latium about 500 BC. Immediately after the fall of the Roman monarchy, amid Porsenna's conquest of Rome, his defeat by the Latins, and his subsequent withdrawal, the plain of Latium began to be threatened by surrounding hill tribes (Sabines, Aequians, and Volscians), who experienced overpopulation and tried to acquire more land. Thus Rome's external affairs during the fifth century largely revolved around its military assistance to the Latin League to hold back these invaders. Many details in Livy's account of this fighting are, however, unreliable. In order to have a literary theme worthy of Rome's later greatness, Livy's annalistic sources had described these conflicts in the most grandiose terms. Yet the armies, military ranks, castrametation (i.e., techniques in making and fortifying encampments), and tactics described belong to the late republic, not the Rome of the fifth century.

made all assembly days eligible for legal business. If debt played a role in the secession, the Hortensian law may have been designed to reduce the backlog of lawsuits in the praetor's court in Rome.

ROMAN EXPANSION IN ITALY

Toward the end of the fifth century, while Rome and the Latins were still defending themselves against the Volscians and the Aequians, the Romans began to expand at the expense of Etruscan states. Rome's incessant warfare and expansion during the republic has spawned modern debate about the nature of Roman imperialism. Ancient Roman historians, who were often patriotic senators, believed that Rome always waged just wars in self-defense, and they wrote their accounts accordingly, distorting or suppressing facts that did not fit this view. The modern thesis of Roman defensive imperialism, which followed this ancient bias, is now largely discredited. Only the fighting in the fifth century BC and the later wars against the Gauls can clearly be so characterized.

Rome's relentless expansion was more often responsible for provoking its neighbours to fight in self-defense. Roman consuls, who led the legions into battle, often advocated war because victory gained them personal glory. Members of the centuriate assembly, which decided war and peace, may sometimes have voted for war in expectation that it would lead to personal enrichment through seizure and distribution of booty.

The evidence concerning Roman expansion during the early republic is poor, but the fact that Rome created 14 new rustic tribes during the years 387–241 BC suggests that population growth could have been a driving force. Furthermore, Romans living on the frontier may have strongly favoured war against restless neighbours, such as Gauls and Samnites. The animal husbandry of the latter involved seasonal migrations between summer uplands and winter lowlands, which caused friction between them and settled Roman farmers.

Though the Romans did not wage wars for religious ends, they often used religious means to assist their war effort. The fetial priests were used for the solemn official declaration of war. According to fetial law, Rome could enjoy divine favour only if it waged just wars—that is, wars of self-defense. In later practice, this often simply meant that Rome maneuvered other states into declaring war upon it. Then Rome followed with its declaration, acting technically in self-defense; this strategy had the effect of boosting Roman morale and sometimes swaying international public opinion.

Rome's first major war against an organized state was fought with Fidenae (437–426 BC), a town located just upstream from Rome. After it had been conquered, its land was annexed to Roman territory. Rome next fought a long and difficult war against Veii, an important Etruscan city not far from Fidenae. Later Roman historians portrayed the war as having lasted 10 years (406–396 BC), patterning it after the mythical Trojan War of the Greeks. After its conquest, Veii's tutelary goddess, Queen Juno, was solemnly summoned to Rome. The city's territory was annexed, increasing Roman territory by 84 percent and forming four new rustic tribes.

During the wars against Fidenae and Veii, Rome increased the number of military tribunes with consular power from three to four and then from four to six. In 406 BC Rome instituted military pay, and in 403 BC it increased the size of its cavalry. The conquest of Veii opened southern Etruria to further Roman expansion. During the next few years, Rome proceeded to found colonies at Nepet and Sutrium and forced the towns of Falerii and Capena to become its allies. Yet, before Roman strength increased further, a marauding Gallic tribe swept down from the Po River valley, raided Etruria, and descended upon Rome. The Romans were defeated in the battle of the Allia River in 390 BC, and the Gauls captured and sacked the city. They departed only after they had received ransom in gold. Henceforth the Romans greatly feared and respected the potential strength of the Gauls. Later Roman historians, however, told patriotic tales about the commanders Marcus Manlius and Marcus Furius Camillus in order to mitigate the humiliation of the defeat.

Roman power had suffered a great reversal, and 40 years of hard fighting in Latium and Etruria were required to restore it fully. The terms of the second treaty between Rome and Carthage (348 BC) show Rome's sphere of influence to be about the same as it had been at the time of the first treaty in 509, but Rome's position in Latium was now far stronger.

THE SAMNITE WARS

During the 40 years after the second treaty with Carthage, Rome rapidly rose to a position of hegemony in Italy south of the Po valley. Much of the fighting during this time consisted of three wars against the Samnites, who initially were not politically unified but coexisted as separate Oscan-speaking tribes of the central and southern Apennines. Rome's expansion was probably responsible for uniting these tribes militarily to oppose a common enemy. Both the rugged terrain and the tough Samnite soldiers proved to be formidable challenges, which forced Rome to adopt military innovations that were later important for conquering the Mediterranean.

Despite its brevity (343–341 BC), the First Samnite War resulted in the major acquisition to the Roman state of the rich land of Campania with its capital of Capua. Roman historians modeled their description of the war's beginning on the Greek historian Thucydides' account of the outbreak of the Peloponnesian War between Athens and Sparta. Nevertheless, they were probably correct in stating that the Campanians, when fighting over the town of Capua with the Samnites, allied themselves with Rome in order to utilize its might to settle the quarrel. If so, this may have been the first of many instances in which Rome went to war after being invited into an alliance by a weaker state already at war. Once invited in, Rome usually absorbed the allied state after defeating its adversary. In any event, Campania now somehow became firmly attached to Rome; it may have been granted Roman citizenship without the right to vote in Rome (*civitas sine suffragio*). Campania was a major addition to Rome's strength and manpower.

The absorption of Campania provoked the Latins to take up arms against Rome to maintain their independence. Since the Gallic sack of Rome in 390 BC, the city had become increasingly dominant within the Latin League. In 381 BC Tusculum was absorbed by being given Roman citizenship. In 358 BC Rome created two more rustic tribes from territory captured along the Volscian coast. The Latin War (340–338 BC) was quickly decided in Rome's favour. Virtually all of Latium was given Roman citizenship and became Roman territory, but the towns retained their local governments. The large states of Praeneste and Tibur maintained nominal independence by becoming Rome's military allies. Thus the Latin League was abolished; but the legal rights that the Latins had enjoyed among themselves were retained by Rome as a legal status, the Latin right (*ius Latii*), and used for centuries as an intermediate step between non-Roman status and full Roman citizenship.

Rome was now the master of central Italy and spent the next decade organizing and pushing forward its frontier through conquest and colonization. The Romans soon confronted the Samnites of the middle Liris (modern Liri) River valley, sparking the Second, or Great, Samnite War (326–304 BC). During the first half of the war Rome suffered serious defeats, but the second half saw Rome's recovery, reorganization, and ultimate victory. In 321 BC a Roman army was trapped in a narrow canyon near the Caudine Forks and compelled to surrender, and Rome was forced to sign a five-year treaty. Later Roman historians, however, tried to deny this humiliation by inventing stories of Rome's rejection of the peace and its revenge upon the Samnites.

In 315 BC, after the resumption of hostilities, Rome suffered a crushing defeat at Lautulae. Ancient sources state that Rome initially borrowed hoplite tactics from the Etruscans (used during the sixth or fifth centuries BC) but later adopted the manipular system of the Samnites, probably as a result of Samnite success at this time. The manipular formation resembled a checkerboard pattern, in which solid squares of soldiers were separated by empty square spaces. It was far more flexible than the solidly massed hoplite formation, allowing the army to maneuver better on rugged terrain. The system was retained throughout the republic and into the empire.

During these same years Rome organized a rudimentary navy, constructed its first military roads (construction of the Via Appia was begun in 312 BC and of the

Via Valeria in 306), and increased the size of its annual military levy as seen from the increase of annually elected military tribunes from 6 to 16. During the period 334–295 BC, Rome founded 13 colonies against the Samnites and created six new rustic tribes in annexed territory. During the last years of the war, the Romans also extended their power into northern Etruria and Umbria. Several successful campaigns forced the cities in these areas to become Rome's allies. The Great Samnite War finally ended in Rome's victory. During the final phase of this war, Rome, on another front, concluded its third treaty with Carthage (306 BC), in which the Carthaginians acknowledged all of Italy as Rome's sphere of influence.

The Third Samnite War (298–290 BC) was the last desperate attempt of the Samnites to remain independent. They persuaded the Etruscans, Umbrians, and Gauls to join them. Rome emerged victorious over this formidable coalition at the battle of Sentinum in 295 and spent the remainder of the war putting down lingering Samnite resistance. They henceforth were bound to Rome by a series of alliances.

THE PYRRHIC WAR, 280–275 BC

Rome spent the 280s BC putting down unrest in northern Italy, but its attention was soon directed to the far south as well by a quarrel between the Greek city of

Portrait of King Pyrrhus, the famed Greek general who staged a multiyear battle, known as the Pyrrhic War, with Rome and its allies. Hulton Archive/Getty Images

Thurii and a Samnite tribe. Thurii called upon the assistance of Rome, whose naval operations in the area provoked a war with the Greek city of Tarentum. As in previous conflicts with Italian peoples, Tarentum summoned military aid from mainland Greece, calling upon King Pyrrhus of Epirus, one of the most brilliant generals of the ancient world. Pyrrhus arrived in southern Italy in 280 BC with 20 elephants and 25,000 highly trained soldiers. After defeating the Romans at Heraclea and stirring up revolt among the Samnites, he offered peace terms that would have confined Roman power to central Italy. When the Senate wavered, Appius Claudius, an aged blind senator, roused their courage and persuaded them to continue fighting.

Pyrrhus again defeated the Romans in 279 at Asculum. His losses in the two battles numbered 7,500 (almost one-third of his entire force). When congratulated on his victory, Pyrrhus, according to Plutarch, replied " . . . that one other such would utterly undo him." This type of victory has since been referred to as Pyrrhic victory. Pyrrhus then left Italy and aided the Greeks of Sicily against Carthage; he eventually returned to Italy and was defeated by the Romans in 275 BC at Beneventum. He then returned to Greece, while Rome put down resistance in Italy and took Tarentum itself by siege in 272.

Rome was now the unquestioned master of Italy. Roman territory was a broad belt across central Italy, from sea to sea. Latin colonies were scattered throughout the peninsula. The other peoples of Italy were bound to Rome by a series of bilateral alliances that obligated them to provide Rome with military forces in wartime. According to the Roman census of 225 BC, Rome could call upon 700,000 infantry and 70,000 cavalry from its own citizens and allies. The conquest of Italy engendered a strong military ethos among the Roman nobility and citizenry, provided Rome with considerable manpower, and forced it to develop military, political, and legal institutions and practices for conquering and absorbing foreign peoples. The Pyrrhic War demonstrated that Rome's civilian army could wage a successful war of attrition against highly skilled mercenaries of the Mediterranean world.

CHAPTER 2

THE MIDDLE REPUBLIC (264–133 BC)

Rome's rapidly expanding sphere of hegemony brought it almost immediately into conflict with non-Italian powers. In the south, the main opponent was Carthage. In violation of the treaty of 306, which (historians tend to believe) had placed Sicily in the Carthaginian sphere of influence, Rome crossed the straits of Messana (between Italy and Sicily) embarking on war. (Rome's wars with Carthage are known as the "Punic Wars"; the Romans called the Carthaginians Poeni [Phoenicians], from which derived the adjective "Punic.")

FIRST PUNIC WAR (264–241 BC)

The proximate cause of the first outbreak was a crisis in the city of Messana (Messina). A band of Campanian mercenaries, the Mamertinians, who had forcibly established themselves within the town and were being hard pressed in 264 by Hieron II of Syracuse, applied for help to both Rome and Carthage. The Carthaginians, arriving first, occupied Messana and effected a reconciliation with Hieron. The Roman commander, nevertheless, persisted in forcing his troops into the city; he succeeded in seizing the Carthaginian admiral during a parley and induced him to withdraw. This aggression involved Rome in war with Carthage and Syracuse.

A Roman war galley with infantry on deck; in the Vatican Museums. Alinari/Art Resource, New York

Operations began with their joint attack upon Messana, which the Romans easily repelled. In 263 the Romans advanced with a considerable force into Hieron's territory and induced him to seek peace and alliance with them. In 262 they besieged and captured the Carthaginian base at Agrigentum on the south coast of the island. The first years of the war left little doubt that Roman intentions extended beyond the protection of Messana.

In 260 the Romans built their first large fleet of standard battleships. At Mylae (Milazzo), off the north Sicilian coast, their admiral Gaius Duilius defeated a Carthaginian squadron of more maneuverable ships by grappling and boarding. This left Rome free to land a force on Corsica (259) and expel the Carthaginians, but it did not suffice to loosen their grasp on Sicily. A large Roman fleet sailed out in 256, repelled the entire Carthaginian fleet off Cape Ecnomus (near modern Licata), and established a fortified camp on African soil at Clypea (Kélibia in Tunisia). The Carthaginians, whose citizen levy was utterly disorganized, could neither keep the field against the invaders nor prevent their subjects from revolting. After one campaign they were ready to sue for peace, but the terms offered by the Roman commander Marcus Atilius Regulus were intolerably harsh. Accordingly, the Carthaginians equipped a new army in which cavalry and elephants formed the strongest arm. In 255 they offered battle to Regulus, who had taken up position with an inadequate force near Tunis, outmaneuvered him, and destroyed the bulk of his army. A second Roman fleet, which reached Africa after defeating the full Carthaginian fleet off Cape Hermaeum (Cape Bon), withdrew all the remaining troops.

The Romans now directed their efforts once more against Sicily. In 254 they captured the important fortress of Panormus (Palermo), but when Carthage moved reinforcements onto the island, the war again came to a standstill. In 251 or 250 the Roman general Caecilus Metellus at last staged a pitched battle near Panormus, in which the enemy's force was effectively crippled. This victory was followed by a siege of the chief Punic base at Lilybaeum (Marsala), together with Drepanum (Trapani), by land and sea. In the face of resistance, the Romans were compelled to withdraw in 249; in a surprise attack upon Drepanum the Roman fleet under the command of admiral Publius Claudius Pulcher lost 93 ships. This was the Romans' only naval defeat in the war. Their fleet, however, had suffered a series of grievous losses by storm and was now so reduced that the attack upon Sicily had to be

suspended. At the same time, the Carthaginians, who felt no less severely the financial strain of the prolonged struggle, reduced their forces and made no attempt to deliver a counterattack.

In 242 Rome resumed operations at sea. A fleet of 200 warships was equipped and sent out to renew the blockade of Lilybaeum. The Carthaginians hastily assembled a relief force, but in a battle fought off the Aegates, or Aegusae (Aegadian) Islands, west of Drepanum, their fleet was caught at a disadvantage and was largely sunk or captured (March 10, 241). This victory, by giving the Romans undisputed command of the sea, rendered certain the ultimate fall of the Punic strongholds in Sicily. The Carthaginians accordingly opened negotiations and consented to a peace by which they ceded Sicily and the Lipari Islands to Rome and paid an indemnity of 3,200 talents. The protracted nature of the war and the repeated loss of ships resulted in an enormous loss of life and resources on both sides.

BETWEEN THE FIRST AND SECOND PUNIC WARS (241–218 BC)

The loss of naval supremacy not only deprived the Carthaginians of their predominance in the western Mediterranean but exposed their overseas empire to disintegration under renewed attacks by Rome. Even the Greek historian Polybius, an admirer of Rome, considered the subsequent Roman actions against Carthage aggressive and unjustified. A gross breach of the treaty was perpetrated when a Roman force was sent to occupy Sardinia, whose insurgent garrison had offered to surrender the island (238). To the remonstrances of Carthage the Romans replied with a declaration of war and only withheld their attack upon the cession of Sardinia and Corsica and the payment of a further indemnity.

From this episode it became clear that Rome intended to use the victory to the utmost. To avoid further infringement of its hegemony, Carthage had little choice but to respond with force. The recent complications of foreign and internal strife had indeed so weakened the Punic power that the prospect of renewing the war under favourable circumstances seemed remote. Yet Hamilcar Barca sought to rebuild Carthaginian strength by acquiring a dominion in Spain where Carthage might gain new wealth and manpower. Invested with an unrestricted foreign command, he spent the rest of his life founding a Spanish empire (237–228). His work was continued by his son-in-law Hasdrubal and his son Hannibal, who was placed at the head of the army in 221. These conquests aroused the suspicions of Rome, which in a treaty with Hasdrubal confined the Carthaginians to the south of the Ebro River. At some point Rome also entered into relations with Saguntum (Sagunto), a town on the east coast, south of the Ebro.

To the Carthaginians it seemed that once again Rome was expanding its interests into their sphere of hegemony. In 219 Hannibal laid siege to Saguntum and carried the town in spite of stubborn defense. The Romans responded with an ultimatum demanding that the Carthaginians surrender Hannibal or go to war. The Carthaginian council supported Hannibal and accepted the war.

SECOND PUNIC WAR (218–201 BC)

It seemed that the superiority of the Romans at sea ought to have enabled them to choose the field of battle. They decided to send one army to Spain and another to Sicily and Africa. But before their preparations were complete, Hannibal began the series of operations that dictated the course of the war for the greater part of its duration. He realized that as long as the Romans commanded the resources of an undivided Italian confederacy, no foreign attack could overwhelm them beyond recovery. Thus he conceived the plan of cutting off their source of strength by carrying the war into Italy and causing a disruption of the league. His chances of ever reaching Italy seemed small, for the sea was guarded by the Roman fleets and the land route was long and arduous.

But the very boldness of his enterprise contributed to its success; after a six months' march through Spain and Gaul and over the Alps, which the Romans were nowhere in time to oppose, Hannibal arrived (autumn 218) in the plain of the Po with 20,000 foot soldiers and 6,000 horses, the pick of his African and

Spanish levies. At the end of the year, Hannibal, by superior tactics, repelled a Roman army on the banks of the Trebbia River, inflicting heavy losses, and thus made his position in northern Italy secure.

In 217 the land campaign opened in Etruria, into which the invading army, largely reinforced by Gauls, penetrated via an unguarded pass. A rash pursuit by the Roman field force led to its being entrapped on the shore of Lake Trasimene (Trasimeno) and destroyed with a loss of at least 15,000 men. This catastrophe left Rome completely uncovered; but Hannibal, having resolved not to attack the capital before he could collect a more overwhelming force, directed his march toward the south of Italy, where he hoped to stir up the peoples who had formerly been the most stubborn enemies of Rome. The Italians, however, were slow everywhere to join the Carthaginians. A new Roman army under the dictator Quintus Fabius Maximus ("Cunctator") dogged Hannibal's steps on his forays through Apulia and Campania and prevented him from acquiring a permanent base of operations.

The eventful campaign of 216 was begun by a new, aggressive move on the

The Carthaginian general Hannibal proved a formidable adversary during the Second Punic War. Henry Guttmann/Hulton Archive/Getty Images

part of Rome. An exceptionally strong field army, variously estimated at between 48,000 and 85,000 men, was sent to crush the Carthaginians in open battle. On a level plain near Cannae in Apulia, Hannibal deliberately allowed his centre to be driven in by the numerically superior Romans, while Hasdrubal's cavalry wheeled around so as to take the enemy in flank and rear. The Romans, surrounded on all sides, were practically annihilated, and the loss of citizens was perhaps greater than in any other defeat that befell the republic.

The effect of the battle on morale was no less momentous. The southern Italian peoples seceded from Rome, the leaders of the movement being the people of Capua, at the time the second greatest town of Italy. Reinforcements were sent from Carthage, and several neutral powers prepared to throw their weight into the scale on Hannibal's behalf. But the great resources of Rome, though terribly reduced in respect to both men and money, were not yet exhausted. In northern and central Italy the insurrection spread but little and could be sufficiently guarded against with small detachments. In the south the Greek towns of the coast remained loyal, and the numerous Latin colonies continued to render important service by interrupting free communication between the rebels and detaining part of their forces.

In Rome itself the crisis gave way to a unanimity unparalleled in the annals of the republic. The guidance of operations was henceforth left to the Senate, which, by maintaining a persistent policy until the conflict was brought to a successful end, earned its greatest title to fame. But it also produced a severe strain, released through cruel religious rites, which were an embarrassment to later Roman authors. The disasters were interpreted as evidence of divine wrath at Roman impiety, to be propitiated by punishment (burial alive) of two offending Vestal Virgins and by the human sacrifice of a Gallic and Greek man and woman.

The subsequent campaigns of the war in Italy assumed a new character. Though the Romans contrived at times to raise 200,000 men, they could spare only a moderate force for field operations. Their generals, among whom the veterans Fabius and Marcus Claudius Marcellus frequently held the most important commands, rarely ventured to engage Hannibal in the open and contented themselves with observing him or skirmishing against his detachments. Hannibal, whose recent accessions of strength were largely discounted by the necessity of assigning troops to protect his new allies or secure their wavering loyalty, was still too weak to undertake a vigorous offensive. In the ensuing years the war resolved itself into a multiplicity of minor engagements, which need not be followed in detail. In 216 and 215 the chief seat of war was Campania, where Hannibal, vainly attempting to establish himself on the coast, experienced a severe repulse at Nola.

In 214 the main Carthaginian force was transferred from Apulia in hopes of capturing Tarentum (Taranto), a suitable harbour by which Hannibal might have secured his overseas communications. In 213–212 the greater part of Tarentum and other cities of the southern seaboard at last came into Hannibal's power, but in the meantime the Romans were suppressing the revolt in Campania and in 212 were strong enough to place Capua under blockade. They severely defeated a Carthaginian relief force and could not be permanently dislodged even by Hannibal himself. In 211 Hannibal made a last effort to relieve his allies by a feint upon Rome itself, but the besiegers refused to be drawn away from their entrenchments, and eventually Capua was starved into surrender. The Romans in 209 gained a further important success by recovering Tarentum. Though Hannibal still won isolated engagements, he was slowly being driven back into the extreme south of the peninsula.

In 207 the arrival of a fresh invading force produced a new crisis. Hasdrubal, who in 208–207 had marched overland from Spain, appeared in northern Italy with a force scarcely inferior to the army that his brother had brought in 218. After levying contingents of Gauls and Ligurians, he marched down the east coast with the object of joining his brother in central Italy for a direct attack upon Rome itself. By this time the steady drain of men and money was telling so severely upon the confederacy that some of the most loyal allies protested their inability to render further help. Nonetheless, by exerting a supreme effort, the Romans raised their war establishment to the highest total yet attained and sent a strong field army against each Carthaginian leader. Before reaching Hannibal, Hasdrubal was met in northern Italy by the army of Marcus Livius Salinator, reinforced by part of Gaius Claudius Nero's army. The battle on the banks of the Metaurus (Metauro) River was evenly contested until Nero, with a dexterous flanking movement, cut off the enemy's retreat. The bulk of Hasdrubal's army was destroyed, and he himself was killed. His head was tossed into his brother's camp as an announcement of his defeat.

The campaign of 207 decided the war in Italy. Though Hannibal still maintained himself for some years in southern Italy, this was chiefly due to the exhaustion of Rome. In 203 Hannibal, in accordance with orders received from home, sailed back to Africa; and another expedition under his brother Mago, which had sailed to Liguria in 205 and endeavoured to rouse the slumbering discontent of the people in Cisalpine Gaul and Etruria, was forced to withdraw.

CAMPAIGNS IN SICILY AND SPAIN

Concurrently with the great struggle in Italy, the Second Punic War was fought on several other fields. To the east King Philip V of Macedon began the First Macedonian War (214–205) in concert with the Carthaginians, when the Roman power seemed to be breaking up after Cannae. Although this compelled the Romans to stretch their already severely strained resources still further by sending troops to Greece, the diversions

Roman diplomacy provided for Philip in Greece and the maintenance of a Roman patrol squadron in the Adriatic Sea prevented any effective cooperation between Philip and Hannibal.

Agriculture in Italy had collapsed, and the Romans had to look to Sardinia and Sicily for their food supply. Sardinia was attacked by Carthaginians in 215, but a small Roman force was enough to repel the invasion. In Sicily the death of Hieron II, Rome's steadfast friend, in 215 left the realm of Syracuse to his inexperienced grandson Hieronymus. The young prince abruptly broke with the Romans, but before hostilities commenced he was assassinated. The Syracusan people now repudiated the monarchy and resumed their republican constitution. When the Romans threatened terrible punishment, the Syracusans found it necessary to cooperate with the Carthaginians.

The Roman army and fleet under Marcus Claudius Marcellus, which speedily appeared before the town, were completely baffled by the mechanical contrivances that the Syracusan mathematician Archimedes had invented in 213 for the defense of the city. Meanwhile, the revolt against Rome spread in the interior of the island, and a Carthaginian fleet gained control of towns on the south coast. In 212 Marcellus at last broke through the defense of Syracuse and, in spite of the arrival of a Carthaginian relief force, took control of the whole town in 211. By the end of 210 Sicily was wholly under the power of Rome.

The conflict in Spain was second in importance only to the Italian war. From this country the Carthaginians drew large supplies of troops and money that might serve to reinforce Hannibal; hence it was in the interest of the Romans to challenge their enemy within Spain. Though the force that Rome at first spared for this war was small in numbers and rested entirely upon its own resources, the generals Publius Cornelius and Gnaeus Cornelius Scipio, by skillful strategy and diplomacy, not only won over the peoples north of the Ebro and defeated the Carthaginian leader Hasdrubal Barca in his attempts to restore communication with Italy but also carried their arms along the east coast into the heart of the enemy's domain.

But eventually the Roman successes were nullified by a rash advance. Deserted by their native contingents and cut off by Carthaginian cavalry, among which the Numidian prince Masinissa rendered conspicuous service, the Roman generals were killed and their troops destroyed (211).

Disturbances in Africa prevented the Punic commanders from exploiting their success. Before long the fall of Capua enabled Rome to transfer troops from Italy to Spain; and in 210 the best Roman general of the day, the young son and namesake of Publius Scipio, was placed in command by popular vote, despite his youth and lack of the prerequisite senior magistracies. He signalized his arrival by a bold and successful coup de main upon the great arsenal of Carthago Nova (Cartagena) in 209. Though after an engagement at Baecula (Bailen; 208) he was unable to prevent Hasdrubal Barca from marching away to Italy, Scipio profited by his opponent's departure to push back the remaining hostile forces the more rapidly. A last effort by the Carthaginians to retrieve their losses with a fresh army was frustrated by a great Roman victory at Ilipa, near Sevilla (Seville), and by the end of the year 206 the Carthaginians had been driven out of Spain.

THE WAR IN AFRICA

In 205 Scipio, who had returned to Rome to hold the consulship, proposed to follow up his victories by an attack on the home territory of Carthage. Though the presence of Hannibal in Italy deterred Fabius and other senators from sanctioning this policy, Scipio gradually overbore all resistance. He built up a force, which he organized and supplemented in Sicily, and in 204 sailed across to Africa. He was met there by a combined levy of Carthage and King Syphax of Numidia and for a time was penned to the shore near Utica. But in the spring he extricated himself by a surprise attack on the enemy's camp, which resulted in the total loss of the allied force by sword or fire.

In the campaign of 203, a new Carthaginian force was destroyed by Scipio on the Great Plains 75 miles (120.7 km) from Utica, their ally Syphax was captured, and the renegade Masinissa was reinstated in the kingdom from which Syphax had recently expelled him. These disasters induced the Carthaginians to sue for peace; but before the moderate terms that Scipio offered could be definitely accepted, a sudden reversal of opinion caused them to recall Hannibal's army for a final trial of war and to break off negotiations. In 202 Hannibal assumed command of a composite force of citizen and mercenary levies reinforced by a corps of his veteran Italian troops.

After negotiations failed, Scipio and Hannibal met in the Battle of Zama. Scipio's force was somewhat smaller in numbers but well trained throughout and greatly superior in cavalry. His infantry, after evading an attack by the Carthaginian elephants, cut through the first two lines of the enemy but was unable to break the reserve corps of Hannibal's veterans. The battle was ultimately decided by the cavalry of the Romans and their new ally Masinissa, who by a maneuver recalling the tactics of Cannae took Hannibal's line in the rear and destroyed it.

The Carthaginians again applied for peace and accepted the terms that Scipio offered. They were compelled to cede Spain and the Mediterranean islands still in their hands, to surrender their warships, to pay an indemnity of 10,000 talents within 50 years, and to forfeit their independence in affairs of war and foreign policy.

The Second Punic War, by far the greatest struggle in which either power engaged, had thus ended in the complete

During the Battle of Zama, Hannibal's elephants were easily outmaneuvered by the Roman cavalry. The Romans eventually claimed victory. Pushkin Museum, Moscow, Russia/The Bridgeman Art Library/Getty Images

triumph of Rome, although not because of any faultiness in the Carthaginians' method of attack. Carthage could only hope to win by invading Italy and using the enemy's home resources against him. The failure of Hannibal's brilliant endeavour was ultimately due to the stern determination of the Romans and to the nearly inexhaustible manpower from their Italian confederacy, which no shock of defeat or strain of war could entirely disintegrate. Although Rome and its allies suffered casualties of perhaps one-fifth of their adult male population, they continued fighting. For Polybius, the

Second Punic War illustrated the superiority of the strong Roman constitution over Hannibal's individual genius.

THE ESTABLISHMENT OF ROMAN HEGEMONY IN THE MEDITERRANEAN WORLD

Just before the Second Punic War, Rome had projected its power across the Adriatic Sea against the Illyrians. As noted, Philip V of Macedon in turn had joined the Carthaginians for a time during the war in an attempt to stem the tide of Roman expansion but had agreed to terms of peace with Rome's allies, the Aetolians, in 206 and then with Rome in the Peace of Phoenice of 205.

Immediately after the Second Punic War, the Roman Senate moved to settle affairs with Philip, despite the war-weary centuriate assembly's initial refusal to declare war. Historians have debated Rome's reasons for this momentous decision, with suggestions ranging from a desire to protect Athenians and other Greeks from Philip out of philhellenism to fear of a secret alliance between Philip and the Seleucid king Antiochus III. Yet these suggestions are belied by the fact that Rome later treated the Greek cities callously and that no fear is apparent in Rome's increasing demands on Philip and in its refusal to negotiate seriously with him through the course of the war. Rather, the Second Macedonian War (200–196) fits the long pattern of Roman readiness to go to war in order to force ever more distant neighbours to submit to superior Roman power.

ROMAN EXPANSION IN THE EASTERN MEDITERRANEAN

In the winter of 200–199, Roman legions marched into the Balkans under the command of Publius Sulpicius Galba. During the next two years there was no decisive battle, as the Romans gathered allies among the Greeks—not only their previous allies, the Aetolians, but also Philip's traditional allies, the Achaeans, who recognized Roman military superiority. The consul of 198, Titus Quinctius Flamininus,

took over the command and defeated Philip at the battle of Cynoscephalae in 197. The terms of settlement allowed Philip to remain king of Macedon but stipulated payment of an indemnity and restrictions on campaigning beyond the borders of his kingdom. Flamininus then sought to win the goodwill of the Greeks with his famous proclamation of their liberation at the Isthmian Games of 196. To lend credibility to this proclamation, he successfully argued against senatorial opposition for the withdrawal of Roman troops from all Greece, including the strategically important "Fetters" (the key garrisons of Acrocorinth, Chalcis, and Demetrias).

Even before the Romans withdrew, the seeds had been sown for their reentry into the East. As an active king, Antiochus III set out to recover the ancestral possessions of his kingdom on the western coast of Anatolia and in Thrace. In response to the Roman demand that he stay out of Europe, the king attempted to negotiate. When the Romans showed little interest in compromise, Antiochus accepted the invitation of Rome's former allies, the Aetolians, who felt they had not been duly rewarded with additional territory after the victory over Philip, to liberate the Greeks. Upon crossing into Greece, however, the king found no enthusiasm among the other Greeks for a war of liberation and was defeated at Thermopylae in 191 by legions under the command of Manius Acilius Glabrio.

Antiochus returned home to gather a larger army. In 190 Lucius Cornelius

Scipio was elected consul in Rome and was authorized to recruit a force for a campaign against Antiochus. Accompanying Lucius as a legate was his brother, the great general Scipio Africanus. In an attempt to avert war, Antiochus offered to accept the earlier Roman terms, only to find that the Romans had now extended their demands to keep Antiochus east of the Taurus Mountains of Anatolia. Unable to accept, Antiochus fought and lost to Scipio's army at Magnesia ad Sipylum in the winter of 190–189. In the following Treaty of Apamea (188), the Seleucid kingdom was limited to Asia east of the Taurus range and was required to pay an indemnity of 15,000 talents and to give up its elephants and all but 10 ships. Rome punished its opponents, the Aetolians, and rewarded its supporters, notably Pergamum and Rhodes, which were granted new territories, including Greek cities, at the expense of "the liberation of the Greeks." The consul of 189, Gnaeus Manlius Vulso, came east with reinforcements, took command of the legions, and proceeded to plunder the Galatians of Anatolia on the pretext of restoring order.

The withdrawal of Roman legions this time did not entail the withdrawal of a Roman presence from the Hellenistic East. On the contrary, according to Polybius, the Romans now "were displeased if all matters were not referred to them and if everything was not done in accordance with their decision." Continuing jealousies and disputes in the Greek world offered Rome opportunities to adjudicate and ultimately to intervene once again. In the Peloponnese the Achaean League was at odds with Sparta, wishing to bring Sparta into the league and to suppress the radical social program of its king, Nabis. Flamininus in 195 supported the independence of Sparta, but in 192 the Achaean leader, Philopoemen, induced Sparta to join the league with a promise of no interference in its internal affairs. When an infringement of the promise prompted the Spartans to secede, Philopoemen in 188 led an Achaean army to take Sparta, kill the anti-Achaean leaders, and force the city back into the league. Although the Senate heard complaints, it took no immediate action. Then, in 184, the Senate reasserted its own terms for settlement but was circumvented by Philopoemen, who reached a separate agreement with the Spartans. The independent-minded Philopoemen died the following year in a campaign by the league to suppress a revolt of Messene. His death led to a change of leadership, as the pro-Roman Callicrates (regarded by Polybius as a sycophant) began a policy of obeying Rome's every wish.

Meanwhile, tensions between Rome and Philip were increasing. Philip had supported Rome's war with Antiochus in the hope of recovering Thessalian and Thracian territory, but in this he was disappointed by the Romans. They did, however, return Philip's younger son, Demetrius, taken to Rome as a hostage in 197—a reward with tragic consequences. During his years as a hostage, Demetrius had made senatorial friendships, which aroused suspicions at home that the Romans would prefer to see Demetrius rather than his elder brother, Perseus, succeed Philip. Philip ordered the death of Demetrius in 181 and then died in 179, leaving his throne to Perseus, the last king of Macedon.

Perseus's activism started a stream of complaints to the Senate from neighbouring Greek powers from 175 onward. The king's real intentions are unclear; perhaps Polybius was right that he wished to make the Romans "more cautious about delivering harsh and unjust orders to Macedonians." The Senate listened to the unfavourable interpretations of Perseus's enemies, who claimed that the king's actions revealed an intent to attack Rome. Like his father, Perseus campaigned to extend Macedonian power to the northeast and south and marched through Greece as far as Delphi. He solicited alliances with the Achaean League and other Greek states, which some of the leaders hostile to Rome would have liked to accept. He arranged dynastic marriages with other Hellenistic kings, taking the daughter of Seleucus IV as his wife and giving the hand of his sister to Prusias II of Bithynia. Although these actions could have been viewed as the behaviour expected of a Hellenistic monarch, Eumenes of Pergamum suggested to the Senate that Perseus was preparing for war against Rome. After the Senate decided on war, it sent Quintus Marcius Philippus to propose a truce and to give Perseus false hopes of negotiation in order to allow the consul of 171, Publius Licinius Crassus, to land his army on the Illyrian coast unhindered—a ploy decried by some older senators as "the new wisdom."

Perseus's initial success against the Roman army in Thessaly in 171 did not alter the massive imbalance of power; the Romans again refused the king's offer to negotiate. Over the next three years Roman commanders devoted more effort to plunder than to the defeat of Perseus. In a notorious incident, the praetor Lucius Hortensius anchored his fleet at Abdera, a city allied with Rome, and demanded supplies; when the Abderitans asked to consult the Senate, Hortensius sacked the town, executed the leading citizens, and enslaved the rest. When complaints reached the Senate, weak attempts were made to force the Roman commanders to make restitution. In 168 the experienced Lucius Aemilius Paullus was reelected consul and sent out to restore discipline. He quickly brought the Third Macedonian War to an end by defeating Perseus in the Battle of Pydna in June 168. Perseus was deposed, and Macedonia was divided into four republics, which were forbidden to have relations with one another; they paid tribute to Rome at half the rate they had previously paid to the king.

In 167 Rome proceeded to punish those who had sided with Perseus (such as the Illyrian Genthius), those whose loyalty had wavered (such as Eumenes), and even those who had contemplated acting as mediators in the war (such as the Rhodians). In Illyria, Paullus, on instructions from the Senate, swept through the countryside enslaving 150,000 inhabitants from 70 Epirote towns. In Achaea, 1,000 leading men suspected of Macedonian sympathies were taken as hostages to Rome. (Among them was Polybius, who befriended the noble Scipionic family and wrote his great history of the rise of Rome with the aid of privileged access to the views of the senatorial leadership.) Eumenes was refused a hearing before the Senate on his visit to Italy; his fall from favour prompted his enemies to dispute his territory, and in 164 a Roman embassy in Anatolia publicly invited complaints against the king. Rhodes had thrived as the leading trade centre of the eastern Mediterranean, using its considerable resources to control piracy; now Rome undermined its economy and power by making the island of Delos a free port, thereby depriving Rhodes of its income from harbour dues. Territory in Lycia and Caria on the mainland, granted to Rhodes in 189, was now taken away. But the far harsher proposal in the Senate to declare Rhodes an enemy and to destroy it was opposed by senior senators such as Cato the Censor and was voted down. As a result of the weakening of Rhodes, piracy became rampant in the eastern Mediterranean (the young Julius Caesar was captured by pirates). During the next century Roman senators did not find the political will to suppress the piracy, perhaps in part because it served their interests; pirates supplied tens of thousands of slaves for their Italian estates and disrupted the grain trade, thus raising prices for their produce in Rome.

The arrangements of 167 served the Roman policy of weakening the powers of the eastern Mediterranean. In the previous year Rome had also intervened to stop Seleucid expansion into Egypt. In a famous episode, the Roman ambassador Gaius Popillius Laenas delivered to Antiochus IV the Senate's demand that the king withdraw from Egypt. When the king requested time for consultation, Popillius "drew a circle around the king with a stick he was carrying and told him not to leave the circle until he gave his response. The king was astonished at this occurrence and the display of superiority, but, after a brief time, said he would do all the Romans demanded."

The power vacuum fostered by the Romans was not ultimately conducive to stability. An adventurer, Andriscus, claiming to be descended from the Macedonian dynasty, was able to enter the Macedonian republics without serious resistance. He was successful enough in raising an army to defeat the first Roman force sent against him in 149 under the command of the praetor Publius Iuventius Thalna (who was killed). A second Roman army under Quintus Caecilius Metellus defeated the pretender in 148. With the death of Callicrates, leadership of the Achaean League passed to Critolaus and Diaeus, outspoken proponents of Greek independence from Rome. In 147 a Roman embassy was sent to intervene in the affairs of the league by supporting the secession of Sparta and also by calling for the detachment of Corinth and Argos from the league. The embassy provoked a violent reply. When further negotiations were blocked by Critolaus, Rome declared war on the Achaeans in 146, citing as reason the ill-treatment of their embassy. Metellus (now with the appellation of "Macedonicus"), having delayed with his army, marched against Critolaus and defeated him in Locris. Then Lucius Mummius Archaicus, consul of 146, took over the command and defeated Diaeus and the remaining Achaeans. The Senate ordered Mummius to teach a lesson to the Greeks: the venerable city of Corinth was sacked, its treasures taken to Rome, and its buildings burned to the ground.

The nature of Roman domination in the East began to change decisively after these wars: in place of influence through embassies, arbitration of disputes, and the occasional military incursion came direct rule. Macedonia was annexed as a province, to be governed and taxed by a Roman proconsul, who also watched over the Greek cities to the south, where the leagues were disbanded. Farther east, the kingdom of Pergamum was added as the province of Asia, as a bequest to the Roman people from Attalus III in 133.

ROMAN EXPANSION IN THE WESTERN MEDITERRANEAN

If Roman military intervention in the east was sporadic in the second century, campaigning in northern Italy and Spain was nearly continuous. During Hannibal's invasion of Italy, the Insubres and Boii, Gallic peoples in the Po valley, had joined the Carthaginians against Rome. In 200 the Gauls and Ligurians combined forces and sacked the Latin colony of Placentia in an attempt to drive the Romans out of their lands. In the following years consular armies repeatedly attacked the Gauls. In 194 Lucius Valerius Flaccus won a decisive victory over the Insubres; in 192 the leading Boii under severe pressure went over to the Roman side, signaling the coming defeat of their tribe. Following their victories, the Romans sent thousands of new colonists to the Po valley to reinforce the older colonies of Placentia and Cremona (190) and to establish new colonies, notably Bononia (189) and Aquileia (181).

During the same period the Romans were at war with the Ligurian tribes of the northern Apennines. The serious effort began in 182, when both consular armies and a proconsular army were sent against the Ligurians. The wars continued into the 150s, when victorious generals celebrated two triumphs over the Ligurians. Here also the Romans drove many natives off their land and settled colonies in their stead (e.g., Luna and Luca in the 170s).

As a result of the Second Punic War, Roman legions had marched into Spain against the Carthaginians and remained there after 201. The Romans formalized their rule in 197 by creating two provinces, Nearer and Further Spain. They also exploited the Spanish riches, especially the mines, as the Carthaginians had done. In 197 the legions were

Cato the Censor was a Roman statesman noted for his conservative and anti-Hellenic policies. His accounts of life in the Roman Empire also made him the first Latin prose writer of importance. Hulton Archive/Getty Images

His comments show that he prided himself on his bravery and lack of greed as compared with other Roman commanders. Yet his narrative must overstate the extent and decisiveness of his success because fighting persisted for years to come, as later Roman governors sought to extend Roman control over more Spanish peoples—the Celtiberians of northeastern Spain, the Lusitanians of modern-day Portugal, and the Vettones and Vaccaei of northwestern Spain. In 177 Tiberius Sempronius Gracchus celebrated a triumph over the Celtiberians. The size of the Roman forces was probably then reduced from four to two legions; from 173 to 155 there was a lull in the regular campaigning. During these decades Spanish peoples brought complaints to Rome about corrupt governors.

Annual warfare resumed in Spain in 154, being perhaps in part a violent reaction to a corrupt administration, and dragged on until 133. Labeled a "fiery war" (really wars), these struggles acquired a reputation for extreme cruelty; they brought destruction to the native population (e.g., 20,000 Vaccaei were killed in 151 after giving themselves up to Lucius Licinius Lucullus) and made recruiting legionaries in Italy difficult. In Further Spain the

withdrawn, but a Spanish revolt against the Roman presence led to the death of one governor and required that the two praetorian governors of 196 be accompanied by a legion each. The situation was serious enough for the consul of 195, Cato the Censor, to be sent to Spain with two legions.

From Cato comes the earliest extant firsthand account of Roman conquest.

Lusitanian leader Viriathus enjoyed some successes, including the surrender of a Roman army in 141–140 and a favourable treaty with Rome, but the next governor of the province, Quintus Servilius Caepio, arranged for his assassination in 139. Two years later in Nearer Spain, the Numantines also forced the surrender of an army under Gaius Hostilius Mancinus; the Senate later disavowed the agreement of equal terms and handed Mancinus, bound and naked, over to the Spaniards to absolve themselves of responsibility before the gods. The wars in Spain were brought to a conclusion in 133 by Publius Cornelius Scipio Aemilianus, who took Numantia after a long siege, enslaved the population, and razed the city.

It was Scipio Aemilianus (b. 185/184) who in the previous decade had imposed a similar final solution on Carthage in the Third Punic War (149–146). After the Second Punic War, Carthage had recovered to the point that in 191 it offered to repay the remainder of the 50-year tribute of 200 talents per year in one lump sum. Rome's refusal of the offer suggests that beyond its monetary value the tribute had the symbolic importance of signifying subjection. Carthage's neighbour, the Numidian king Masinissa, had been granted as a reward for his support of Rome at the Battle of Zama his paternal kingdom and the western Numidian kingdom ruled by Syphax. During the next half century Masinissa periodically tried to exploit his favour in Rome by encroaching on Carthaginian territory.

Initially, the Carthaginians submissively sought the arbitration of Rome in these disputes, but more often than not Roman judgment went in favour of Masinissa. After a series of losses, the Carthaginians in 151 decided to act on their own and raised an army to ward off the Numidian attacks. When a Roman delegation observed the Carthaginian army raised in breach of the treaty of 201, Rome was provided with the casus belli for a declaration of war in 149; Polybius, however, claims that the Senate had decided on this war "long before." The elderly Cato had been ending his speeches in the Senate since 153 with the notorious exhortation that "Carthage must be destroyed." Carthage desperately and pathetically tried to make amends, executing the generals of the expedition against the Numidians, surrendering to Rome, and handing over hostages, armour, and artillery. Only then did the Romans deliver their final demand: Carthage must be abandoned and the population moved to a new site inland. Such extreme terms could not be accepted.

The war against Carthage, with its prospects of rich booty, presented no recruiting problems for the Romans: huge land and naval forces were sent out under both consuls of 149, Lucius Marcius Censorinus and Manius Manilius. The imbalance of resources meant that the outcome was never in doubt, but the fortifications of Carthage delayed the Roman victory. The young Scipio Aemilianus was elected consul for 147, and by popular vote he was assigned the task of bringing the war to an end. He blockaded the city by land and sea, inflicting terrible suffering. Finally, in 146, the Roman army took Carthage, enslaved its remaining 50,000 inhabitants, burned the buildings to the ground, and ritually sowed the site with salt to guarantee that nothing would ever grow there again. Carthaginian territory was annexed as the province of Africa.

EXPLANATIONS OF ROMAN EXPANSION

As one of the decisive developments in western history, Roman expansion has invited continual reinterpretation by historians. Polybius, who wrote his history in order to explain to other Greeks the reasons for Roman success, believed that after their victory over Hannibal the Romans conceived the aim of dominating all before them and set out to achieve it in the Second Macedonian War. If one accepts the Roman view that they fought only "just wars"—that is, only when provoked—then Roman conquest emerges as "one of the most important accidents in European history," as Rome had to defend itself from threats on all sides. Historians have suggested other motives for empire, such as a desire to profit from war, an interest in commercial expansion, or a love of the Greeks, who asked for protection against Hellenistic monarchs.

Major historical phenomena of this kind rarely receive final, decisive interpretations, but several assertions may be ventured. Some of the interpretations are anachronistic impositions on the ancient world; ancient testimony, for example, gives no support to commercial or mercantile explanations. Cultural and economic interpretations seem more appropriate. Roman culture placed a high value on success in war: *virtus* (courage and qualities of leadership) was displayed, above all, in war, and the triumph, a parade through Rome celebrating a major victory over an enemy, was the honour most highly prized by the senatorial generals who guided Roman decisions about war and peace. Moreover, these leaders, and the whole Roman people, were fully aware of the increasing profits of victory; in the 2nd century commanders and soldiers, as well as the city itself, were enriched by the glittering booty from Africa and the Greek East.

Yet, it is rightly pointed out, Roman intervention in the East was sporadic, not systematic, and the Romans did not annex territory in the Balkans, Anatolia, or North Africa for more than 50 years after their initial victories. The latter point, however, is not telling, since the Romans regarded defeated states allied to them as part of their *imperium*, whether or not they were under Roman provincial administration. The sporadic timing of the wars would seem to support the Romans' claim that they only reacted, justly, to provocations. But attention to the individual provocations should not blind the historian to the larger pattern of Roman behaviour.

From 218 the Romans annually fielded major armies decade after decade.

Rome was able to go to war every year in response to provocations only because it chose to define its interests and make alliances farther and farther afield. Polybius, as noted, reveals how the Romans were the masters of manipulation of circumstances to force opponents to behave in a way they could interpret as provocative. Therefore, the Roman interpretation of "just wars" and the Polybian interpretation of a universal aim to conquer need not be contradictory. The concept of "just war" may have justified any given war but does not explain the perpetual Roman readiness to go to war. For that the historian must look to Polybius's universal aim or to general political, social, economic, and cultural features of Rome. Finally, it must be remembered that in some instances it was clearly the Roman commander who provoked the war in order to plunder and to win a triumph (e.g., Licinius Lucullus, governor of Nearer Spain, in 151).

BEGINNINGS OF PROVINCIAL ADMINISTRATION

Rome dominated its Latin and Italian neighbours by incorporating some into the Roman citizen body and by forming bilateral alliances with most of the Italian city-states. After the Punic Wars, Rome undertook to rule newly acquired territories directly as subject provinces. In 241 Sicily became Rome's first province, followed by Sardinia-Corsica in 238, and Spain, divided into two provinces, in 197. After a 50-year hiatus, Macedonia and Africa were annexed in 146, and the province of Asia (northwestern Anatolia) in 133. In principle, each province was to be administered in accordance with its *lex provinciae*, a set of rules drawn up by the conquering commander and a senatorial embassy. The *lex provinciae* laid down the organization of taxation, which varied from province to province.

The provincial administrative apparatuses were minimal and unprofessional, as the Romans relied heavily on the local elites as mediators. Each year a senatorial magistrate was sent out to govern with nearly unfettered powers. Because initially the governors were usually praetors, the addition of new provinces required the election of more praetors (increased to four in 227 and to six in 197). The assignments to provinces were done by lot. The governor took with him one of the quaestors to oversee the finances of provincial government and senatorial friends and relatives to serve as deputies and advisors (*legati*). Among the humbler functionaries assisting the governor were scribes to keep records and lictors with fasces (bundles of rods and axes) to symbolize gubernatorial authority and to execute sentences pronounced by the governor in criminal cases.

The governor's main duties were to maintain order and security and to collect revenues. The former often entailed command of an army to ward off external threats and to suppress internal disorders such as banditry. When not commanding his army, the governor spent his time hearing legal cases and arbitrating disputes. During the republic, revenue collection was left to private companies of *publicani* , so called because they won by highest bid the contract to collect the revenues. It was the governor's responsibility to keep the *publicani* within the bounds of the *lex provinciae* so that they did not exploit the helpless provincials too mercilessly, but this was difficult. Governors expected to make a profit from their term of office, and some collaborated with the *publicani* to strip the provinces of their wealth.

TRANSFORMATION DURING THE MIDDLE REPUBLIC

The Greek historian Polybius admired Rome's balanced constitution, discipline, and strict religious observance as the bases of the republic's success and stability. Yet Rome's very successes in the second century undermined these features, leading to profound changes in the republic's politics, culture, economy, and society.

CITIZENSHIP AND POLITICS IN THE MIDDLE REPUBLIC

The Romans organized their citizenry in a way that permitted expansion. This was regarded as a source of strength by contemporaries such as Philip V, who noted that Rome replenished its citizen ranks with freed slaves. The extension of citizenship continued in the early 2nd century, as in the grant of full citizen rights to Arpinum, Formiae, and Fundi in

188. Yet Rome's glittering successes made such openness ever more problematic. For one, the city attracted increasing numbers of Latins and allies, who wished to use their ancient right to migrate and take up Roman citizenship. The depletion of Latin and Italian towns prompted protests until, in 177, Rome took away the right of migration and forced Latin and Italian migrants to return to their hometowns to register for military service. Such measures were sporadically repeated in the following years.

In addition, the flood of slaves into Rome from the great conquests increased the flow of foreign-born freedmen into the citizen body. Sempronius Gracchus (father of the famous tribunes) won senatorial approbation as censor in 168 by registering the freedmen in a single urban tribe and thus limiting their electoral influence. Despite these efforts, the nature and meaning of Roman citizenship were bound to change, as the citizen body became ever more diffuse and lived dispersed from Rome, the only place where the right of suffrage could be exercised.

Polybius greatly admired Rome's balanced constitution, with its elements of monarchy (magistrates), aristocracy (Senate), and democracy (popular assemblies). According to Greek political theory, each form of constitution was believed to be unstable and susceptible to decline until replaced by another. Yet Rome's system of balance, Polybius thought, was a check on the cycle of decline. By forcing the Roman constitution into the mold of Greek political theory, however, he exaggerated the symmetry of checks and balances. In reality, the Senate enjoyed a period of steady domination through the first two-thirds of the 2nd century, having emerged from the Second Punic War with high prestige. Only occasionally did the developing tensions and contradictions surface during these decades.

Politics during the period was largely a matter of senatorial families competing for high office and the ensuing lucrative commands. Because offices were won in the centuriate and tribal assemblies, senators had to cultivate support among the *populus*. Yet the system was not as democratic as it might appear. Senators with illustrious names and consular ancestors dominated the election to the highest offices, increasing their share of the consulates from about one-half to two-thirds during the second century. These proportions can be interpreted in two ways: the Senate was not a closed, hereditary aristocracy but was open to new families, who usually rose through the senatorial ranks in the course of generations with the patronal support of established families. Yet a small circle of prominent families (e.g., the Aemilii, Claudii, and Cornelii) were disproportionately successful, surprisingly so in view of the popular electoral process. Since the campaigning was not oriented toward issues, the great families were able to maintain their superiority over the centuries by their inherited resources: their famous names, their wealth, and their clienteles of voters.

While aristocratic electoral competition was tradition during the republic, this period began to exhibit the escalation in competitiveness that was later fatal to the republic. For example, Publius Cornelius Scipio Africanus emerged from the Second Punic War as the Roman whose *dignitas* (prestige) far surpassed that of his peers. Nonetheless, a number of senators attacked him and his brother Lucius Cornelius with legal charges until he finally retired from Rome to end his life at his Campanian villa at Liternum. For younger senators, however, Scipio's spectacular achievement was something to emulate. The ambitious young Flamininus moved swiftly through the senatorial *cursus honorum* ("course of honors") to win the consulship and command against Philip V at the age of 30.

Such cases prompted laws to regulate the senatorial *cursus*: iteration in the same magistracy was prohibited, the praetorship was made a prerequisite for the consulship, and in 180 the *lex Villia annalis* (Villian law on minimum ages) set minimum ages for senatorial magistrates and required a two-year interval between offices. The consulship (two elected to it per year) could be held from age 42, the praetorship (six per year) from age 39, and the curule aedileship from 36. Patricians, still privileged in this area, were probably allowed to stand for these offices two years earlier. The senatorial career was preceded by 10 years of military service, from age 17, and formally began with a quaestorship, the most junior senatorial magistracy (eight per

Scipio Africanus's victory over Hannibal in the Battle of Zama brought the Second Punic War to an end. Hulton Archive/Getty Images

year), at age 30 or just under. The offices between the quaestorship and praetorship, the aedileship (4 per year) and the plebeian tribunate (10 per year), were not compulsory but provided opportunities to win popularity among the voters by staging aedilician games and supporting popular causes, respectively. Here again, excess elicited restraint, and legal limits were placed on the lavishness of the games. More broadly, from 181 legislation designed to curb electoral bribery was intermittently introduced.

The problems of electoral competition did not disappear. In the late 150s second consulships were prohibited altogether, but within decades the rules were broken. Scipio Aemilianus, grandson by adoption of Scipio Africanus, challenged the system. Returning from the Carthaginian campaign to Rome to stand for the aedileship, he was elected instead to the consulship, even though he was underage and had not held the prerequisite praetorship. He was then elected to a second consulship for 134. Scipio had no subversive intent, but his career set the precedent for circumventing the *cursus* regulations by appeal to the popular assemblies.

While the second century was a time of heated competition among senators, it was generally a period of quiescence of the plebs and their magistrates, the tribunes. Nevertheless, signs of the upheaval ahead are visible. For one, the long plebeian struggle against arbitrary abuse of magisterial power continued. A series of Porcian laws were passed to protect citizens from summary execution or scourging, asserting the citizen's right of appeal to the assembly (*ius provocationis*). A descendant of the Porcian clan later advertised these laws on coins as a victory for freedom. Moreover, the massive annual war effort provoked occasional resistance to military service. In 193 the tribunes started to investigate complaints about overly long military service. Interpreting this as a challenge to magisterial authority, the Senate responded with a declaration of an emergency levy, and the tribunes stopped their activity. In 151 the tribunes tried to protect some citizens from the levy for the unpopular war in Spain. A confrontation between the tribunes and the recruiting consuls ensued, in which the tribunes briefly imprisoned the consuls until a compromise relieved the crisis. The scene of tribunes taking consuls to jail was repeated in 138 during a period of renewed difficulties over recruiting.

Since the Hortensian law of 287, the plebs had the constitutional power to pass laws binding on the entire state without senatorial approval. During the next century and a half few attempts were made to use the power for purposes of major reform against the Senate's will, in part because the plebeian tribunes, as members of the senatorial order, generally shared the Senate's interests and in part because the plebeians benefited from Rome's great successes abroad under senatorial leadership. Yet senatorial fear of unbridled popular legislative power is perceptible in the Aelian and Fufian law of about 150. This law, imperfectly known from later passing references, provided that a magistrate holding a legislative assembly could be prevented from passing a bill on religious grounds by another magistrate claiming to have witnessed unfavourable omens in a procedure called *obnuntiatio*. In addition, the days of the year on which legislative assemblies could be held were reduced.

As conservative senators worked to restrain the democratic element in the political processes, the plebeians sought to expand their freedom. Voting in electoral and judicial assemblies had been public, allowing powerful senators more easily to manage the votes of their clients. The Gabinian law (139) and Cassian law (137) introduced secret written ballots into the assemblies, thus loosening the control of patrons over their clients. Significantly, the reform was supported by Scipio Aemilianus, the sort of senator who stood to benefit by attracting the clients of other patrons through his personal popularity. These reforms, together with the changing composition of the electorate in the city, carried the potential, soon to be realized, for more volatile assemblies.

CULTURE AND RELIGION

Expansion brought Rome into contact with many diverse cultures. The most important of these was the Greek culture in the eastern Mediterranean with its highly refined literature and learning.

Rome responded to it with ambivalence: although Greek *doctrina* was attractive, it was also the culture of the defeated and enslaved. Indeed, much Greek culture was brought to Rome in the aftermath of military victories, as Roman soldiers returned home not only with works of art but also with learned Greeks who had been enslaved. Despite the ambivalence, nearly every facet of Roman culture was influenced by the Greeks, and it was a Greco-Roman culture that the Roman empire bequeathed to later European civilization.

As Roman aristocrats encountered Greeks in southern Italy and in the East in the third century, they learned to speak and write in Greek. Scipio Africanus and Flamininus, for example, are known to have corresponded in Greek. By the late republic it became standard for senators to be bilingual. Many were reared from infancy by Greek-speaking slaves and later tutored by Greek slaves or freedmen. Nonetheless, despite their increasing fluency in Greek, senators continued to insist on Latin as the official language of government; visiting dignitaries from the East addressing the Senate in Greek had their speeches translated—as a mark of their subordination.

Because Greek was the lingua franca of the East, Romans had to use Greek if they wished to reach a wider audience. Thus the first histories by Romans were written in Greek. The patrician Fabius Pictor, who, as noted above, founded the Roman tradition of historiography during the Second Punic War, wrote his annalistic history of Rome in Greek partly in order to influence Greek views in favour of Rome, and he emphasized Rome's ancient ties to the Greek world by incorporating in his history the legend that the Trojan hero Aeneas had settled in Latium. Because Roman history was about politics and war, the writing of history was always judged by Romans to be a suitable pastime for men of politics—i.e., for senators such as Fabius.

Rome had had a folk tradition of poetry in the native Saturnian verse with a metre based on stress, but not a formal literature. Lucius Livius Andronicus was regarded as the father of Latin literature, a fact that illustrates to what extent the development of Roman literature was bound up with conquest and enslavement. Livius, a native Greek speaker from Tarentum, was brought as a slave to Rome, where he remained until his death (c. 204). Becoming fluent in Latin, he translated the Homeric *Odyssey* into Latin in Saturnian verse. Thus Latin literature began with a translation from Greek into the native metre. Livius reached wider audiences through his translations of Greek plays for public performance. Gnaeus Naevius, the next major figure (c. 270–c. 201), was again not a native Roman but an Oscan speaker from Campania. In addition to translating Greek drama, he wrote the first major original work in Latin, an epic poem about the First Punic War. Naevius's successors, Quintus Ennius from Calabria (239–169) and Titus Maccius Plautus from Umbria (c. 254–184), transformed the Latin poetic genres by importing Greek metrical forms based on the length of syllables rather than on stress. Ennius was best known for his epic history of Rome in verse, the *Annales*, but he also wrote tragedies and satires. Plautus produced comedies adapted from Greek New Comedy. He is the only early author whose work is well represented in the corpus of surviving literature (21 plays judged authentic by Marcus Terentius Varro, Rome's greatest scholar). None of the plays of his younger contemporaries, Caecilius Statius (*c.* 210–168) and Marcus Pacuvius (*c.* 220–130), survive, nor do the once highly esteemed tragedies of Lucius Accius (170–*c.* 86). The six extant comedies of Terence (Publius Terentius Afer; *c.* 190–159) provide a sense of the variation in the comic tradition of the 2nd century. These authors also were outsiders, coming from the Celtic Po valley, Brundisium, Umbria, and North Africa, respectively. Thus, while assorted foreigners, some of servile origin, established a Latin literature by adapting Greek genres, metrical forms, and content, native Roman senators began to write history in Greek.

Other forms of Greek learning were slower to take root in Rome. Later Romans remembered that a Greek doctor established a practice in Rome for the first time just before the Second Punic War, but his reputation did little to stimulate Roman interest in the subject. Like doctors, Greek philosophers of the second century were regarded with interest and suspicion. In the early third century Romans had erected in public a statue of Pythagoras, a sixth-century Greek philosopher who had founded communities of philosophers in southern Italy. In the mid-second century some senators displayed an interest in philosophy. Scipio Aemilianus, Gaius Laelius (consul 140), and Lucius Furius Philus (consul 136) were among those who listened to the lectures of the three leaders of the Athenian philosophical schools visiting Rome on a diplomatic mission in 155—the academic Carneades, the peripatetic Critolaus, and the stoic Diogenes. On an official visit to the East in 140, Scipio included in his entourage the leading stoic Panaetius. In the same period, another stoic, Blossius of Cumae, was said to have influenced the reforming tribune Tiberius Sempronius Gracchus. Yet the philosophical influence should not be exaggerated; none of these senators was a philosopher or even a formal student of philosophy.

Moreover, the sophisticated rhetoric of the philosophers—in 155 Carneades lectured in favour of natural justice one day and against it the next—was perceived by leading Romans such as Cato the Censor as subversive to good morals. At his urging the Senate quickly concluded the diplomatic business of Carneades, Critolaus, and Diogenes in 155 and hurried them out of Rome. This was part of a broader pattern of hostility to philosophy: in 181 the (spurious) Books of Numa, falsely believed to have been influenced by Pythagoras, were burned, and the following decades witnessed several expulsions of philosophers from the city. In comedies of the period, the discipline was held up for ridicule.

The hostility toward philosophy was one aspect of a wider Roman sense of unease about changing mores. Cato, a "new man" (without senatorial ancestors) elected consul (195) and censor (184), represented himself as an austere champion of the old ways and exemplifies the hardening Roman reaction against change under foreign influence. Although Cato knew Greek and could deploy allusions to Greek literature, he advised his son against too deep a knowledge of the literature of that "most worthless and unteachable race." Cato despised those senatorial colleagues who ineptly imitated Greek manners. He asserted the value of Latin culture in the role of father of Latin prose literature. His treatise on estate management, the *De agricultura* (c. 160), has survived with its rambling discourse about how to run a 200-*iugera* (124-acre) farm, including advice on everything from buying and selling slaves to folk medicine. Cato's greater, historical work, the *Origines*, survives only in fragments: it challenged the earlier Roman histories insofar as it was written in Latin and emphasized the achievements of the Italian peoples rather than those of the few great senatorial families of Rome (whose names were conspicuously omitted).

Elected censor in 184 to protect Roman mores, Cato vowed "to cut into pieces and burn like a hydra all luxury and voluptuousness." He expelled seven men from the Senate on various charges of immorality and penalized through taxation the acquisition of such luxuries as expensive clothing, jewelry, carriages, and fancy slaves. The worry about luxury was widespread, as evidenced by the passage of a series of sumptuary laws supported by Cato. During the depths of the Second Punic War the Oppian law (215) was passed to meet the financial crisis by restricting the jewelry and clothing women were allowed to wear. In 195, after the crisis, the law was repealed despite Cato's protests. Later sumptuary laws were motivated not by military crisis but by a sense of the dangers of luxury: the Orchian law (182) limited the lavishness of banquets; the Fannian law (161) strengthened the Orchian provisions, and the Didian law (143) extended the limits to all Italy. A similar sense of the dangers of wealth may also have prompted the *lex Voconia* (169), which prohibited Romans of the wealthiest class from naming women as heirs in their wills.

The laws and censorial actions ultimately could not restrain changes in Roman mores. Economic conditions had been irreversibly altered by conquest; the magnitude of conspicuous consumption is suggested by a senatorial decree of 161 that restricted the weight of silver tableware in a banquet to 100 pounds—10 times the weight for which Publius Cornelius Rufinus was punished in 275. Moreover, the very competitiveness that had traditionally marked the senatorial aristocracy ensured the spread of cultural innovations and new forms of

Seventeenth-century painter Nicolas Poussin captured the ribald spirit of Bacchic worship in A Bacchanalian Revel before a Herm. National Gallery, London, UK/The Bridgeman Art Library/Getty Images

conspicuous consumption among the elite. In contrast to the austere Cato, other senators laid claim to prestige by collecting Greek art and books brought back by conquering armies, by staging plays modeled on Greek drama, and by commissioning literary works, public buildings, and private sculptural monuments in a Greek style.

Whereas the influence of Greek high culture was felt principally in a small circle of elite Romans who had the wealth to acquire Greek art and slaves and the leisure and education to read Greek authors, the influence of religions from the eastern Mediterranean was perceived as potentially subversive to a far wider audience. Polybius praised the Romans for their conscientious behaviour toward the gods. Romans were famous for their extreme precision in recitation of vows and performance of sacrifices to the gods, meticulously repeating archaic words and actions centuries after their original meanings had been forgotten. Guiding these state cults were priestly colleges, and priestly offices such as of pontifex and augur were filled by senators, whose dominance in politics was thus replicated in civic religion.

In earlier centuries Rome's innate religious conservatism was, however, counterbalanced by an openness to foreign gods and cults. As Rome incorporated new peoples of Italy into its citizen body, it accepted their gods and religious practices. Indeed, among the most authoritative religious texts, consulted in times of crisis or doubt, were the prophetic Sibylline Books, written in Greek and imported from Cumae. The receptivity appears most pronounced in the third century: during its final decades temples were built in the city for Venus Erycina from Sicily and for the Magna Mater, or Great Mother, from Pessinus in Anatolia; games were instituted in honour of the Greek god Apollo (212) and the Magna Mater after the war. The new cults were integrated into the traditional structure of the state religion, and the "foreignness" was controlled (i.e., limits were placed on the orgiastic elements in the cult of the Great Mother performed by her eunuch priests).

The openness, never complete or a matter of principle, tilted toward resistance in the early second century. In 186 Roman magistrates, on orders from the Senate, brutally suppressed Bacchic worship in Italy. Associations of worshipers of the Greek god Bacchus (Dionysus) had spread across Italy to Rome. Their members, numbering in the thousands, were initiated into secret mysteries, knowledge of which promised life after death. They also engaged in orgiastic worship. The secrecy soon gave rise to reports of the basest activities, such as uncontrolled drinking, sexual promiscuity, forgery of wills, and poisoning of kin. According to Livy, more than 7,000 were implicated in the wrongdoing, many of whom were tried and executed. The consuls destroyed the places of Bacchic worship throughout Italy. For the future, the (extant) senatorial decree prohibited men from acting as priests in the cult, banned secret meetings, and required the praetor's and Senate's authorization of ceremonies to be performed by gatherings of more than five people.

The terms of the decree provide a sense of what provoked the harsh senatorial reaction. It was not that the Bacchic cult spread heretical beliefs about the gods; Roman civic religion was never based on theological doctrine with pretensions to exclusive truth. Rather, the growing secret cult led by male priests threatened the traditionally dominant position of senators in state religion. The decree did not aim to eliminate Bacchic worship but to bring it under the supervision of senatorial authorities. The following centuries witnessed sporadic official actions against foreign cults. It happens to be recorded that a praetor of 139 removed private altars built in public areas and expelled astrologers and Jews from the city. Thus the reaction to eastern religions paralleled that to Greek philosoph. Both were perceived as new ways of thinking that threatened to undermine traditional mores and the relations of authority implicit in them.

ECONOMY AND SOCIETY

It seems certain that the economy and society of Italy were transformed in the wake of Rome's conquest of the Mediterranean world, even though the changes can be described only incompletely and imprecisely, owing to the dearth of reliable information for the preceding centuries. Romans of the first century BC believed that their ancestors had been a people of small farmers in an age uncorrupted by wealth. Even senators who performed heroic feats were said to have been of modest means—men such as Lucius Quinctius Cincinatus, who was said to have laid down his plow on his tiny farm to serve as dictator in 458 BC. Although such legends present an idealized vision of early Rome, it is probably true that Latium of the fifth and fourth centuries was densely populated by farmers of small plots. Rome's military strength derived from its superior resources of manpower levied from a pool of small landowning citizens (*assidui*). A dense population is also suggested by the emigration from Latium of scores of thousands as colonists during the fourth and third centuries. The legends of senators working their own fields seem implausible, but the disparity in wealth was probably much less noticeable than in the late republic. The fourth-century artifacts uncovered by archaeologists display an overall high quality that makes it difficult to distinguish a category of luxury goods from the pottery and terracottas made for common use.

War and conquest altered this picture; yet certain fundamental features of the economy remained constant. Until its fall, the Roman Empire retained agriculture as the basis of its economy, with probably four-fifths of the population tilling the soil. This great majority continued to be needed in food production because there were no labour-saving technological breakthroughs. The power driving agricultural and other production was almost entirely supplied by humans and animals, which set modest limits to economic growth. In some areas of Italy, such as the territory of Capena in southern Etruria, archaeologists have found traditional patterns of settlement and land division continuing from the fourth to the end of the first century—evidence that the Second Punic War and the following decades did not bring a complete break with the past.

Economic change came as a result of massive population shifts and the social reorganization of labour rather than technological improvement. The Second Punic War, and especially Hannibal's persistent presence in Italy, inflicted a considerable toll, including loss of life on a staggering scale, movement of rural populations into towns, and destruction of agriculture in some regions. Although the devastation has been overestimated by some historians, partial depopulation of the Italian countryside is evident from the literary and archaeological records: immediately after the war enough land stood vacant in Apulia and Samnium to settle between 30,000 and 40,000 of Scipio's veterans, while areas of Apulia, Bruttium, southern Campania, and south-central Etruria have yielded no artifacts indicating settlement in the postwar period.

Populations have been known to show great resilience in recovering from wars, but the Italian population was given no peace after 201. In subsequent decades Rome's annual war effort required a military mobilization unmatched in history for its duration and the proportion of the population involved. During the 150 years after Hannibal's surrender, the Romans regularly fielded armies of more than 100,000 men, requiring on average about 13 percent of the adult male citizens each year. The attested casualties from 200 to 150 add up to nearly 100,000. The levy took Roman peasants away from their land. Many never returned. Others, perhaps 25,000, were moved in the years before 173 from peninsular Italy to the colonies of the Po valley. Still others, in unknown but considerable numbers, migrated to the cities. By the later second century some Roman leaders perceived the countryside to be depopulated.

To replace the peasants on the land of central and southern Italy, slaves were imported in vast numbers. Slavery was well established as a form of agricultural labour before the Punic Wars (slaves must have produced much of the food during the peak mobilization of citizens from 218 to 201). The scale of slavery, however, increased in the second and first centuries as a result of conquests. Enslavement was a common fate for the defeated in ancient warfare: the Romans enslaved 5,000 Macedonians in 197; 5,000 Histri in 177; 150,000 Epirotes in 167; 50,000 Carthaginians in 146; and in 174 an unspecified number of Sardinians, but

so many that "Sardinian" became a byword for "cheap" slave. These are only a few examples for which the sources happen to give numbers. More slaves flooded into Italy after Rome destabilized the eastern Mediterranean in 167 and gave pirates and bandits the opportunity to carry off local peoples of Anatolia and sell them on the block at Delos by the thousands. By the end of the republic Italy was a thoroughgoing slave society with well over one million slaves, according to the best estimates. No census figures give numbers of slaves, but slaveholding was more widespread and on a larger scale than in the antebellum American South, where slaves made up about one-third of the population. In effect, Roman soldiers fought in order to capture their own replacements on the land in Italy, although the shift from free to servile labour was only a partial one.

The influx of slaves was accompanied by changes in patterns of landownership, as more Italian land came to be concentrated in fewer hands. One of the punishments meted out to disloyal allies after the Second Punic War was confiscation of all or part of their territories. Most of the *ager Campanus* and part of the Tarentines' lands—perhaps two million acres in total—became Roman *ager publicus* (public land), subject to rent. Some of this property remained in the hands of local peoples, but large tracts in excess of the 500-*iugera* limit were occupied by wealthy Romans, who were legally *possessores* (i.e., in possession of the land, although not its owners) and as such paid a nominal rent to the Roman state. The trend toward concentration continued during the second century, propelled by conquests abroad. On the one side, subsistence farmers were always vulnerable in years of poor harvests that could lead to debt and ultimately to the loss of their plots. The vulnerability was exacerbated by army service, which took peasants away from their farms for years at a time. On the other side, the elite orders were enriched by the booty from the eastern kingdoms on a scale previously unimaginable. Some of the vast new wealth was spent on public works and new forms of luxury, and part was invested to secure future income. Land was the preferred form of investment for senators and other honourable men: farming was regarded as safer and more prestigious than manufacture or trade. For senators, the opportunities for trade were limited by the Claudian law of 218 prohibiting them from owning large ships. Wealthy Romans thus used the proceeds of war to buy out their smaller neighbours. As a result of this process of acquisition, most senatorial estates consisted of scattered small farms. The notorious *latifundia*, the extensive consolidated estates, were not widespread. Given the dispersion of the property, the new landlord was typically absentee. He could leave the working of the farms in the hands of the previous peasant owners as tenants, or he could import slaves.

The best insights into the mentality of the estate-owning class of this period come from Cato's *De agricultura*. Although based on Greek handbooks discussing estate management, it reflects the assumptions and thinking of a second-century senator. Cato envisaged a medium-sized, 200-*iugera* farm with a permanent staff of 11 slaves. As with other Roman enterprises, management of the farm was left to a slave bailiff, who was helped by his slave wife. While Cato, like the later agricultural writers Varro and Lucius Junius Columella, assumed the economic advantage of a slave work force, historians today debate whether estates worked by slaves were indeed more profitable than smaller peasant farms. Cato had his slaves use much the same technology as the peasants, although a larger estate could afford large processing implements, such as grape and olive crushers, which peasants might have to share or do without. Nor did Cato bring to bear any innovative management advice; his suggestions aimed to maximize profits by such commonsense means as keeping the slave work force occupied all year round and buying cheap and selling dear. Nevertheless, larger estates had one significant advantage in that the slave labour could be bought and sold and thus more easily matched to labour needs than was possible on small plots worked by peasant families.

Cato's farm was a model representing one aspect of the reality of the Italian countryside. Archaeologists have discovered the villas characteristic of the Catonian estate beginning to appear in Campania in the second century and later in other areas. The emergence of slave agriculture did not exclude the continuing existence in the area of peasants as owners of marginal land or as casual day labourers or both. The larger estates and the remaining peasants formed a symbiotic relationship, mentioned by Cato: the estate required extra hands to help during peak seasons, while the peasants needed the extra wages from day labour to supplement the meagre production of their plots. Yet in many areas of Italy the villa system made no inroads during the republic, and traditional peasant farming continued. Other areas, however, underwent a drastic change: the desolation left by the Second Punic War in the central and southern regions opened the way for wealthy Romans to acquire vast tracts of depopulated land to convert to grazing. This form of extensive agriculture produced cattle, sheep, and goats, herded by slaves. These were the true *latifundia*, decried as wastelands by Roman imperial authors such as the elder Pliny.

The marketplace took on a new importance as both the Catonian estate and the *latifundium* aimed primarily to produce goods to sell for a profit. In this sense, they represented a change from peasant agriculture, which aimed above all to feed the peasant's family. The buyers of the new commodities were the growing cities—another facet of the complex economic transformation. Rome was swelled by migrants from the countryside and became the largest city of preindustrial Europe, with a population of about one million in the imperial era; other Italian cities grew to a lesser extent.

The mass of consumers created new, more diverse demands for foodstuffs from the countryside and also for manufactured goods. The market was bipolar, with the poor of the cities able to buy only basic foodstuffs and a few plain manufactured items and the rich demanding increasingly extravagant luxury goods. The limitations of the poor are reflected in the declining quality of humble temple offerings. The craftsmen and traders produced mainly for the rich minority. The trading and artisanal enterprises in Rome were largely worked by slaves and freedmen imported to Rome by the wealthy. Although honourable, freeborn Romans considered it beneath their dignity to participate directly in these businesses, they willingly shared in the profits through ownership of these slaves and through collection of rents on the shops of humbler men. Thus, manufacturing and trading were generally small-scale operations, organized on the basis of household or family. Roman law did not recognize business corporations with the exception of publican companies holding state contracts; nor were there guilds of the medieval type to organize or control production. Unlike some later medieval cities, Rome did not produce for export to support itself; its revenues came from booty, provincial taxes, and the surplus brought from the countryside to the city by aristocratic Roman landlords. Indeed, after 167 provincial revenues were sufficient to allow for the abolition of direct taxes on Roman citizens.

Building projects were the largest enterprises in Rome and offered freeborn immigrants jobs as day labourers. In addition to the private building needed to house the growing population, the early and middle second century witnessed public building on a new scale and in new shapes. The leading senatorial families gained publicity by sponsoring major new buildings named after themselves in the Forum and elsewhere. The Basilica Porcia (built during Marcus Porcius Cato's censorship of 184), the Basilica Aemilia et Fulvia (179), and the Basilica Sempronia (170–169) were constructed out of the traditional tufa blocks but in a Hellenized style.

New infrastructures were required to bring the necessities of life to the growing population. The Porticus Aemilia (193), a warehouse of 300,000 square feet on the banks of the Tiber, illustrates how the new needs were met with a major new building technology, concrete construction. Around 200 BC in central Italy it was discovered that a wet mixture of crushed stone, lime,

An entablature, or horizontal molding, from the Basilica Aemilia et Fulvia hints at the grandeur of this public building, constructed in 179 BC. Manuel Cohen/Getty Images

and sand (especially a volcanic sand called *pozzolana*) would set into a material of great strength. This construction technique had great advantages of economy and flexibility over the traditional cut-stone technique: the materials were more readily available, the concrete could be molded into desired shapes, and the molds could be reused for repetitive production. The Porticus Aemilia, for example, consisted of a series of roughly identical arches and vaults—the shapes so characteristic of later Roman architecture. The new technology also permitted improvements in the construction of the aqueducts needed to increase the city's water supply.

The economic development outside of Rome encompassed some fairly large-scale manufacturing enterprises and export trade. At Puteoli on the Bay of Naples the ironworks industry was organized on a scale well beyond that of the household, and its goods were shipped beyond the area. Puteoli flourished during the republic as a port city, handling imports destined for Rome as well as exports of manufactured goods and processed agricultural products. In their search for markets, the large Italian landowners exported wine and olive oil to Cisalpine Gaul and more distant locations. Dressel I amphoras, the three-foot pottery jars carrying these products, have been found in substantial quantities in Africa and Gaul. Yet the magnitude of the economic development should not be exaggerated: the ironworks industry was exceptional, and most pottery production continued to be for local use.

SOCIAL CHANGES

Major social changes and dislocations accompanied the demographic shifts and economic development. Relations between rich and poor in Rome had traditionally been structured by the bond existing between patron and client. In the daily morning ritual of the *salutatio*, humble Romans went to pay their respects in the houses of senators, who were obligated to protect them. These personal relationships lent stability to the social hierarchy. In the second century, however, the disparity between rich and poor citizens grew. While this trend increased the personal power of individual senators, it weakened the social control of the elite as a whole; the poor had become too numerous to be controlled by the traditional bond of patron and client.

Until the end of the 170s the impoverishment of humble citizens had been counterbalanced to some extent by the founding of colonies, because dispossessed peasants were given new lands in outlying regions. During the middle decades of the second century, however, colonization ceased, and the number of dispossessed increased, to judge from the declining number of small landowners in the census. The problem created by a growing proletariat was recognized by a few senators. Gaius Laelius, probably during his consulship of 140, proposed a scheme of land redistribution to renew the class of small-holders, but it was rejected by the Senate.

Some of the dispossessed went to Rome, where, together with the increasing numbers of slaves and freedmen, they contributed to the steadily growing population. This density led to the miseries associated with big cities, which were exacerbated by the absence of regulation. By 200 BC the pressure of numbers necessitated apartment buildings of three stories. Constructed without a building code, these structures were often unsound and prone to collapse. Moreover, closely placed and partly made of wood, they were tinderboxes, ever ready to burst into flame. The population density also increased the vulnerability to food shortages and plagues. In 188 fines were levied against dealers for withholding grain, attesting to problems of supply. The 180s and 170s witnessed repeated outbreaks of plague. The state, which could use its power to increase the grain supply, was helpless against diseases. In general, the republican state developed few new institutions to manage the growing urban problems. Until the reign of Augustus, matters were left to the traditional authority of urban magistrates, who were unaided by a standing fire brigade or police force. Consequently, Rome held an increasing potential for social discontent and conflicts without a corresponding increase in means of control.

The family, regarded by Romans as a mainstay of the social order, also was affected by the wider economic and social transformations of the second century BC. In the early republic the family had formed a social, economic, and legal unity. The woman generally married into her husband's family and came under his legal authority (or that of his father if he was still alive), and her dowry merged with the rest of the estate under the ownership of the husband. The husband managed the family's affairs outside the house, while the wife was custodian within. Marriage was an arrangement for life; divorces were rare and granted only in cases of serious moral infractions, such as adultery or wine-tippling on the part of the wife. The children of the couple were subject to the father's nearly absolute legal powers (*patria potestas*), including the power of life and death, corporal punishment, and a monopoly of ownership of all property in the family. The father's power lasted until his death or, in the case of a daughter, until her marriage. When the father died, his sons, his wife, and his unmarried daughters became legally independent, and all inherited equal shares of the family's property unless otherwise specified in a will. The imperial authors idealized the early republic as a time of family harmony and stability, which was lost through the corruption of the later republic.

When family life emerged into the full light of history in the second century BC, it had changed in significant ways. A form of marriage, commonly called "free marriage," was becoming prevalent. Under this form, the wife no longer came into her husband's power or property regime but remained in that of her father; upon her father's death she became independent with rights to own and dispose of property. But she was not a member of the family of her husband and children and had no claim to inheritance from them, even though she lived with them in the same house. Because many women inherited part of their fathers' estates, they could use their independent fortunes to exert influence on husbands, children, and people outside the house. In the same period, divorce became far more common. Moral infractions were no longer needed to justify divorce, which could be initiated by either side. Frequent divorce and remarriage went hand in hand with the separation of marital property. There is plausibility in the suggestion that these changes were brought on by a desire of the women's fathers to avoid having their daughters' portions of the larger family estates slip irrevocably into the hands of their husbands. Although the changes in law and practice were not motivated by any movement to emancipate women, the result was that propertied women of the late republic, always excluded from the public sphere of male citizens, came to enjoy a degree of freedom and social power unusual before the 20th century.

Slaves came to permeate the fabric of family life and altered relationships within the household. They were regularly assigned the tasks of child-rearing, traditionally the domain of the mother, and of education, until then the responsibility of both the father and the mother. Whereas children had acquired the skills needed for their future roles by observing their parents in a kind of apprenticeship, in wealthy houses sons and, to a lesser extent, daughters were now given a specialized education by slaves or freedmen. The management of aristocratic households was entrusted to slaves and freedmen, who served as secretaries, accountants, and managers. The wife was no longer needed as custodian of the household, though domestic guardianship remained an element in the idealization of her role. Later moralists attributed a decline in Roman virtue and discipline to the intrusion of slaves into familial relationships and duties.

ROME AND ITALY

During the middle republic the peoples of Italy began to coalesce into a fairly homogeneous and cohesive society. Polybius, however, does not give insight into this process, because, living in Rome, he too little appreciated the variety of Italian cultures under Roman sway, from the Gallic peoples in the mountains of the north to the urbane Greeks on the southern coasts. Other evidence, though meagre, nonetheless suggests several processes that contributed to the increasing cohesion.

First, the Romans built a network of roads that facilitated communication across Italy. The first great road was the Via Appia, which was laid out by Appius Claudius Caecus in 312 to connect Rome to Capua. Between the First and Second Punic Wars roads were built to the north: the Via Aurelia (241?) along the Tyrrhenian coast, the Via Flaminia (220) through Umbria, and the Via Clodia through Etruria. Then, in the second century, Roman presence in the Po valley was consolidated by the Via Aemilia (187) from Ariminum on the Adriatic coast to the Latin colony of Placentia and by the Via Postumia (148) running through Transpadane Gaul to Aquileia in the east and Genua in the west.

Second, internal migration—Italians moving to Rome and Romans being sent to Latin colonies throughout Italy—promoted social and cultural homogeneity. Some of these colonies were set alongside existing settlements; others were founded on new sites. The colonies re-created the physical and social shape of Rome; the town plans and architecture, with forums including temples to Jupiter, were modeled on those of Rome. The imposition of a Latin colony on the Greek city of Paestum in Lucania (273) entailed the implantation of a Roman-style forum in the centre of the existing city in a way that rudely intruded on the old sanctuary of Hera. The initial system governing the distribution of land to Latin colonists aimed to replicate the Roman social hierarchy differentiated by wealth. It is recorded of the colonists sent to Aquileia in 181 that the 3,000 infantrymen each received 50 *iugera* (31 acres), the centurions 100 *iugera* (62 acres), and

Via Appia, or Appian Way was the first and most famous of the ancient Roman roads, running from Rome to Campania and southern Italy. Shutterstock.com

the cavalrymen 140 *iugera* (86 acres). The unifying effect of the colonies is evident in Paestum's notable loyalty to Rome during the Second Punic War.

Third, although Rome did not seek to govern Italy through a regular administration, it influenced local affairs through formal bonds of personal friendship (*amicitia*) and hospitality (*hospitium*) between the Roman elite and their local counterparts. Through these ties the leading men of Italy were gradually drawn into the ruling class in Rome. The most prominent example of the second century is that of Gaius Marius of Arpinum, who, only two generations after his town had received full citizen rights, began his meteoric senatorial career under the patronage of the great Roman nobles, the Metelli.

Fourth, the regular military campaigns brought together Romans and Italians of all classes under the command of Roman magistrates. The Italian troops appear to have been levied in a fashion similar to the one used for the Romans, which would have required a Roman-style census as a means of organizing the local citizenries. In the absence of direct administration, military service was the context in which Italians most regularly experienced Roman authority.

Fifth, Rome occasionally deployed its troops in Italy to maintain social order. Rome suppressed an uprising of serfs in Etruscan Volsinii in 265 and a sedition in Patavium in 175. When the massive influx of slaves raised the spectre of rebellions across Italy, Roman troops were deployed to put down uprisings: in 195, 5,000 slaves were executed in Latin Setia; in 196 the praetor was sent with his urban legion to Etruria to fight a pitched battle in which many slaves were killed; and the praetor of 185 dealt with rebellious slaves in Apulia, condemning 7,000 to death. The later slave revolt in Sicily (*c.* 135–132) was not contained so effectively and grew to include perhaps 70,000. The slaves defeated the first consular army sent in 134; the efforts of two more consuls were required to restore order. The revolts, unusual for their frequency and size, are not to be explained by abolitionist programs (nonexistent in antiquity) nor by maltreatment. The causes lay in the enslavement and importation of entire communities with their native leadership and in the free reign given to slave shepherds who roamed armed around the countryside serving as communication lines between slave plantations. These uprisings made it clear that the social fabric of Italy, put under stress by the transformations brought about by conquest, had to be protected by Roman force.

While the exercise of Roman authority and force was sometimes resented by Italians, Rome's power made its mores and culture worthy of imitation. The Latin language and Roman political institutions slowly spread. A request from the old Campanian city of Cumae in 180 that it be allowed to change its official language from Oscan to Latin was a sign of things to come.

CHAPTER 3

THE LATE REPUBLIC (133–31 BC)

The fall of Carthage and Corinth did not mark even a temporary end to warfare. War and military glory still were an essential part of the Roman aristocratic ethos and, hence, of Roman political life during the later years of the Roman Republic.

AFTERMATH OF VICTORIES

Apart from major wars still to come, small wars on the frontiers of Roman power—never precisely fixed—continued to provide an essential motive in Roman history: in Spain, Sardinia, Illyria, and Macedonia, barbarians could be defeated and triumphs won. Thus the limits of Roman power were gradually extended and the territories within them pacified, while men of noble stock rivaled the *virtus* of their ancestors and new men staked their own competing claims, winning glory essential to political advancement and sharing the booty with their officers and soldiers. Cicero could still depict it as a major disgrace for Lucius Piso (consul; 58 BC) that he had won no triumph in the traditionally "triumphal" province of Macedonia. Nonetheless, the coincidence of the capture of Corinth and Carthage was even in antiquity regarded as a turning point in Roman history: it was the end (for the time being) of warfare against civilized powers, in which the danger was felt to be greater and the glory and the booty were superior to those won against barbarian tribes.

Changes in Provincial Administration

The first immediate effect was on the administration of the empire. The military basis of provincial administration remained: the governor (as he is called) was in Roman eyes a commander with absolute and unappealable powers over all except Roman citizens, within the limits of the territory (his *provincia*) assigned to him (normally) by the Senate. He was always prepared—and in some provinces expected—to fight and win. But it had been found that those unlimited powers were often abused and that Senate control could not easily be asserted at increasing distances from Rome. For political and perhaps for moral reasons, excessive abuse without hope of a remedy could not be permitted.

Hence, when the decision to annex Carthage and Macedonia had been made in principle (149 BC), a permanent court (the *quaestio repetundarum*) was established at Rome to hear complaints against former commanders and, where necessary, to assure repayment of illegal exactions. No penalty for offenders was provided, and there was no derogation from the commander's powers during his tenure. Nevertheless, the step was a landmark in the recognition of imperial responsibility, and it was also to have important effects on Roman politics.

Another result of the new conquests was a major administrative departure. When Africa and Macedonia became *provinciae* to be regularly assigned to

commanders, it was decided to break with precedent by not increasing the number of senior magistrates (praetors). Instead, prorogation—the device of leaving a magistrate in office *pro magistratu* ("in place of a magistrate") after his term had expired, which had hitherto been freely used when emergencies had led to shortages of regular commanders—was established as part of the administrative system: thenceforth, every year at least two praetors would have to be retained as promagistrates. This was the beginning of the dissociation between urban magistracy and foreign command that was to become a cardinal principle of the system of Sulla and of the developed Roman Empire.

Social and Economic Ills

It is not clear to what extent the temporary end of the age of major wars helped to produce the crisis of the Roman Republic. The general view of thinking Romans was that the relaxation of external pressures led to internal disintegration. (This has happened in other states, and the view is not to be lightly dismissed.) Moreover, the end of large-scale booty led to economic recession in Rome, thus intensifying poverty and discontent. But the underlying crisis had been building up over a long period.

THE REFORM MOVEMENT OF THE GRACCHI (133–121 BC)

From the state's point of view, the chief effect was a decline in military manpower.

The minimum property qualification for service was lowered and the minimum age (17) ignored. Resistance became frequent, especially to the distant and unending guerrilla war in Spain.

THE PROGRAM AND CAREER OF TIBERIUS SEMPRONIUS GRACCHUS

Tiberius Gracchus, grandson of Scipio Africanus and son of the Gracchus who had conquered the Celtiberians and treated them well, was quaestor in Mancinus's army when it faced annihilation. On the strength of his family name, he personally negotiated the peace that saved it. When the Senate—on the motion of his cousin Scipio Aemilianus, who later finished the war—renounced the peace, Tiberius felt aggrieved. He joined a group of senior senators hostile to Aemilianus and with ideas on reform.

Elected tribune for 133, in Scipio's absence, Tiberius attempted to find a solution for the social and military crisis, with the political credit to go to himself and his backers. Tiberius had no intention of touching private property. His idea was to enforce the legal but widely ignored limit of 500 *iugera* (309 acres) on occupation of public land and to use the land thus retrieved for settling landless citizens, who would both regain a secure living and be liable for service. The slave war in Sicily, which had lasted several years and had threatened to spread to Italy, had underlined both the danger of using large numbers of slaves on the land

and the need for a major increase in military citizen manpower.

Tiberius's proposal was bound to meet with opposition in the Senate, which consisted of large landowners. On the advice of his eminent backers, he took his bill, which made various concessions to those asked to obey the law and hand back excess public land, straight to the Assembly of the Plebs, where it found wide support. This procedure was not revolutionary; bills directly concerning the people appear to have been frequently passed in this way. But his opponents persuaded another aristocratic tribune, Marcus Octavius, to veto the bill. Tiberius tried the constitutional riposte—an appeal to the Senate for arbitration. The Senate was unwilling to help, and Octavius was unwilling to negotiate over his veto—an action apparently unprecedented, though not (strictly speaking) unconstitutional. Tiberius had to improvise a way out of the impasse. He met Octavius's action with a similarly unprecedented retort and had Octavius deposed by the Assembly. He then passed his bill in a less conciliatory form and had himself, his father-in-law, and his brother appointed commissioners with powers to determine boundaries of public land, confiscate excess acreage, and divide it in inalienable allotments among landless citizens.

As it happened, envoys from Pergamum had arrived to inform the Senate that Attalus III had died and made the Roman people his heirs (provided the cities of his kingdom were left free). Tiberius, at whose house the envoys were lodging, anticipated Senate debate and had the inheritance accepted by the people and the money used to finance his agrarian schemes.

Tiberius's opponents now charged him with aiming at tyranny, a charge that many may well have believed. Redistribution of land was connected with demagogic tyranny in Hellenistic states, and Tiberius's subsequent actions had been high-handed and beyond the flexible borderline of what was regarded as *mos majorum* (constitutional custom). Fearing prosecution once his term in office was over, he now began to canvass for a second tribunate—another unprecedented act, bound to reinforce fears of tyranny. The elections took place in an atmosphere of violence, with nearly all his tribunician colleagues now opposed to him. When the consul Publius Scaevola, on strict legal grounds, refused to act against him, Publius Scipio Nasica, the chief pontiff, led a number of senators and their clients to the Assembly, and Tiberius was killed in a resulting scuffle. Widespread and bloody repression followed in 132. Thus political murder and political martyrdom were introduced into Roman politics.

The reign of brothers Tiberius and Gaius Gracchus was marked by dissension and charges of tyranny. Réunion des Musées Nationaux/Art Resource, NY

The land commission, however, was allowed to continue because it could not easily be stopped. Some evidence of its activities survives. By 129, perhaps running out of available land held by citizens, it began to apply the Gracchan law to public land held by Italian individuals or communities. This had probably not been envisaged by Tiberius, just as he did not include noncitizens among the beneficiaries of distributions. The Senate, on the motion of Scipio Aemilianus, upheld the Italians' protests, transferring decisions concerning Italian-held land from the commission to a consul. This seriously hampered the commission's activities. Marcus Fulvius Flaccus, chairman of the commission and consul in 125, tried to solve the problem by offering the Italians the citizenship (or alternatively the right to appeal against Roman executive acts to the Roman people) in return for bringing their holdings of public land under the Gracchan law. This aroused fears of uncontrollable political repercussions. Flaccus was ordered by the Senate to fight a war in southern France (where he gained a triumph) and had to abandon his proposal. There is no sign of widespread Italian interest in it at this time, though the revolt of the Latin colony Fregellae (destroyed 125) may be connected with its failure.

THE PROGRAM AND CAREER OF GAIUS SEMPRONIUS GRACCHUS

In 123 Gaius Gracchus, a younger brother of Tiberius, became tribune. He had served on Tiberius's land commission and had supported Flaccus's plan. Making the most of his martyred brother's name, Gaius embarked on a scheme of general reform in which, for the first time in Rome, Greek theoretical influences may be traced. Among many reforms—including provision for a stable and cheap wheat price and for the foundation of colonies (one on the site of Carthage), to which Italians were admitted—two major ideas stand out. The first was to increase public revenues (both from the empire and from taxes) and pass the benefit on to the people. The second was to raise the wealthiest nonsenators (particularly the equites, holders of the "public horse"and next to senators in social standing) to a position from which, without actually taking part in the process of government, they could watch over senatorial administration and make it more responsible. The idea was evoked by Tiberius's death.

As early as 129 a law compelled senators to surrender the "public horse" (which hitherto they had also held) and possibly in other ways enhanced the group consciousness and privileges of the equites. Regarding the increase of public revenue, Gaius put the *publicani* (public contractors, hitherto chiefly concerned with army and building contracts and with farming minor taxes) in charge of the main tax of Asia—a rich province formed out of Attalus's inheritance, which would henceforth provide Rome with the major part of its income. This was expected both to reduce senatorial corruption and to improve efficiency. Gaius also put eminent nonsenators (probably defined by wealth, but perhaps limited to the equites, or equestrian class) in charge of the *quaestio repetundarum*, whose senatorial members had shown too much leniency to their colleagues, and he imposed severe penalties on senators convicted by that court.

Finally, in a second tribunate, he hoped to give citizenship to Latins and Latin rights to other Italians, with the help of Flaccus who, though a distinguished former consul, took the unique step of becoming tribune. But a consul and a tribune of 122 together persuaded the citizen voters that it was against their interests to share the privileges of citizenship: the bill was defeated, and Gaius failed in his attempt to be re-elected once more. In 121, preparing (as private citizens) to use force to oppose the cancellation of some of their laws, Gaius and Flaccus were killed in a riot, and many of their followers were executed.

During the next decade the measures benefiting the people were largely abolished, though the Gracchan land distributions, converted into private property, did temporarily strengthen the Roman citizen peasantry. The provisions giving power to wealthy nonsenators could not be touched, for political

War Against Jugurtha

On the whole, Roman historians were no more interested in internal factional politics than in social or economic developments, so the struggles of the aristocratic families must be pieced together from chance information. It would be mere paradox to deny the importance in republican Rome, as in better known aristocratic republics, of family feuds, alliances, and policies, and parts of the picture are known—e.g., the central importance of the family of the Metelli, prominent in politics for a generation after the Gracchi and dominant for part of that time. In foreign affairs the client kingdom of Numidia—loyal ever since its institution by Scipio Africanus—assumed quite unwarranted importance when a succession crisis developed there soon after 120.

As a bastard, Jugurtha, relying on superior ability and aristocratic Roman connections, sought to oust his two legitimate brothers from their shares of the divided kingdom. Rome's usual diplomatic methods failed to stop Jugurtha from disposing of his brothers, but the massacre of Italian settlers at Cirta by his soldiers forced the Senate to declare war (112).

The war was waged reluctantly and ineffectively, with the result that charges of bribery were freely bandied about by demagogic tribunes taking advantage of suspicion of aristocratic political behaviour that had smoldered ever since the Gracchan crisis. Significantly, some eminent men, hated from those days, were now convicted of corruption. The Metelli, however, emerged unscathed, and Quintus Metellus, consul in 109, was entrusted with the war in Africa. He waged it with obvious competence but failed to finish it, and thus gave Gaius Marius, a senior officer, his chance.

reasons, and they survived as the chief effect of Gaius's tribunates. The court seems to have worked better than before, and, during the next generation, several other standing criminal courts were instituted, as were occasional ad hoc tribunals, always with the same class of jurors. In 106 a law adding senators to the juries was passed, but it remained in force for only a short time.

THE CAREER OF GAIUS MARIUS

Marius, born of an equestrian family at Arpinum, had attracted the attention of Scipio Aemilianus as a young soldier and, by shrewd political opportunism, had risen to the praetorship and married into the patrician family of the Julii Caesares. Though Marius had deeply offended the Metelli, once his patrons, his considerable military talents had induced Quintus Metellus to take him to Africa as a *legatus*. Marius intrigued against his commander in order to gain a consulship; he was elected (chiefly with the help of the equites and antiaristocratic tribunes) for 107 and was given charge of the war by special vote of the people. He did little better than Metellus had, but in 105 his quaestor Lucius Sulla, in delicate and dangerous negotiations, brought about the capture of Jugurtha, opportunely winning the war for Marius and Rome.

During the preceding decade a serious threat to Italy had developed in the north. Starting in 125, several Roman commanders had fought against Ligurian and Gallic tribes in southern France and

had finally established a Roman sphere of influence there. A road had been built linking Italy with Spain, and some garrison posts probably secured it. Finally, a colony was settled at Narbonne, an important road junction (c. 118). But, unwilling to extend administrative responsibilities, the Senate had refused to establish a regular *provincia*. Then some migrating German tribes, chief of them the Cimbri, after defeating a Roman consul, invaded southern France, attracting native sympathy and finding little effective Roman opposition. Two more consular armies suffered defeat, and in October 105 a consul and proconsul with their forces were destroyed at Orange. There was panic in Rome, allayed only by the firm action of the other consul, Publius Rutilius Rufus.

At this moment news of Marius's success in Africa arrived, and he was at once dispensed from legal restrictions and again elected consul for 104. After a brilliant triumph that restored Roman morale, he took over the army prepared and trained by Rutilius. He was reelected consul year after year, while the German tribes delayed attacking Italy. Finally, in 102–101, he annihilated them at Aquae Sextiae (Aix-les-Bains) and, with his colleague, Quintus Catulus, on the Campi Raudii (near the Po delta). Another triumph and a sixth consulship (in 101) were his reward.

In his first consulship, Marius had taken a step of great (and probably unrecognized) importance: aware of the difficulties long endemic in the traditional

Gaius Marius, carried in victory on the shoulders of his troops. Marius capitalized on an impressive war record to win political office, eventually gaining consul status. The Bridgeman Art Library/Getty Images

system of recruitment, he had ignored property qualifications in enrolling his army and, as a result, had recruited ample volunteers among men who had nothing to lose. This radical solution was thenceforth generally imitated, and conscription became confined to emergencies (such as the Social and Civil wars). He also enhanced the importance of the legionary eagle (the standard), thus beginning the process that led to each legion's having a continuing corporate identity. At the same time, Rutilius introduced arms drill and reformed the selection of senior officers. Various tactical reforms in due

course led to the increasing prominence of the cohort (one-tenth of a legion) as a tactical unit and the total reliance on non-Roman auxiliaries for light-armed and cavalry service. The precise development of these reforms cannot be traced, but they culminated in the much more effective armies of Pompey and Caesar.

Marius's African army had been unwilling to engage in another war, and Marius preferred to use newly levied soldiers (no longer difficult to find). But neither he nor the Senate seemed aware of any responsibilities to the veterans. In 103 a tribune, Lucius Saturninus, offered to pass a law providing land in Africa for them in return for Marius's support for some anti-oligarchic activities of his own. Marius agreed, and the large lots distributed to his veterans (both Roman and Italian) turned out to be the beginning of the Romanization of Africa. In 100, with the German wars ended, Saturninus again proved a welcome ally, arranging for the settlement of Marius's veterans in Gaul. An incidental effect was the departure of Marius's old commander and subsequent enemy, Quintus Metellus, who refused to recognize the validity of Saturninus's law and, choosing martyrdom, went into exile. But this time Saturninus exacted a high price. With his ally, the praetor Gaius Glaucia, he introduced laws to gain the favour of plebs and equites and proceeded to provide for the settlement of veterans of wars in Macedonia and Sicily in the same way as for those of Marius's war. He planned to seek reelection for 99, with Glaucia illegally gaining the consulship. Violence and even murder were freely used to accomplish these aims.

Marius now had to make a choice. Saturninus and Glaucia might secure him the continuing favour of the plebs and perhaps the equites, though they might also steal it for themselves. But as the saviour of his country and six times consul, he now hoped to become an elder statesman (*princeps*), accepted and honoured by those who had once looked down on him as an upstart. To this end he had long laboured, dealing out favours to aristocrats who might make useful allies. This was the reward Marius desired for

his achievement; he never thought of revolution or tyranny. Hence, when called on to save the state from his revolutionary allies, he could not refuse. He imprisoned them and their armed adherents and did not prevent their being lynched.

Despite having saved the oligarchy from revolution, he received little reward. He lost the favour of the plebs while the oligarchs, in view of both his birth and his earlier unscrupulous ambition, refused to accept him as their equal. Metellus was recalled. This was a bitter blow to Marius's prestige, and he preferred to leave Rome and visit Asia.

Before long a face-saving compromise was found, and Marius returned; but in the 90s he played no major part. Though he held his own when his friends and clients were attacked in the courts, his old aristocratic protégés now found more promising allies. Sulla is typical: closely associated with Marius in his early career, he was by 91 ready to take the lead in attacking Marius and (significantly) found eager support. The oligarchy could not forgive Marius.

EVENTS IN ASIA

In foreign affairs, the 90s were dominated by Asia, Rome's chief source of income. Mithradates VI, king of Pontus, had built a large empire around the Black Sea and was probing and intriguing in the Roman sphere of influence. Marius had met him and had given him a firm warning, which was temporarily effective. Mithradates had proper respect for Roman power.

Scheming to annex Cappadocia, he had been thwarted by the Senate's instructing Sulla, as proconsul, to install a pro-Roman king there in 96–95. (It was on this occasion that Sulla received a Parthian embassy—the first contact between the two powers.) But dissatisfaction in the Roman province of Asia gave new hope to Mithradates. Ineffectively organized after annexation and corrupt in its cities' internal administration, it was soon overrun with Italian businessmen and Roman tax collectors. When the Senate realized the danger, it sent its most distinguished jurist, Quintus Mucius Scaevola (consul in 95 and *pontifex maximus*), on an unprecedented mission to reorganize Asia (94).

Scaevola took Publius Rutilius Rufus—jurist, stoic philosopher, and former consul—with him as his senior officer, and after Scaevola's return, Rutilius remained behind, firmly applying the new principles they had established. This caused an outcry from businessmen, whose profits Scaevola had kept within bounds; he was prosecuted for "extortion" in 92 and convicted after a trial in which Roman *publicani* and businessmen unscrupulously used their power among the class that provided criminal juries. The verdict revealed the breakdown of Gaius Gracchus's system: The class he had raised to watch over the Senate now held irresponsible power, making orderly administration impossible and endangering the empire. Various leading senators were at once vexatiously prosecuted, and political chaos threatened.

DEVELOPMENTS IN ITALY

The 90s also saw dangerous developments in Italy. In the second century BC, Italians as a whole had shown little desire for Roman citizenship and had been remarkably submissive under exploitation and ill treatment. The most active of their governing class flourished in overseas business, and the more traditionally minded were content to have their oligarchic rule supported by Rome. Their admission to citizenship had been proposed as a by-product of the Gracchan reforms.

By 122 it had become clear that the Roman people agreed with the oligarchy in rejecting it. The sacrifices demanded of Italy in the Numidian and German wars probably increased dissatisfaction among Italians with their patently inferior status. Marius gave citizenship to some as a reward for military distinction—illegally, but his standing (*auctoritas*) sufficed to defend his actions. Saturninus admitted Italians to veteran settlements and tried to gain citizenship for some by full admission to Roman colonies. The censors of 97–96, aristocrats connected with Marius, shared his ideas and freely placed eminent Italians on the citizen registers. This might have allayed dissatisfaction, but the consuls of 95 passed a law purging the rolls and providing penalties for those guilty of fraudulent arrogation. The result was insecurity and danger for many leading Italians. By 92 there was talk of violence and conspiracy among desperate men.

It was in these circumstances that the eminent young noble, Marcus Livius Drusus, became tribune for 91 and hoped to solve the menacing accumulation of problems by means of a major scheme of reforms. He attracted the support of the poor by agrarian and colonial legislation and tried to have all Italians admitted to citizenship and to solve the jury problem by a compromise: the courts would be transferred to the Senate, and 300 equites would be admitted to it. (To cope with the increase in business it would need this expansion in size.)

Some leading senators, frightened at the dangerous situation that had developed, gave weighty support. Had Drusus succeeded, the poor and the Italians might have been satisfied; the equites, deprived of their most ambitious element by promotion, might have acquiesced; and the Senate, always governed by the prestige of the noble *principes* rather than by votes and divisions, could have returned, little changed by the infusion of new blood, to its leading position in the process of government. But Drusus failed. Some members of each class affected were more conscious of the loss than of the gain, and an active consul, Lucius Philippus, provided leadership for their disparate opposition. After much violence, Drusus's laws were declared invalid. Finally, he himself was assassinated. The Italians now rose in revolt (the Social War), and in Rome a special tribunal, manned by the Gracchan jury class, convicted many of Drusus's supporters until the Senate succeeded in suspending its sittings because of the military danger.

The first year of the Social War (90) was dangerous. The tribes of central and southern Italy, traditionally among the best soldiers in Rome's wars, organized in a confederacy for the struggle that had been forced upon them. Fortunately all but one of the Latin cities—related to Rome by blood and tradition and specially favoured by Roman law—remained loyal. Their governing class had for some time had the privilege of automatically acquiring Roman citizenship by holding local office. Moreover, Rome now showed its old ability to act quickly and wisely in emergencies: the consul Lucius Caesar passed a law giving citizenship to all Italians who wanted it. The measure came in time to head off major revolts in Umbria and Etruria, which accepted at once.

CIVIL WAR AND THE RULE OF LUCIUS SULLA

In 89 BC the war in central Italy was won, and Gnaeus Pompeius Strabo celebrated a triumph. Attention now turned to the East, where Mithradates had taken advantage of Rome's troubles to expel the kings of Cappadocia and Bithynia. A Roman embassy restored them, and he withdrew. However, when the envoys incited Bithynian incursions into his territory, Mithradates launched a major offensive; he overran the two kingdoms and invaded Roman territory, where he attracted the sympathy of the natives by executing thousands of Italians and defeating and capturing the Roman commanders in the area.

In Rome, various men, including Marius, had hoped for the Eastern command. But it went to Lucius Sulla, elected consul for 88 after distinguished service in the Social War. Publius Sulpicius, a tribune in that year and an old friend of Drusus, tried to continue the latter's policy of justice to the Italians by abolishing the gerrymandering that in practice deprived the new citizens of an effective vote. Finding the oligarchy firmly opposed, he gained the support of Marius (who still commanded much loyalty) for his plans by having the Eastern command transferred to him. After much street-fighting, the consuls escaped from Rome, and Sulpicius's bills were passed.

Sulla's response was totally unforeseen. He appealed to the army he had led in the Social War, which was still engaged in mopping-up operations in Campania, and persuaded them to march on Rome. He occupied the city and executed Sulpicius; Marius and others escaped. Significantly, Sulla's officers left him. It was the first time a private army of citizens had occupied Rome—an effect of Marius's army reform, which had ended by creating a "client army" loyal chiefly to its commander, and of the Social War, which had made the use of force within Italy seem commonplace. The end of the republic was foreshadowed.

Having cowed Rome into acquiescence and having passed some legislation, Sulla left for the East. Cinna, one of the consuls of 87, at once called for the overthrow of Sulla's measures. Resisted by his colleague Octavius, he left Rome to collect an army and, with the help of Marius, occupied the city after a siege. Several leading men were killed or condemned to death, Sulla and his supporters were outlawed, and (after Marius's death early in 86) another commander was sent to Asia. The policy now changed to one of reconciliation: the Social War was wound up, and the government gained wide acceptance until Cinna was killed by mutinous soldiers (84).

Sulla meanwhile easily defeated Mithradates' forces in two battles in Boeotia, took Athens, which under a revolutionary regime had declared for Mithradates, and cleared the king's army out of Greece. While negotiating with Cinna's government, Sulla also entered upon negotiations with Mithradates and, when he heard of Cinna's death, quickly made peace and an alliance with Mithradates, driving the government's commander in Asia to suicide. After wintering his troops in the rich cities of Asia, Sulla crossed into Greece and then into Italy, where his veteran army broke all resistance and occupied Rome (82). Sulla was elected dictator and, while Italy and all the provinces except Spain were quickly reduced, began a reign of terror (the "proscriptions"), in which hundreds of his enemies or those of his adherents were killed without trial, while their property went to enrich him and his friends. Wherever in Italy he had met resistance, land was expropriated and given to his soldiers for settlement.

While the terror prevailed, Sulla used his powers to put through a comprehensive program of reform (81). Although he had twice taken Rome with a private proletarian army, he had earlier had connections with the inner circles of the oligarchy, and after Cinna's death some eminent men who had refused to collaborate with Cinna joined Sulla. By the time Sulla's success seemed certain, even most of those who had collaborated were on his side, and he was acclaimed as the defender of the nobility who had defeated an illegal revolutionary regime. His reforms aimed chiefly at stabilizing Senate authority by removing alternative centres of power.

The tribunate was emasculated, the censors' powers were reduced, provincial governors were subjected to stricter Senate control, and the equites, who had been purged of Sulla's opponents by the proscriptions, were deprived of some symbols of dignity and made leaderless by the inclusion of 300 of Sulla's chief supporters in the Senate. The jury reform of Gaius Gracchus, seen by some leading senators as the prime cause of political disintegration, could now be undone, and the criminal courts could once more become a monopoly of senators.

Sulla's measures were by no means merely reactionary. His program was basically that of Marcus Drusus. His overriding aim was the restoration of stable government, and this could only come from the Senate, directed by the *principes* (former consuls and those they chose to consult). Sulla accepted and even extended recent developments where they seemed useful: the Italians retained full citizenship; the system of standing criminal courts was expanded; the practice of praetors normally spending their year of office in Rome and then going to provinces for a second year was extended to consuls and became an integral part of his system. To prevent long command of armies (which might lead to careers like his own), Sulla increased the number of praetors so that, in principle and in normal circumstances, each province might have a new governor every year. As for the overriding problem of poverty, his contribution to solving it was to settle tens of thousands of his veterans on land confiscated from enemies in Italy; having become landowners, the veterans would be ready to defend the social order, in which they now had a stake, against the dispossessed.

At the beginning of 80 Sulla laid down his dictatorship and became merely consul, with the senior Metellus (Quintus Metellus Pius), a relative of his wife, as his colleague. The state of emergency was officially ended. At the end of the year, after seeing to the election of two reliable consuls, Sulla retired to Campania as a private citizen; he hoped that the restored oligarchy would learn to govern the state he had handed over to them. In 78 Marcus Lepidus, an ambitious patrician whom Sulla disliked and distrusted, was elected consul. Sulla did not intervene. Within a few months, Sulla was dead. Lepidus at once attacked his system, using the grievances of the

After initiating sweeping reforms—some wrought by force and bloodshed—Sulla voluntarily gave up his dictatorship and receded from public life. Hulton Archive/ Getty Images

hatred because of cold-blooded duplicity during the troubles of 88 and 87. After Strabo's death, young Pompey, who had served under him and inherited his dubiously won wealth, was protected by Cinna's government against his father's enemies. Following in his father's footsteps, he deserted the government after Cinna's death, raised a force among his father's veterans in central Italy, and helped to conquer Italy and, in a lightning campaign, Sicily and the province of Africa for Sulla. Although not old enough to hold any regular magistracy (he was born in 106), he had, from these military bases, blackmailed Sulla into granting him a triumph (81) and had married into the core of the Sullan oligarchy. Out of pique against Sulla, he had supported Lepidus's election for 78, but he had too great a stake in the Sullan system to permit Lepidus to overthrow it.

Meanwhile a more serious challenge to the system had arisen in Iberia. Quintus Sertorius, a former praetor of tough Sabine gentry stock, had refused to follow most of his social betters in joining Sulla; instead he had left for Spain, where he claimed to represent the legitimate government. Although acting throughout as a Roman proconsul, with a "counter-Senate" of eminent Roman citizens, Sertorius won

expropriated as a rallying cry and his province of Gaul as a base. But he was easily defeated by his former colleague Quintus Catulus, assisted by young Gnaeus Pompeius (Pompey).

THE EARLY CAREER OF POMPEY

Pompey was the son of Gnaeus Pompeius Strabo, who had triumphed after the Social War but had incurred general the enthusiastic support of the native population by his fairness, honesty, and charisma, and he soon held most of the Iberian Peninsula, defending it successfully even against a large force under Quintus Metellus Pius. When the consuls of 77 would have nothing to do with this war, Pompey was entrusted by the Senate, through the efforts of his eminent friends and sponsors, with the task of assisting Metellus. The war dragged on for years, with little glory for the Roman commanders. Although Sertorius had many sympathizers in Italy, superior numbers and resources finally wore him down, and he was assassinated by a Roman officer. Pompey easily defeated the remnants of Sertorius's forces in 72.

The death of Nicomedes IV of Bithynia (74) led to another major war. Like Attalus of Pergamum, Nicomedes left his kingdom to Rome, and this provoked Mithradates, who was in contact with Sertorius and knew of Rome's difficulties, to challenge Rome again. The Eastern command again led to intrigues in Rome. The command finally went to Lucius Lucullus, a relative of Sulla and consul in 74, who hoped to build up a countervailing power in the East.

At the same time, Marcus Antonius, father of the later Triumvir, was given a

Early in his career, during his joint consulate with Crassus, the great statesman and general Pompey managed to substantially repeal Sulla's political reforms. Pompey was first an associate, then an opponent, of Julius Caesar. Hulton Archive/Getty Images

command against the pirates in the eastern Mediterranean (whom his father had already fought in 102–100), partly, perhaps, as further reinsurance against Pompey. With Italian manpower heavily committed, a minor slave rising led by Spartacus (73) assumed threatening dimensions, until Marcus Crassus (an old

Sullan and profiteer in the proscriptions) volunteered to accept a special command and defeated the slaves. At this point (71) Pompey returned from Spain with his army, crucified the remnants of the slave army, and claimed credit for the victory.

POMPEY AND CRASSUS

Pompey and Crassus now confronted each other, each demanding the consulship for 70, though Pompey had held no regular magistracy and was not a senator. Agreeing to join forces, both secured it.

During their consulship, the political, though not the administrative, part of the Sullan settlement was repealed. The tribunes' powers were fully restored, criminal juries were divided between senators and wealthy nonsenators, and, for the first time since Sulla, two censors—both supporters of Pompey—were elected. The censors purged the Senate and, in compiling the registers, at last fully implemented the Italians' citizenship.

The year 70 also saw the prosecution of Verres (son of a "new man" and Sullan profiteer), who had surpassed the liberal Roman conventions in exploiting his province of Sicily. For future impunity he relied on his aristocratic connections (especially the Metelli and their friends), his fortune, and the known corruptibility of the Sullan senatorial juries. But Verres was unlucky. First, he had ill-treated some of Pompey's important Sicilian clients, thus incurring Pompey's displeasure. Next, his case coincided with the anti-Sullan reaction of 70. Finally, the Sicilians succeeded in persuading Cicero—an ambitious young "new man" from Arpinum hoping to imitate the success of his fellow citizen Marius by means of his rhetorical ability—to undertake the prosecution. Despite obstruction from Verres' friends, Cicero collected massive evidence against him, presented his case to fit into the political context of the year, and obtained Verres' conviction as an act of expiation for the shortcomings of the Sullan order.

The year 70 thus marked the loss of control by the Sullan establishment. The nobility (families descended from consuls) continued to gain most of the consulships, with the old patriciate (revived by Sulla after a long decline) stronger than for generations. The Senate still supervised administration and made ordinary political decisions, and the system continued to rely essentially on *mos majorum* (constitutional custom) and *auctoritas* (prestige)—potent forces in the status society of the Roman Republic. The solid bases of law and power that Sulla had tried to give it had been surrendered, however. The demagogue—tribune or consul—could use the legal machinery of the popular assembly (hence such men are called *populares*), while the commander could rely on his army in the pursuit of private ambition. The situation that Sulla had tried to remedy now recurred, made worse by his intervention. His massacres and proscriptions had weeded out the defenders of lawful government, and his rewards had gone to the timeservers and the unscrupulous. The large infusion of equites into the Senate had intensified the effect. While eliminating the serious friction between the two classes, which had made the state ungovernable by 91, it had filled the Senate with men whose tradition was the opposite of that sense of mission and public service that had animated the best of the aristocracy. Few men in the new ruling class saw beyond self-interest and self indulgence.

One result was that massive bribery and civil disorder in the service of ambition became endemic. Laws were repeatedly passed to stop them, but they remained ineffective because few found it in their interest to enforce them. Exploitation of the provinces did not decrease after Verres. Governors (still with unlimited powers) feathered their own nests and were expected to provide for all their friends. Extortion cases became a political ritual, with convictions impossible to obtain. Cicero, thenceforth usually counsel for the defense, presented hair-raising behaviour as commonplace and claimed it as acceptable. The Senate's traditional opposition to annexation faded out. Pompey made Syria into a province and added a large part of Pontus to Bithynia (inherited in 74 and occupied in 70). The demagogue Clodius annexed Cyprus—driving its king to suicide—to pay for his massive grain distributions in Rome. Caesar, finally, conquered Gaul by open aggression and genocide and bled it white for the benefit of his friends and his ambitions. Crassus would have done the same with Parthia, had he succeeded.

Opposition to all this in the Senate, where it appeared, was based on personal or political antagonism. If the robber barons were attacked on moral grounds, it was because of the use they made of their power in Rome.

Politically, the 60s lay under the shadow of Pompey. Refusing to take an ordinary province in 69, he waited for his chance. It came in 67 when his adherent Gabinius, as tribune, secured him, against the opposition of all important men, an extraordinary command with unprecedented powers to deal with the pirates. Pompey succeeded within a few months where Antonius and others had failed. The equites and the people were delighted because trade, including Rome's food imports, would now be secure. Meanwhile Lucullus had driven Mithradates out of Anatolia and into Armenia; but he had offended Roman businessmen by strict control and his own soldiers and officers by strict discipline. Faced with mutinies, he suffered a reverse and became vulnerable to attacks in Rome. In 66 another tribunician law appointed Pompey, fresh from his naval victories, to take over supreme command in the East, which he did at once, studiously insulting his predecessor. He quickly defeated Mithradates and procured his death, then spent some time in a total reorganization of the East, where Asia (the chief source of revenue) was protected by three further provinces and a ring of client states beyond the frontier. The whole of the East now stood in his *clientela* (clientship), and most of it owed him money as well. He returned by far the wealthiest man in Rome.

POLITICAL SUSPICION AND VIOLENCE

Meanwhile Roman politics had been full of suspicion and violence, much of it stirred up by Crassus who, remembering 71, feared Pompey's return and tried to make his own power impregnable. There was much material for revolution, with poverty (especially in the country, among families dispossessed by Sulla) and debt (among both the poor and the dissolute rich) providing suitable issues for unscrupulous *populares*. One such man, the patrician Catiline, after twice failing to gain the consulship by traditional bribery and intrigue, put himself at the head of a movement planning a coup d'état in Rome to coincide with an armed rising in Italy (late 63). Cicero, as consul, defeated these efforts and, relying on the doubtful legality of a Senate vote in support, had Catiline's eminent Roman associates executed. Catiline himself fell in a desperate battle.

For Cicero—the "new man" who had made his way to the top by his own oratorical and political skill, obliging everyone by unstinting service, representing Pompey's interests in Rome while avoiding offense to Pompey's enemies—this was the climax of his life. Like his compatriot Marius, he had saved the state for its rulers: he had taken resolute action when those rulers were weak and vacillating; and, like Marius, he got small thanks

for it. Pompey was miffed at having to share his fame with a municipal upstart, and eminent gentlemen could not forgive that upstart for having driven patricians to their death.

Pompey's return was peaceful. Like Marius, he wanted recognition, not tyranny. He dismissed his army, to the surprise of Crassus and others, and basked in the glory of his triumph and the honours voted to him. But having given up power, he found himself caught in a net of constitutional obstruction woven by his politically experienced enemies and was unable to have either of his principal demands met: land for his veterans and the ratification of his arrangements in the East. It was at this point that Caesar returned from Spain.

Gaius Julius Caesar, descended (as he insisted) from kings and gods, had shown talent and ambition in his youth: he opposed Sulla but without inviting punishment, married into the oligarchy but advocated popular causes, vocally defended Pompey's interests while aiding Crassus in his intrigues and borrowing a fortune from him, flirted with Catiline but refused to dabble in revolution, then worked to save those whom Cicero executed. In 63 he won a startling success: defeating two distinguished *principes*, he, who had not yet been praetor, was elected *pontifex maximus*—a post of supreme dignity, power, and patronage. Despite some cynicism among Roman aristocrats toward the state religion, its ceremonial was kept up and was a recognized means of political manipulation;

surplus sufficient to pay off his debts. On returning to Rome, he naturally hoped for the consulship of 59; but his enemies, by legal chicanery, forced him to choose between standing for office and celebrating a triumph. He gave up the triumph and easily became consul.

THE FINAL COLLAPSE OF THE ROMAN REPUBLIC (59–44 BC)

For his consulship Caesar fashioned an improbable alliance. His skill in having won the trust of both Crassus and Pompey enabled him to unite these two enemies in his support. Crassus had the connections, Pompey had the soldiers' vote, and Caesar was consul and *pontifex maximus*.

The combination that Caesar had fashioned (often misleadingly called the "first Triumvirate") was invincible, especially since the consul Caesar had no scruples about countering legal obstruction with open force. Pompey got what he wanted, as did Crassus, whose immediate need was a concession to the Asian tax farmers, in whose companies he probably had much of his capital. In return, Caesar got a special command in Cisalpine Gaul and Illyricum for five years by vote of the people; the

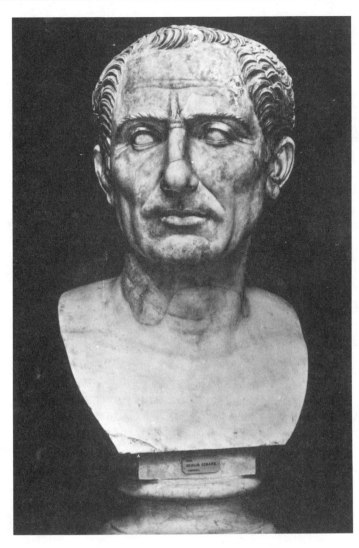

Julius Caesar is credited with laying the foundations for the Roman imperial system and changing the course of Greco-Roman history. Hulton Archive/Getty Images

thus priesthoods could give more lasting power than magistracies, in addition to the cachet of social success. Young Caesar was now head of the hierarchy. After his praetorship (62), Caesar successfully governed Spain, clearing a

Senate itself, on Pompey's motion, extended it to Transalpine Gaul. Marriage alliances sealed the compact, chief of them Pompey's marriage to Caesar's daughter Julia.

Caesar left for Gaul, but Rome was never the same. The shadow of the alliance hung over it, making the old-style politics impossible. In 58 Publius Clodius, another aristocratic demagogue, was tribune and defended Caesar's interests. Cicero had incurred Clodius's enmity and was now sacrificed to him: he was driven into exile as having unlawfully executed citizens in 63. By 57 Caesar's allies had drifted back into rivalry. Pompey secured Cicero's return, and Cicero at once tried to break up the alliance by attracting Pompey to the Senate's side. Just when he seemed about to succeed, the three dynasts secretly met and revived their compact (56). Rome had to bow once more.

In 55 Pompey and Crassus were consuls, and the contents of their secret agreement were slowly revealed. Caesar, whom his enemies had made efforts to recall, was prolonged in his command for five years and (it later appeared) had been promised another consulship straight after, to secure him against prosecution and give him a chance of another army command. Pompey was given a special command over all of Spain, which he exercised through deputies while he himself remained just outside Rome to keep an eye on the city. Crassus, who now needed glory and new wealth to equal those of his allies, was to attack Parthia

with a large army. Thus the three dynasts would practically monopolize military power for the foreseeable future.

Cicero, among others, had to submit and was thenceforth their loyal spokesman. After his achievement of 63 he had dreamed of leading a coalition of all "right-thinking" men in Italy in defending the traditional oligarchy, but he had found little support among the oligarchy. He now used this fact to rationalize his surrender. His brother took service in Gaul under Caesar.

The dynasts' pact did not even bring peace. Clodius, as tribune, had created a private army, and there was no state force to counter it. Pompey could have done it by calling his soldiers in, but the Senate did not trust him enough to request this, and Pompey did not wish to parade himself as an unashamed tyrant. Other men formed private armies in opposition to Clodius, and one Milo at last managed to have him killed after a scuffle (52). By then, however, Roman politics had radically and unexpectedly changed.

POLITICAL MANEUVERS

Julia died in 54, breaking the ties between Caesar and Pompey. Caesar pressed Pompey to renew them, but Pompey held off, preserving his freedom of action. Crassus's Parthian campaign ended in disaster and in Crassus's death (53). By 52 Pompey and Caesar stood face to face, still nominally friends but with no personal link between them and no common interests. Caesar, by conquering the whole of Gaul, had almost equaled Pompey's prestige and, by his utterly ruthless way of waging war, Pompey's wealth. Unlike Pompey, he used his wealth to dispense patronage and buy useful friends.

At this point Pompey cautiously offered the oligarchy his support. It had much to give him that he wanted—control of the administrative machine, respectability, and the seal of public approval. Its leaders (even the intransigent young Cato, who had led opposition to the three individually long before their alliance and to their joint oppression of the state ever since) now recognized that acceptance of Pompey's terms and surrender to his protection was their only chance of survival. Pompey at once turned firmly against Milo, who presented a political threat. If Milo could use the force that had killed Clodius to keep firm control of Rome, he—an ambitious man of known conservative views—might in due course offer an alternative and more trustworthy champion to the oligarchy.

But he was not yet ready. Pompey forced them to make their choice at once, and they chose Pompey in preference. He was made sole consul and had Milo convicted by an intimidated court. Meanwhile he had made a marriage alliance with the noblest man in Rome, Quintus Metellus Scipio, who became his colleague in the consulship. The state had captured Pompey (or vice versa), and Caesar stood alone in opposition to both of them. During the next two years there were a series of maneuvers. The Senate leaders,

with Pompey's silent support, worked for Caesar's recall, which would have meant his instantly sharing the fate of Milo, while Caesar and his agents in Rome tried to strike some bargain that would ensure his safety and his future in politics. Finally, Pompey declared himself, and, early in 49, the Senate voted to outlaw Caesar. Two tribunes supporting him (one of them Mark Antony) had to flee. By the time they reached him, Caesar had already crossed the Rubicon: he now had a cause.

CIVIL WAR

Pompey had exuded confidence over the outcome if it came to war. In fact, however, Caesar's veterans were unbeatable, and both men knew it. To the disgust of his followers, Pompey evacuated Rome, then Italy. His plan was to bottle Caesar up in Italy and starve him out. But Caesar, in a lightning sweep, seized Massilia and Spain from Pompey's commanders, then crossed into Greece, where a short campaign ended in Pompey's decisive defeat at Pharsalus (48). Pompey fled to Egypt, where he was assassinated by a man hoping thus to curry Caesar's favour. This was by no means the end of the war. Almost at once Caesar was nearly trapped at Alexandria, where he had intervened in a succession dispute; but he escaped and installed Cleopatra on the throne, for personal as well as political reasons. In Africa the Pompeian forces and their native allies were not defeated until Caesar himself moved against them and annihilated them at Thapsus. Cato, disdaining the victor's pardon, committed suicide at Utica (46). In Spain, where Pompey's name was still powerful, his sons organized a major rising, which Caesar himself again had to defeat at Munda (45) in the bloodiest battle of the war. By the time he returned, he had only a few months to live.

THE DICTATORSHIP AND ASSASSINATION OF CAESAR

In Rome the administrative machine had inevitably been disrupted, and Caesar had always remained in control, as consul or as dictator. Those who had feared proscriptions, or hoped for them, were proved wrong. Some of Caesar's enemies had their property confiscated, but it was sold at fair value; most were pardoned and suffered no loss. One of these was Cicero, who, after much soul-searching, had followed his conscience by joining Pompey before Pharsalus.

Poverty and indebtedness were alleviated, but there was no wholesale cancellation of debts or redistribution of property, and many of Caesar's adherents were disappointed. Nor was there a general reform of the republic. (Caesar's only major reform was of the calendar; indeed, the Julian calendar proved adequate for centuries.) The number of senators and magistrates was increased, the citizenship was more freely given, and the province of Asia was relieved of some of its tax burden. But Caesar had no plan for reforming the system—not even to the extent that Sulla had tried to do, for Sulla had at least

planned for his own retirement. For a time, honourable men, such as Cicero, hoped that the "Dictator for Settling the Constitution" (as Caesar called himself) would produce a real constitution—some return to free institutions. By late 45 that hope was dead. Caesar was everywhere, doing everything to an almost superhuman degree. He had no solution for the crisis of the republic except to embody it in himself and none at all for the hatred of his peers, which he knew this was causing. He began to accept more and more of the honours that a subservient Senate invidiously offered, until finally he reached a position perilously close to kingship (an accursed term in Rome) and even deification.

Whether he passed those hazy boundary lines is much debated and not very important. He had put himself in a position in which no Roman ought to have been and which no Roman aristocrat could tolerate. As a loyal friend of his was later to say: "With all his genius, he saw no way out." To escape the problem or postpone it, he prepared for a Parthian war to avenge Crassus—a project most likely to have ended in similar disaster. Before he could start on it, about 60 men—former friends and old enemies, honourable patriots and men with grievances—struck him down in the Senate on March 15, 44 BC.

THE TRIUMVIRATE AND OCTAVIAN'S ACHIEVEMENT OF SOLE POWER

Brutus and Cassius, the organizers of the conspiracy, expected all Romans to

Caesar was launching a series of political and social reforms when he was assassinated by a group of nobles in the Senate House on March 15—the infamous Ides of March. Hulton Archive/Getty Images

rejoice with them in the rebirth of "freedom." But to the Roman people the freedom of the governing class had never meant very much. The armies (especially in the west) were attached to Caesar and the Senate was full of Caesarians at all levels, cowed but biding their time. Mark Antony, the surviving consul whom Brutus had been too scrupulous to assassinate with his master, gradually gained control of the city and the official machinery, and the "liberators" withdrew to the East.

But a challenger for the position of leader of the Caesarians soon appeared in the person of Octavian, Caesar's son by adoption and now his heir. Although not yet 20, Octavian proved an accomplished politician. He attracted loyalty as a Caesarian while cooperating against Antony with the Senate, which, under Cicero's vigorous leadership, now turned against the consul. Cicero hoped to fragment and thus defeat the Caesarian party, with the help of Brutus and Cassius, who were making good progress in seizing control of the eastern provinces and armies. In 43 the two consuls (both old Caesarian officers) and Octavian defeated Antony at Mutina, and success seemed imminent. But the consuls died, and

Octavian demanded and, by armed force, obtained the consulship.

The armies of Italy, Spain, and Gaul soon showed that they would not fight against one another. Octavian, Antony, and Lepidus (the senior Caesarian with an army) now had themselves appointed "Triumvirs for Settling the Constitution" for five years and secured control of Italy by massive proscriptions and confiscations (Cicero, Antony's chief enemy, was among the first to die). They then defeated and killed Brutus and Cassius at Philippi (42) and divided the Roman world among themselves, with Lepidus, a weak man accidentally thrust into prominence, getting the smallest share. Octavian, who was to control Italy, met armed opposition from Antony's brother and wife, but they got no help from Antony and were defeated at Perusia (41).

Octavian and Antony sealed their alliance with a marriage compact. Antony married Octavia, Octavian's sister. Octavian then confronted Pompey's son Sextus Pompeius, who had seized control of the islands off Italy. After much diplomatic maneuvering (including another meeting with Antony), Octavian attacked and defeated Sextus; when Lepidus tried to reassert himself, Octavian crushed him and stripped him of his office of Triumvir (while with conspicuous piety leaving him the chief pontificate, now an office without power). Octavian now controlled the West and Antony the East, still officially as Triumvirs (their term of office had been

extended), even though Lepidus had been eliminated in 36.

Each of the two leaders embarked on campaigns and reorganization in his half—Octavian in Illyricum, Antony particularly on the Parthian frontier. But Antony now married Cleopatra and tried to make Egypt his military and political base. In a war of propaganda, Octavian gradually convinced the western provinces, Italy, and most of the Roman upper class that Antony was sacrificing Roman interests, trying to become a Hellenistic king in Alexandria, and planning to rule the Roman world from there with Cleopatra. In 32, though he now held no legal position, Octavian intimidated most of Antony's remaining aristocratic friends into joining him, made the whole West swear allegiance to himself, and in 31, as consul, crossed into Greece to attack Antony. On September 2 he defeated Antony and Cleopatra in a naval battle at Actium. Although in itself not a major victory, it was followed by the disintegration of Antony's forces, and Antony and Cleopatra finally committed suicide in Alexandria (30).

INTELLECTUAL LIFE OF THE LATE REPUBLIC

The late Roman Republic, despite its turmoil, was a period of remarkable intellectual ferment. Many of the leading political figures were men of serious intellectual interests and literary achievement; foremost among them were Cicero,

Caesar, Cato, Pompey, and Varro, all of them senators. The political upheaval itself leavened intellectual life; imperial senators were to look back to the late republic as a time when great political struggles stimulated great oratory, something the more ordered world of the emperors could no longer do.

The seeds of intellectual development had been sown in the late third and early second centuries; the flowering came in the last generation of the republic. As late as the 90s BC the Romans still appear relatively unsophisticated. Greek intellectuals were absorbed in debates among themselves, giving only passing nods to Romans by dedicating untechnical works to them. In 92 the censors issued an edict closing down the schools of Latin rhetoric in Rome. Serious students such as Cicero had to go east in the 80s to receive their higher education from leading Greek philosophers and rhetoricians.

The centre of intellectual life began to shift toward the West after the 90s. As a result of the Mithradatic wars, libraries were brought from the East to Italy. The Hellenistic kingdoms, which had provided the patronage for much intellectual activity, were dismantled by Pompey and Octavian, and Greek intellectuals increasingly joined the retinues of great Roman senators such as Pompey. Private Roman houses, especially senatorial villas on the Bay of Naples, became the focus of intellectual life; it was there that libraries were reassembled and Greek teachers kept as dependents.

Roman traditions favoured the development of certain disciplines, creating a pattern that was distinct from the Greek. Disciplines related to the public life of senators prospered—notably oratory, law, and history; certain fields of study were judged fit for diversions in leisure hours, and still others were considered beneath the dignity of an honourable Roman. Areas such as medicine and architecture were left to Greeks and others of lower status, and mathematics and the sciences aroused little interest. Greek slaves especially played an important role in the intellectual life of the late republic, serving in roles as diverse as teachers, copyists of manuscripts, and oral readers to aristocrats.

By the beginning of the imperial era the maturing of Roman intellectual culture was evident. Caesar had commissioned Varro to organize the first public library in Rome, and Greek scholars such as the geographer Strabo moved west to pursue their studies in Rome.

GRAMMAR AND RHETORIC

The education of the Roman elite was dominated by training in language skills, grammar, and rhetoric. The *grammatici*, who taught grammar and literature, were lower-class and often servile dependents. Nevertheless, they helped to develop a Roman consciousness about "proper" spelling and usage that the elite adopted as a means of setting themselves off from humbler men. This interest in language was expressed in Varro's work on words and grammar, *De Lingua Latina* (43?), with its prescriptive tone. Rhetoric, though a discipline of higher status, was still taught mainly by Greeks in Greek. The rhetoricians offered rules for composition: how to elaborate a speech with ornamentation and, more important, how to organize a work through the dialectical skills of definition and division of the subject matter into analytical categories. The Romans absorbed these instructions so thoroughly that the last generation of the republic produced an equal of the greatest Greek orators in Cicero. The influence on Roman culture of dialectical thinking, instilled through rhetoric, can hardly be overstated; the result was an increasingly disciplined, well-organized habit of thinking. This development can be seen most clearly in the series of agricultural works by Roman authors: whereas Cato's second-century *De agricultura* is rambling and disorganized, Varro's three books on *Res rusticae* (37), with their division of soils into 99 types, seem excessively organized.

LAW AND HISTORY

Roman law, although traditional in content, was also deeply influenced by Greek dialectic. For centuries the law had been passed down orally by pontifical priests. It emerged as an intellectual discipline only in the late republic, when men who saw themselves as legal specialists began to write treatises aimed at organizing existing law into a system, defining principles and concepts, and then applying those principles systematically. Quintus Mucius Scaevola was a pivotal figure: a pontifex in the traditional role, he published the first systematic legal treatise, *De iure civili*, in the 80s. Cicero credited his contemporary Servius Sulpicius Rufus with being the jurist who transformed law into a discipline (*ars*).

The decisive events of the late republic stimulated the writing of history. The first extant historical works in Latin (rather than in Greek) date from this period: Sallust's *Bellum Iugurtinum* (*Iugurthine War*) and *Bellum Catilinae* (*Catilinarian Conspiracy*) and Caesar's memoirs about his Gallic and civil wars. The rapid changes also prompted antiquarian studies as Roman senators looked back to archaic institutions and religious rituals of the distant past to legitimize or criticize the present. Varro's 41 books (now lost) on *Antiquitates terum humanarum et divinarum* ("Antiquities of things human and divine") were influential in establishing the traditions of early Rome for future generations.

PHILOSOPHY AND POETRY

Philosophy and poetry were suitable as pastimes for senators; few, however, were as serious about philosophy as the younger Cato and Cicero. Even Cicero's philosophical works were not technical treatises by Greek standards. Rather, they

One of Rome's greatest poets, Virgil wrote poems that expressed his sorrow regarding the political and social upheaval all around him. Hulton Archive/Getty Images

were written by humbler men and are now lost. A survey of their names and titles, however, shows that stoicism was not yet the dominant philosophical school it later became. More in evidence were the Epicureans, peripatetics, and academics. There also were revivals of Aristotelian and Pythagorean studies in this period.

The best-known poets of the late republican and civil war periods came from well-to-do Italian families. Catullus from Verona (*c.* 84–*c.* 54) had a reputation as *doctus* (learned) for his exquisitely crafted poems full of literary allusions in the Alexandrian style. Far from cumbersome, however, were many of his short, witty poems that challenged traditional Roman mores and deflated senatorial pretensions.

Rome's greatest poets, Virgil (70–19) and Horace (65–8), were born during the republic, came of age during the civil wars, and survived to celebrate the victory of their patron, Augustus. Virgil's *Eclogues* one and nine, written during the civil wars, poignantly evoke the suffering of the great upheaval that ironically inspired Rome's highest intellectual and artistic achievements.

were presented as dialogues among leading senators in their leisure. Similarly, Lucretius's *De rerum natura* ("*On the Nature of Things*"; 50s) offered, in verse, a nontechnical explanation of Epicureanism. The technical philosophical works

CHAPTER 4

THE EARLY ROMAN EMPIRE (31 BC–AD 193)

Actium left Octavian the master of the Roman world. This supremacy, successfully maintained until his death more than 40 years later, made him the first of the Roman emperors. Suicide removed Antony and Cleopatra and their potential menace in 30 BC, and the annexation of Egypt with its Ptolemaic treasure brought financial independence. With these reassurances Octavian could begin the task of reconstruction.

THE CONSOLIDATION OF THE EMPIRE UNDER THE JULIO-CLAUDIANS

Law and order had vanished from the Roman state when its ruling aristocrats refused to curb their individual ambitions, and the most corrupt and violent people could gain protection for their crimes by promising their support to those ambitious. Furthermore, the ambitious and the violent together could thus transform a republic based on disciplined liberty into a turbulent cockpit of murderous rivalries.

Good government depended on limits being set to unrestrained aspirations, and Octavian was in a position to impose them. But his military might, although sufficiently strong in 31 BC to guarantee orderly political processes, was itself incompatible with them; nor did he relish the role of military despot. The fate of Julius Caesar, an eagerness to acquire political respectability, and his own esteem for ancestral custom combined to dissuade Octavian from it. He wished to be, in his own words, "the author of the best civilian government possible." His problem was to regularize his own position so as to make it generally acceptable, without simultaneously reopening the door to violent lawlessness. His pragmatic responses not only ensured stability and continuity but also respected republican forms and traditions so far as possible.

THE ESTABLISHMENT OF THE PRINCIPATE UNDER AUGUSTUS

Large-scale demobilization allayed people's fears; regular consular elections raised their hopes. In 29–28 BC Octavian carried out, with Marcus Vipsanius Agrippa, his powerful deputy, the first census of the Roman people since 70; and this involved drawing up an electoral roll for the Centuriate Assembly. Elections followed, and Octavian was inevitably chosen consul. Then, on Jan. 13, 27 BC, he offered to lay down his powers. The Roman Senate rejected this proposal, charging him instead to administer (besides Egypt) Spain, Gaul, and Syria for the next 10 years, while the Senate was to supervise the rest of the empire. Three days later, among other honours, it bestowed upon him the name by which he has ever since been known, Augustus.

As most of the troops still under arms were in the regions entrusted to Augustus's charge, the arrangements of 27 BC hardly affected his military strength. Moreover, so long as he was consul (he was reelected every year until 23 BC), he was civilian head of government as well. In other words, he was still preeminent and all-powerful, even if he had, in his own words, placed the *res*

Gaius Octavius was the first Roman emperor to rule after the republic. The Senate conferred upon him the name Augustus, a title that is meant to convey Octavius's superiority among men. Hulton Archive/Getty Images

publica at the disposal of the Senate and the Roman people. Augustus particularly wished to conciliate the senatorial class, without whose cooperation civilian government was impossible. But his monopolization of the consulship offended the Senate, making a different arrangement clearly necessary. Accordingly, in 23 Augustus made a change; he vacated the consulship and never held it again (except momentarily in 5 BC and again in 2 BC, for a limited, specific purpose).

In its place he received the tribunician power (*tribunicia potestas*). He could not become an actual plebeian tribune, because Julius Caesar's action of making him a patrician had disqualified him for the office. But he could acquire the rights and privileges pertaining to the office; and they were conferred upon him, apparently by the Senate, whose action was then ratified by the popular assembly. He had already been enjoying some of a tribune's privileges since 36; but he now acquired them all and even some additional ones, such as the right to convene the Senate whenever he chose and to enjoy priority in bringing business before it. Through his tribunician power he could also summon the popular assembly and participate fully in its proceedings. Clearly, although no longer consul, he still retained the legal right to authority in civilian affairs.

The arrangement of 23 entailed an additional advantage. The power of the plebeian tribune was traditionally associated with the protection of citizens, and Augustus's acquisition of it was therefore unlikely to rouse resentment. Indeed, Augustus thenceforth shrewdly propagated the notion that if his position in the state was exceptional (which it clearly was), it was precisely because of his tribunician power. Although he held it for only one year at a time, it was indefinitely renewable and was pronounced his for life. Thus, it was both annual and perpetual and was a suitable vehicle for numbering the years of his supremacy. His era (and this is true also of later emperors) was counted officially from the year when he acquired the tribunician power.

The year 23 likewise clarified the legal basis for Augustus's control of his provincia (the region under his jurisdiction) and its armed forces. The Senate invested him with an imperium proconsulare (governorship and high command), and, while this had a time limit, it was automatically renewed whenever it lapsed (usually every 10 years). This proconsular imperium, furthermore, was pronounced valid inside Italy, even inside Rome and the pomerium (the boundary within which only Roman gods could be worshiped and civil magistrates rule), and it was superior (majus) to the imperium of any other proconsul. Thus, Augustus could intervene legally in any province, even in one entrusted to someone else.

The network of favours owed him that Augustus had cultivated within the state, among people of the greatest authority over their own networks, made his position virtually unassailable, but he avoided provoking this high class of his supporters, senatorial and equestrian, by not drawing attention to the most novel and autocratic of the many grants of power he had received, the *imperium proconsulare majus*. Instead, he paraded the tribunician power as the expression of his supreme position in the state.

After 23 no fundamental change in Augustus's position occurred. He felt no need to hold offices that in republican times would have conferred exceptional power (e.g., dictatorship, lifetime censorship, or regular consulship), even though these were offered him. Honours, of course, came his way. In 19 BC he received some consular rights and prerogatives, presumably to ensure that his imperium was in no particular inferior to a consul's. In 12, when Lepidus died, he became *pontifex maximus* (he had long since been elected into all of the priestly colleges). In 8 BC, the eighth month of the year was named after him, and in 2 BC, he was designated *pater patriae* ("father of his country"), a distinction that he particularly esteemed because it suggested that he was to all Romans what a paterfamilias was to his own household. He also accepted special commissions from time to time—e.g., the supervision of the supply of grain and water, the maintenance of public buildings (including temples), the regulation of the Tiber, the superintendence of the police and firefighting services, and the upkeep of Italy's roads. Such behaviour advertised his will and capacity to improve the lives of people dependent on him. Of that capacity, manifest on a grand scale, his tribunician power and proconsular imperium were only the formal expression. He was a charismatic leader of unrivaled prestige (*auctoritas*), whose merest suggestions were binding.

Like an ordinary Roman, he contented himself with three names. His, however, Imperator Caesar Augustus, were absolutely unique, with a magic all their own that caused all later emperors to appropriate them, at first selectively but after AD 69 in their entirety. Thereby they became titles, reserved for the emperor (or, in the case of the name Caesar, for his heir apparent); from them derive the titles emperor, kaiser, and tsar. Yet, as used by Augustus and his first four successors, the words Imperator Caesar Augustus were names, not titles— that is, respectively, praenomen, nomen (in effect), and cognomen. One title that Augustus did have was *princeps* (prince). This, however, was unofficial—a mere popular label, meaning Rome's first citizen—and government documents such as inscriptions or coins do not apply it to Augustus. But because of it the system of government he devised is called the *principate*.

THE ROMAN SENATE AND THE URBAN MAGISTRACIES

Augustus regarded the Senate, whose leading member (*princeps senatus*) he had become in 28, as a body with important functions. It heard fewer overseas embassies than formerly, but otherwise its dignity and authority seemed unimpaired. Its members filled the highest offices, and its decrees, although not formally called laws, were just as binding. The Senate soon became a high court whose verdicts were unappealable. It supervised the older provinces and, nominally, the state finances as well and, in effect, elected the urban magistrates. Formally, even the emperor's powers derived from the Senate.

Nevertheless, it lacked real power. Its provinces contained few troops (and by AD 40 it had ceased to control even these few). Hence, it could hardly dispute Augustus's wishes. In fact, real power rested with Augustus, who superintended state finances and above all controlled membership in the Senate; every senator's career depended on his goodwill. But he valued the Senate as the repository of the true Roman spirit and traditions and as the body representing public opinion. He was considerate toward it, shrewdly anticipated its reactions, and generally avoided contention with it. He regularly kept it informed about his activities; and an imperial council (*Consilium Principis*), which he consulted on matters of policy, in the manner of a republican magistrate seeking the opinion of his advisory committee, consisted of the consuls, certain other magistrates, and 15 senators—not handpicked by him but chosen by lot every six months.

To rid the Senate of unworthy members, he reduced its numbers by successive reviews to about 600 (from the triumviral 1,000 or more). Sons of senators and men of good repute and substance who had served in the army and the *vigintiviri* ("board of twenty," minor magistracy) could become members by being elected, at age 25 or over, to the quaestorship. Their subsequent rank in the Senate depended on what other magistracies they managed to win. These were, in ascending order, the aedileship (or plebeian tribunate), the praetorship, and the consulship. No one disliked by Augustus could expect to reach any of them, while anyone whom he nominated or endorsed was sure of election. Despite the emperor's control, there were usually enough candidates for keen contests.

By AD 5 *destinatio* seems to have been the practice—that is, a special panel of senators and equites selected the praetors and consuls, and the comitia centuriata automatically ratified their choice. In about AD 5, likewise, the consulship was shortened to six months. This not only gratified senators and increased the number of high-ranking qualified officials but also showed that the consuls' duties were becoming largely ceremonial. This was also true, but to a far lesser degree, of the other unpaid magistrates. A senator really made his mark in between his magistracies, when he served in important salaried posts, military or civilian or both, sometimes far from Rome.

THE EQUESTRIAN ORDER

One of the great institutions of the Roman Empire developed because senators were either too proud or too few to fill all the posts open throughout the empire. Some posts were considered menial and went to the emperor's freedmen or slaves. Others were entrusted to equites, and thus it was that the equestrian order developed.

Augustus decided that membership in the order should be open to Roman citizens of means and reputation but not necessarily of good birth. Ultimately, there were thousands of equites throughout the empire. Although this was a lower aristocracy, a good career was available to them. After tours of duty as an army officer (the so-called militiae equestres), an aspiring eques might serve as the emperor's agent (procurator) in various capacities and eventually become one of the powerful prefects (of the fleet, of the vigiles, or fire brigade, of the grain supply, of Egypt, or of the Praetorian Guard). This kind of an equestrian career became standardized only under Claudius I, but Augustus began the system and, by his use of equites in responsible posts, founded the imperial civil service, which later was headed chiefly by them.

The equites also performed another function. The senatorial order had difficulty in maintaining its numbers from its own ranks and depended on recruitment from below, which meant from the equestrian order. Because this order was not confined to Rome or even to Italy, the Senate gradually acquired a non-Italian element. The western provinces were already supplying senators under Augustus.

Members of the equestrian order, called eques, were the Roman equivalent of an English knight. Most were originally part of the military cavalry, later becoming members of a political and administrative class. Hulton Archive/Getty Images

Administration of Rome and Italy

Ordinary Roman citizens who were neither senators nor equites were of lesser consequence. Although still used, the old formula *senatus populusque Romanus* ("the Senate and the Roman people") had changed its meaning; in effect, its populusque Romanus portion now meant "the emperor." The "Roman people" had become the "Italian people," and it was embodied in the person of Augustus, himself the native of an Italian town.

To reduce the risk of popular demonstrations in Rome, the emperor provided grain doles, occasional donatives, and various entertainments; but he allowed the populace no real power. After AD 5 the Roman people's participation in public life consisted in the formality of holding occasional assemblies to ratify decisions made elsewhere. Ultimately, this caused the distinction between the Roman citizens of Italy and the provincial inhabitants of the overseas empire to disappear; under Augustus, however, the primacy of Italy was insistently emphasized.

Indeed, Italy and justice for its inhabitants were Augustus's first cares. Arbitrary triumviral legislation was pronounced invalid after 29 BC, and ordinary Roman citizens everywhere had access to Augustus's own court of appeal (his appellate jurisdiction dated from 30 BC and in effect replaced the republican appeal to the people). His praetorian and urban cohorts provided physical security; his officials assured grain supplies; and he himself, with help from such aides as Agrippa, monumentalized Italian towns. The numerous Augustan structures in Italy and Rome (as he boasted, a city of brick before his time and of marble afterward) have mostly perished, but impressive ruins survive (e.g., aqueduct, forum, and mausoleum in Rome; bridge at Narni; arch at Fano; gate at Perugia). Doubtless their construction alleviated unemployment, especially among the proletariat at Rome.

But economic considerations did not influence Augustus's policies much (customs tariffs, for instance, were for fiscal, not protective, purposes), nor did he build harbour works at Ostia, Rome's port. Italian commerce and industry—notably fine pottery, the so-called *terra sigillata*, and wine—nevertheless flourished in the conditions he created. Public finances, mints, and coinage issues, chaotic before him, were placed on a sound basis, partly by the introduction of a sales tax and of a new levy (inheritance taxes) on Roman citizens—who hitherto had been subject only to harbour dues and manumission charges—and partly by means of repeated subventions to the public treasury (*aerarium Saturni*) from Augustus's own enormous private resources (*patrimonium Caesaris*). To keep the citizen body pure, he made manumission of slaves difficult, and from those irregularly manumitted he withheld the citizenship. His many highways also contributed to Italy's economic betterment.

Augustus's great achievement in Italy, however, was to restore morale and unify the country. The violence and self-aggrandizement of the first century BC had bred apathy and corruption. To reawaken a sense of responsibility, especially in official and administrative circles, Augustus reaffirmed traditional Italian virtues (by laws aimed against adultery, by strengthening family ties, and by stimulating the birth rate) and revived ancestral religion (by repairing temples, building new shrines, and reactivating moribund cults and rituals). To infuse fresh blood and energy into disillusioned Roman society, he promoted the assimilation of Italy: the elite of its municipal towns entered the Roman Senate, and Italy became firmly one with Rome.

ADMINISTRATION OF THE PROVINCES

Sharply distinguished from Italy were the provinces of the empire. From 27 BC on they were of two types. The Senate supervised the long-established ones, the so-called public provinces. Their governors were chosen by lot, usually served for a year, commanded no troops, and were called proconsuls (although only those superintending Asia and Africa were in fact former consuls, the others being former praetors). The emperor supervised all other provinces, and collectively they made up his provincia. He appointed their governors, and these served at his pleasure, none with the title of proconsul because in his own provincia proconsular imperium was wielded by

him alone. These imperial provinces might be "unarmed," but many of them were garrisoned, some quite heavily. Those containing more than one legion were entrusted to former consuls and those with a legion or less to former praetors; in both cases their governors were called legati Augusti pro praetore ("legates of Augustus with authority of a praetor"). There were also some imperial provinces governed not by senators but by equites (usually styled procurators but sometimes prefects); Judaea at the time of Christ's crucifixion was such an equestrian province, Pontius Pilate being its governor. An entirely exceptional imperial province was Egypt, so jealously guarded that no senator could visit it without express permission; its prefect was unique in being an equestrian in command of legions.

The provinces paid tribute, which helped to pay for the armed services, various benefactions to supporters, a growing palace staff, and the public-works programs. Periodical censuses, carefully listing provincial resources, provided the basis for the two direct taxes: tributum soli, exacted from occupiers of provincial soil, and tributum capitis, paid on other forms of property (it was not a poll tax, except in Egypt and in certain backward areas). In addition, the provinces paid indirect taxes, such as harbour dues. In imperial provinces the direct taxes (tributa) were paid to the emperor's procurator, an equestrian official largely independent of the governor. In senatorial provinces, quaestors supervised the finances; but, increasingly, imperial procurators also appeared. The indirect taxes (*vectigalia*) were still collected by publicani, who were now much more rigorously controlled and gradually replaced by imperial civil servants.

To reward his troops after faithful service, Caesar had settled them on lands mostly in the provinces, in veteran towns; and Augustus, for the same reason and to reduce the dangerous military presence in the state generally, resorted to the same procedure on a vast scale. Thus, in the space of a single generation, more than 120 new centres were organized across the empire in an explosion of urbanizing energy never equaled or even approached in later times. In the settlements called *coloniae* all residents were

to be Roman citizens, and the form of government and many other aspects of life specified in their charters bore a thoroughly Roman character. Some coloniae, in further approximation to Italian models, enjoyed exemption from tribute. In the municipia, only those elected as magistrates were awarded Roman citizenship (after Hadrian, in Africa, admission was sometimes extended to the whole of the local senate); but the whole of the local aristocracy in the course of time would be in this way gradually incorporated fully into the state. In municipia, too, charters specified Roman forms of government. Urban centres that were wholly noncitizen, called *civitates*, enjoyed autonomy in their own affairs, under the governor's

EMPEROR WORSHIP

Many individuals and even whole communities, in Italy and elsewhere, spontaneously expressed their thanks for the priceless gift of peace by worshiping Augustus and his family. Emperor worship was also encouraged officially, however, as a focus of common loyalty for the polyglot empire. In the provinces, to emphasize the superiority of Italy, the official cult was dedicated to Roma et Augustus. To celebrate it, representatives from provincial communities or groups of communities met in an assembly (Consilium Provinciae), which incidentally might air grievances as well as satisfactions. This system began in the Greek-speaking provinces, long used to wooing their rulers with divine honours. It penetrated the west only slowly, but from 12 BC an assembly for the three imperial Gallic provinces existed at Lugdunum.

In Italy, the official cult was to the genius Augusti (the life spirit of his family); it was coupled in Rome with the Lares Compitales (the spirits of his ancestors). Its principal custodians (seviri Augustales) were normally freedmen. Both the Senate and the emperor had central control over the institution. The Senate could withhold a vote of posthumous deification, and the emperor could acknowledge or refuse provincial initiatives in the establishment of emperor worship, in the construction for it, or in its liturgical details. The energy, however, that infused emperor worship was to be found almost wholly among the local nobilities.

eye. They paid taxes and administered the rural territory around them. In the west, many of them were eventually granted the status of municipia, and they adopted the originally Italian magistracies (*duoviri* and *aediles*, collectively *quattuorviri*) and senate (*curia* or *ordo*), normally numbering 100 members. The entire West rapidly came under the administration of urban centres of these three forms, without which the central government could never have done its job. Moreover, these centres radiated economic and cultural influence around them and so had an immense effect, particularly on the way of life of the more backward areas. In the east, however, urban centres, though equally important for government purposes, had already been in existence and long settled into their own culture and their own forms of government.

The provinces were generally better off under the empire. Appointment over them as governor was now and henceforth generally granted with the emperor's approval. Because he thought of himself as in some ways the patron and defender of the provincial population, lax or extortionate officials could expect some loss of imperial favour, an end to their careers, or an even more severe punishment.

THE ARMY

It was Augustus's soldiers, however, not his worshipers, who made him all-powerful. Their allegiance, like the name Caesar, was inherited from his "father," the deified Julius. The allegiance was to the emperor personally, through a military oath taken in his name every January 1; and the soldiers owed it after his death to his son or chosen successor. This preference of theirs for legitimacy could not be ignored because they were now a standing army, something that the republic had lacked. Demobilization reduced the 60 legions of Actium to 28, a number hardly sufficient but all that Augustus's prudence or economy would countenance. These became permanent formations, each with its own number and name; the soldiers serving in them were called legionnaries.

Besides the legionnaries there was a somewhat smaller body of auxiliaries, or supporting troops. The two corps together numbered more than a quarter of a million men. To them must be added the garrison of Italy—the praetorian cohorts, or emperor's bodyguard, about 10,000 strong—and the marines of the imperial fleet, which had its main headquarters at Misenum and Ravenna in Italy and subsidiary stations and flotillas on seas and rivers elsewhere (the marines, however, were not reckoned good combat forces). All these troops were long-service professionals—the praetorians serving 16 years; legionaries, 20; auxiliaries, 25; and marines, 28—with differing pay scales, the praetorians' being the highest. In addition to their pay, the men received donatives, shares of booty, and retirement bonuses from a special treasury (*aerarium militare*) established in

An ivory carving depicting Roman soldiers wearing the legions' familiar plumed helmets. Time & Life Pictures/ Getty Images

municipal towns and the auxiliaries from tribal areas. The tendency to use provincials grew, and by the year 100 the Roman imperial army was overwhelmingly non-Italian.

Nevertheless, it helped greatly to Romanize the empire. The legionnaries were Roman citizens from the day they enlisted, if not before, and the auxiliaries (after Claudius anyway) from the day they were discharged; and, though serving soldiers could not legally marry, many had mistresses whose children often became Roman citizens. The troops, other than praetorians and marines, passed their years of service in the "armed" imperial provinces—the auxiliaries in forts near the frontier and the legionaries at some distance from it in camps that showed an increasing tendency, especially after AD 69, to become permanent (some of them, indeed, developed into great European cities). There was no central reserve, because, although desirable for emergencies, it might prove dangerous in peacetime.

AD 6 and maintained out of the sales tax and Roman citizens' death duties. Under Augustus the praetorians were normally Italians, but many legionaries and virtually all auxiliaries were provincials, mainly from the imperial provinces in the west, the legionaries coming from

The officers were naturally Roman citizens. In the legions those of the highest rank (*legati* and *tribuni*) were senators or equites; lower officers (*centuriones*) might enter directly from Italian or provincial municipalities or might rise through the ranks; by the time they retired, if not sooner, many of them were equites. In the auxiliaries the unit commanders (*praefecti*) were equites, often of provincial birth. On retirement the soldiers frequently settled in the provinces where they had served, made friends, and perhaps acquired families. Imperial policy favoured this practice. Thus the army, which had done much to introduce into the provinces Romans of all ranks, with their own way of life, through veteran settlements of the 40s, 30s, and 20s BC, continued in the same role on a more modest and casual scale throughout the Augustan reign and for two centuries or so afterward.

FOREIGN POLICY

After Actium and on two other occasions, Augustus solemnly closed the gates of the shrine of Janus (a gesture of peace) to show that Rome had peace as well as a princeps. These well-publicized gestures were purely temporary; the gates were swiftly reopened. His proconsular imperium made Augustus the arbiter of peace and war, and an ostensible search for defensible frontiers made his a very warlike reign. While the republic had left the limits of Roman territorial claims rather vague and indefinite, he planned conquests stretching to the boundaries defined by nature (deserts, rivers, and ocean shores), not always, however, with immediate annexation in mind. When annexation did occur, it was followed by the construction of solidly built military

roads, paved with thick stone blocks: these also served the official post system (*cursus publicus*) and were provided with rest stages and overnight lodges at regular intervals.

Areas where subjugation looked arduous and where Romanization seemed problematic were left to client kings, dependent on the emperor's support and goodwill and under obligation to render military aid to Rome. Such satellite kingdoms spared Augustus the trouble and expense of maintaining strong defenses everywhere; nevertheless, their ultimate and intended destiny was incorporation as soon as it suited their overlord's convenience. Usually, territory was gained more easily by creating and subsequently incorporating a client kingdom than by launching an expansionist war.

In the south, Augustus found suitable frontiers quickly. In 25 BC an expedition under Aelius Gallus opened the Red Sea to Roman use and simultaneously revealed the Arabian Desert as an unsurpassed and, indeed, unsurpassable boundary. The same year Gaius Petronius, the prefect of Egypt, tightened Rome's grip as far as the First Cataract and established a broad military zone beyond it. The vast region north of the Sahara and the Atlas Mountains was also secured (*c.* 25) after a series of punitive raids against native tribes and the annexation of one client kingdom (Numidia) and the creation of another (Mauretania). Three legions, two in Egypt and one in Africa (a senatorial province), policed the southern shore of the Mediterranean.

In the west, consolidation was extended to the Atlantic. Gaul, Julius Caesar's conquest, was organized as four provinces: senatorial Narbonensis and the imperial three Gauls (Aquitania, Belgica, and Lugdunensis). In Spain, after Agrippa successfully ended in 19 BC the last campaign that Augustus had launched in person in 26, three provinces were formed: senatorial Baetica and imperial Lusitania and Tarraconensis. Three legions enforced Roman authority from Gibraltar to the mouth of the Rhine. Augustus ignored the advice of court poets and others to advance still farther and annex Britain.

In the east, Parthia had demonstrated its power against Crassus and Antony, and Augustus proceeded warily. He retained Antony's ring of buffer client kingdoms, although he incorporated some, including the most celebrated of them, Judaea; he made it a province in AD 6, respecting, however, some of the customs of its Jewish inhabitants. Augustus stationed four legions in Syria and obviously envisaged the Euphrates River and the northern extension of the Arabian Desert as the desirable frontier with Mesopotamia. Farther north, however, no such natural line existed. North of the Black Sea the client kingdom of the Cimmerian Bosporus, under its successive rulers Asander and Polemo, helped to contain southward and westward thrusts by the Scythians, an Iranian people related to the Parthians, and this provided protection in the north for Anatolia and its provinces (senatorial Asia and Bithynia-Pontus and imperial Cilicia and Galatia, the latter a large new province created in 25 BC out of Amyntas's client kingdom).

By a show of force, Augustus's stepson Tiberius, in 20 BC, recovered the standards lost at Carrhae and installed Tigranes as client king of Armenia. Although Augustan propaganda depicted this as a famous victory, strategic considerations inevitably obliged the Parthians, once they settled their internal, dynastic dissensions, to dispute Roman control of Armenia. Thus it can hardly be said that Augustus settled the eastern frontier. Missions were sent to the East repeatedly (Agrippa, 17–13 BC; Gaius Caesar, AD 1–4; Germanicus, 18–19), and Armenia remained a problem for Augustus's successors: Tiberius successfully maintained Roman influence there, but Gaius and Claudius failed to do so, leaving Nero with a difficult situation.

In the north, too, there was difficulty. The Alps and their passes were finally subjugated early in Augustus's reign. This enabled Tiberius and his brother Drusus between 16 and 8 BC to conquer all the way to the great rivers of central Europe. New provinces were created in the Alps and Tyrol (Maritime and Pennine Alps, Raetia, Noricum) and also farther east (Pannonia, Moesia). Stability along the Danube was precariously maintained, under Augustus and later, by means of periodical alliances with Maroboduus and his successors, who ruled Germanic tribes such as the Marcomanni and Quadi in Bohemia to the north of the river, and by the existence of a Thracian client kingdom to the south of its lowest course.

The push across the Rhine began in 12 BC. Although it reached the Elbe, consolidation beyond the Rhine proved elusive. A revolt in Pannonia (AD 6–9) interrupted it, and, in AD 9, German tribes under Arminius annihilated Quinctilius Varus and three legions in the Teutoburg Forest. This disaster reduced the number of legions to 25 (it did not reach 28 again until half a century later), and it disheartened Augustus.

Old and weary, he withdrew to the Rhine and decided against all further expansion, a policy he urged upon his successor. For the watch on the Rhine the military districts of Upper and Lower Germany were created, containing eight legions between them. Another seven garrisoned the Danubian provinces. These figures reveal imperial anxiety for the northern frontier.

ECONOMIC LIFE

Although widespread, Augustus's wars chiefly affected the frontier districts. Elsewhere, peace prevailed. Indeed, never before had so large an area been free of war for so long. This state of affairs helped trade. The suppression of piracy and the use of military roads, which the frontier warfare itself brought into being, provided safe arteries of commerce. Stable currency also aided economic growth. Activity directly connected with the soil predominated; but there were also many establishments, usually small, engaged in manufacturing, and such products as textiles, pottery, tiles, and papyrus were turned out in surprising quantities. Advanced techniques were also known: glassblowing, for example, dates from the Augustan age. Most products were consumed locally, but the specialties or monopolies from any region usually exceeded local needs, and the surplus was sold elsewhere, generating a brisk interchange of goods.

Some traveled great distances, even beyond the empire: trade with India, for example, reached respectable proportions once the nature of the monsoon was understood, and the Red Sea was opened to Roman shipping. Merchants, especially Levantines, traveled everywhere, and fairs were frequent. The Mediterranean world was linked together as never before, and standardization made considerable headway. In Augustus's day Italy was economically the most important part of the empire. It could afford to import on a large scale, thanks partly to provincial tribute but above all to its own large productivity. The eastern provinces, for their part, recovered rapidly from the depredations of the civil wars and were industrially quite advanced. The other provinces were less developed, but they soon ceased being mere suppliers of raw materials; they learned to exploit their natural resources by using new techniques and then began overtaking the more advanced economies of Italy and the Greek-speaking regions. The importance of trade in unifying the empire should not be underestimated.

AUGUSTAN ART AND LITERATURE

In 17 BC Rome held Secular Games, a traditional celebration to announce the entry into a new epoch (*saeculum*). New it was, for, although Augustus preserved what he could of republican institutions, he added much that was his own. His Rome had become very Italian, and this spirit is reflected in the art and literature of his reign. Its greatest writers were native Italians, and, like the ruler whose program they glorified, they used the traditional as the basis for something new. Virgil, Horace, and Livy, as noted above, imitated the writing of classical Greece, but chiefly in form, their tone and outlook being un-Hellenic. It was the glory of Italy and faith in Rome that inspired Virgil's Georgics and Aeneid, Horace's Odes, and the first 10 books of Livy's history.

In Augustan art a similar fusion was achieved between the prevailing Attic and Hellenistic models and Italian naturalism. The sculptured portraits on the Ara Pacis (Altar of the Augustan Peace) of 9 BC, for all their lifelike quality, are yet in harmony with the classical poise of the figures, and they strike a fresh note: the stately converging processions (Rome's imperial family and magistrates on one side; senators, equites, and citizens on the other) became the prototypes for all later processional reliefs. Augustan painting likewise displays a successful combination of Greek and Roman elements, to judge from the frescoes in the house of Livia on the Palatine. In Augustan architecture, decidedly conservative and Hellenic, the potentialities of curving and vaulted spaces that had been revealed in the earlier first century BC were not realized. Building was, however, very active and widespread.

The culture of the age undoubtedly attained a high level of excellence, dominated by the personality of the emperor and his accomplishments. Imperial art had already reached full development, a matter of no small moment, because Rome's political predominance made the spread of its influence inevitable. The Mediterranean world was soon assuming a Roman aspect, and this is a measure of Augustus's extraordinary achievement. Yet it was an achievement with limitations. His professed aim—to promote stability, peace, security, and prosperity—was irreproachable, but perhaps it was also unexciting. Emphasizing conservatism by precept and his own example, he encouraged the simpler virtues of a less sophisticated age, and his success made this sedate but rather static outlook fashionable. People accepted the routine of his continuing rule, at the cost, however, of some loss of intellectual energy and moral fervour. The great literature, significantly, belongs to the years near Actium, when people's imagination still nursed heady visions of Roman victory and Italian destiny. After the Secular Games the atmosphere became more commonplace and produced the frivolities of Ovid and the pedestrian later books of Livy.

The sculpted portraits of imperial house members, including Emperor Augustus, adorn a wall of the Ara Pacis ("Altar of the Augustan Peace"). Roger Viollet/Getty Image

Appraisal of Augustus

Augustus's position as princeps cannot be defined simply. He was neither a Roman king (rex) nor a Hellenistic monarch (basileus), nor was he, as the 19th-century German historian Theodor Mommsen thought, a partner with the Senate in a dyarchy. He posed as the first servant of an empire over which the Roman Senate presided, and it would appear that his claim to have accepted no office inconsistent with ancestral custom was literally true. Proconsular imperium was a republican institution, and, although tribunician power was not, it contained nothing specifically unrepublican. But, while precedents can be cited for Augustus's various powers, their concentration and tenure were absolutely unparalleled. Under the republic, powers like his would have been distributed among several holders, each serving for a limited period with a colleague. Augustus wielded them all, by himself, simultaneously and without any time limit (in practice, at least). This fact made him an emperor, but it did not necessarily make him a military tyrant.

In discharging both military and civilian functions, Augustus was no different from republican consuls or praetors. Admittedly his military power was overwhelming; but, if he chose not to brandish it, the tone of his reign could remain essentially civilian. Constitutional safeguards were indeed lacking; everything was at the emperor's discretion, and even Augustus passed legislation that made anti-imperial behaviour, real or suspected, treasonable (men were, in fact, executed for conspiracy during his reign). But there had been no constitutional safeguards in the republic, under Sulla, Pompey, the triumvirs, or even Julius Caesar. Augustus's improved police services probably made lower-class Romans at least feel safer under him. The senatorial class, however, contained a minority resentful of the sheer undeniable preponderance of the princeps' power, and he was the target of several unsuccessful plots against his life.

The principate was something personal, what the emperor chose to make it, and the relations prevailing between emperor and Senate usually indicated what a reign was like. In Augustus's case they reveal a regime that was outwardly constitutional, generally moderate, and certainly effective. But, as he himself implied at the end of his life, he was a skillful actor in life's comedy. Later emperors lacked his sureness of touch.

When Augustus died, the Senate unhesitatingly pronounced him *divus*—the deified one who had restored peace, organized a standing army to defend the frontiers, expanded those frontiers farther than any previous Roman, improved administrative practices everywhere, promoted better standards of both public and private behaviour, integrated Rome and Italy, embellished Rome, reconciled the provinces, expedited Romanization, and above all maintained law and order while respecting republican traditions.

Augustus's luck was hardly inferior to his statecraft. Despite indifferent health, he headed the Roman state in one capacity or another for 56 years. His rule, one of the longest in European history, consolidated the principate so firmly that what might have been an episode became an epoch. At his death there was practically no one left with any personal memory of the republic, and Augustus's wish came true: he had fashioned a lasting as well as constitutional government. The principate endured with only minor changes for about 200 years.

THE SUCCESSION

Like any great Roman magnate, Augustus owed it to his supporters and dependents to maintain the structure of power that they constituted together and which would normally pass from father to son. In accepting the heritage from Caesar, he had only done the right thing, and he was respected for it by his peers. None of them would have advised him later to dismantle what he had since added to it. When, for instance, he was away from Rome, rather than accepting a diminution in his prerogatives of administration, a senator as city prefect was deputed to represent him. Consequently, Augustus began thinking early about who should follow him. The soldiers' views on legitimacy reinforced his own natural desire to found a dynasty, but he had no son and was therefore obliged to select his successor. Death played havoc with his attempts to do so. His nephew Marcellus, his son-in-law Agrippa, his grandsons Gaius and Lucius (Julia's children by

Agrippa), were groomed in turn; but they all predeceased him. Augustus, finally and reluctantly, chose a member of the republican nobility, his stepson Tiberius, a scion of the ultra-aristocratic Claudii. In AD 4 Augustus adopted Tiberius as his son and had tribunician power and probably proconsular imperium as well conferred upon him. This arrangement was confirmed in 13, and, when Augustus died the following year, Tiberius automatically became emperor.

Tiberius (ruled 14–37), during whose reign Christ was crucified, was a soldier and administrator of proved capability but of a reserved and moody temperament that engendered misunderstanding and unpopularity. Slander blamed him for the death in 19 of his nephew and heir apparent, the popular Germanicus; and, when informers (*delatores*), who functioned at Rome like public prosecutors, charged notables with treason, Tiberius was thought to encourage them. By concentrating the praetorian cohorts in a camp adjoining Rome, he increased the soldiers' scope for mischief-making without building any real security, and in 26 he left Rome permanently for the island of Capreae (Capri), entrusting Rome to the care of the city prefect. Tiberius heeded the aged Augustus's advice and did not extend the empire. (The annexation of Cappadocia, a client kingdom, represented no departure from Augustan policy.) In general he took his duties seriously; however, by administering the empire from Capreae he offended the Senate and was never fully trusted, much less really liked. At his death he was not pronounced divus. His great-nephew, Germanicus's son Gaius, succeeded him.

Gaius (better known by his nickname, Caligula, meaning "Little Boot") ruled from 37 to 41 with the absolutism of a monarch. His short reign was filled with reckless spending, callous murders, and humiliation of the Senate. Gaius's foreign policy was inept. Projected annexation proved abortive in Britain; it touched off heavy fighting in Mauretania. In Judaea and Alexandria, Gaius's contemptuous disregard of Jewish sentiment provoked near rebellion. When assassination ended his tyranny, the Senate contemplated restoration of the republic but was obliged by the Praetorian Guard to recognize Claudius, Germanicus's brother and therefore Gaius's uncle, as emperor.

Claudius I (ruled 41–54) went far beyond Augustus and Tiberius in centralizing government administration and, particularly, state finances in the imperial household. His freedmen secretaries consequently acquired great power; they were in effect directors of government bureaus. Claudius himself displayed much interest in the empire overseas; he enlarged it significantly, incorporating client kingdoms (Mauretania in 42; Lycia, 43; Thrace, 46) and, more important, annexing Britain. Conquest of Britain began in 43, Claudius himself participating in the campaign; the southeast was soon overrun, a colonia established at Camulodunum (Colchester) and a municipium at Verulamium (St. Albans), while Londinium (London) burgeoned into an

important *entrepôt*. Claudius also promoted Romanization, especially in the western provinces, by liberally granting Roman citizenship, by founding coloniae, and by inducting provincials directly into the Senate—he became censor in 47 and added to the Senate men he wanted, bestowing appropriate quaestorian or praetorian rank upon them to spare the maturer ones among them the necessity of holding junior magistracies; lest existing senators take offense, he elevated some of them to patrician status (a form of patronage often used by later emperors).

Claudius's provincial policies made the primacy of Italy less pronounced, although that was hardly his aim. In fact, he did much for Italy, improving its harbours, roads, and municipal administration and draining its marshy districts. The execution of many senators and equites, the insolence and venality of his freedmen, the excessive influence of his wives, and even his bodily infirmities combined to make him unpopular. Nevertheless, when he died (murdered probably by his fourth wife, Julia Agrippina, Augustus's great-granddaughter, who was impatient for the succession of the 16-year-old Nero, her son by an earlier marriage), he was pronounced divus.

Nero (ruled 54–68) left administration to capable advisers for a few years but then asserted himself as a vicious despot. He murdered successively his stepbrother Britannicus, his mother Julia Agrippina, his wife Octavia, and his tutor Seneca. He also executed many

Christians, accusing them of starting the great fire of Rome in 64 (this is the first recorded Christian persecution). In Rome his reliance on particular favourites and his general misgovernment led to a conspiracy by Gaius Calpurnius Piso in 65, but it was suppressed, leading to yet more executions; the victims included the poet Lucan.

The empire was not enlarged under this unwarlike emperor, but it was called upon to put down serious disorders. In Britain in 60–61 the rapacity and brutality of Roman officials provoked a furious uprising under Queen Boudicca; thousands were slaughtered, and Camulodunum, Vernulamium, and Londinium were destroyed. In the east a major military effort under Corbulo, Rome's foremost general, was required (62–65) to reestablish Roman prestige. A compromise settlement was reached, with the Romans accepting the Parthian nominee in Armenia and the Parthians recognizing him as Rome's client king. In 66, however, revolt flared in Judaea, fired by Roman cruelty and stupidity, Jewish fanaticism, and communal hatreds; the prefect of

Portrait of Emperor Nero committing suicide after the Roman army had overrun the city in 68 AD. Hulton Archive/Getty Images

Egypt, Julius Alexander, prevented involvement of the Jews of the Diaspora. An army was sent to Judaea under Titus Flavius Vespasianus to restore order; but it had not completed its task when two provincial governors in the west rebelled against Nero—Julius Vindex in Gallia Lugdunensis and Sulpicius Galba in Hispania Tarraconensis. When the praetorians in Rome also renounced their allegiance, Nero lost his nerve and committed suicide. He brought the Julio-Claudian dynasty to an ignominious end by being the first emperor to suffer *damnatio memoriae*—his reign was officially stricken from the record by order of the Senate.

GROWTH OF THE EMPIRE UNDER THE FLAVIANS AND ANTONINES

Nero's death ushered in the so-called year of the four emperors. The extinction of the Julio-Claudian imperial house robbed the soldiers of a focus for their allegiance, and civil war between the different armies ensued. The army of Upper Germany, after crushing Vindex, urged its commander, Verginius Rufus, to seize the purple for himself. But he elected to support Galba—scion of a republican patrician family claiming descent from Jupiter and Pasiphae—who was recognized as emperor by the Senate. However, the treasury, emptied by Nero's extravagance, imposed a stringent economy, and this bred unpopularity for Galba; his age (73) was also against him,

and unrest grew. Early in January 69 the Rhineland armies acclaimed Aulus Vitellius, commander in Lower Germany; at Rome the praetorians preferred Marcus Salvius Otho, whom Galba had alienated by choosing a descendant of the old republican aristocracy for his successor. Otho promptly procured Galba's murder and obtained senatorial recognition; this ended the monopoly of the purple for the republican nobility.

Otho, however, lasted only three months; defeated at Bedriacum, near Cremona in northern Italy, by Vitellius's powerful Rhineland army, he committed suicide (April 69). The Senate thereupon recognized Vitellius; but the soldiers along the Danube and in the east supported Vespasianus, the commander in Judaea. In a second battle near Bedriacum, the Rhineland troops were defeated in their turn, and on Vitellius's death soon afterward an accommodating Senate pronounced Vespasian emperor.

THE FLAVIAN EMPERORS

On Dec. 22, 69, the Senate conferred all the imperial powers upon Vespasian en bloc with the famous *Lex de Imperio Vespasiani* ("Law Regulating Vespasian's authority"), and the Assembly ratified the Senate's action. This apparently was the first time that such a law was passed; a fragmentary copy of it is preserved on the Capitol in Rome.

Vespasian (ruled 69–79) did not originate from Rome or its aristocracy. His family came from the Sabine municipality Reate, and with his elevation the Italian bourgeoisie came into its own. He and his two sons, both of whom in turn succeeded him, constituted the Flavian dynasty (69–96). Vespasian faced the same difficult task as Augustus—the restoration of peace and stability. The disorders of 69 had taken troops away from the Rhine and Danube frontiers. Thereupon, the Danubian lands were raided by Sarmatians, a combination of tribes who had overwhelmed and replaced the Scythians, their distant kinsmen, in eastern Europe. The assailants were repelled without undue difficulty; but the Sarmatian Iazyges, now firmly in control of the region between the Tisza and Danube rivers, posed a threat for the future.

Developments in the Rhineland were more immediately serious. There in 69 a certain Civilis incited the Batavians serving as auxiliaries in the Roman army to rebel. Gallic tribes joined the movement, and the insurgents boldly overran all but two of the legionary camps along the Rhine. Vespasian sent his relative Petilius Cerealis to deal with the rebels, who, fortunately for Rome, were not united in their aims; by 70 Cerealis had restored order. That same year Vespasian's elder son, Titus, brought the bloody war in Judaea to its end by besieging, capturing, and destroying Jerusalem.

To rehabilitate the public finances, Vespasian introduced new imposts, including a poll tax on Jews, and practiced stringent economies. With the Senate he was courteous but firm. He allowed it little initiative but used it as a reservoir from which to obtain capable administrators. To that end he assumed the censorship and added senators on a larger scale than Claudius had done, especially from the municipalities of Italy and the western provinces. Already before 69 an aristocracy of service had arisen, and the provincialization of the Roman Senate had begun; thereafter this development made rapid headway. Besides the censorship, Vespasian also often held the consulship, usually with Titus as his colleague. His object presumably was to ensure that his own parvenu Flavian house outranked any other. In this he succeeded; the troops especially were ready to accept the Flavians as the new imperial family. On Vespasian's death in 79, Titus, long groomed for the succession, became emperor and immediately had his father deified.

Titus (ruled 79–81) had a brief reign, marred by disasters (the volcanic eruption that buried Pompeii and Herculaneum and another great fire in Rome); but his attempts to alleviate the suffering and his general openhandedness won him such popularity that he was unhesitatingly deified after his early death.

Domitian (ruled 81–96), Titus's younger brother, had never been formally indicated for the succession; but the praetorians acclaimed him, and the Senate ratified their choice. Throughout his reign Domitian aimed at administrative efficiency, but his methods were high-handed. For him the Senate existed merely to supply imperial servants. He also used equites extensively, more than any previous emperor. He held the consulship repeatedly, was censor perpetuus from 85 on, and demanded other extravagant honours. On the whole, his efficiency promoted the welfare of the empire. Above all, he retained the allegiance of the troops. Although scornful of the Senate's dignity, he insisted on his own and mercilessly punished any act of disrespect, real or fancied, toward himself. He became even more suspicious and ruthless when Saturninus, commander in Upper Germany, attempted rebellion in 89. He crushed Saturninus; executions and confiscations ensued, and delatores flourished. The tyranny was particularly dangerous to senators, and it ended only with Domitian's assassination in 96. The Flavian dynasty, like the Julio-Claudian, ended with an emperor whose memory was officially damned.

The disorders in 69 were the cause of some military reforms. Under the Flavians, auxiliaries usually served far from their native hearths under officers of different nationality from themselves. At the same time, the tasks assigned to them came increasingly to resemble those performed by the legionaries. The latter grew less mobile, as camps with stone buildings came to be the rule; and it became common for detachments from a legion (vexillationes), rather than the entire legion, to be used for field operations. This army of a new type proved its mettle in Britain, where the advance halted by Boudicca's revolt was now resumed. Between 71 and 84 three able

governors—Petilius Cerealis, Julius Frontinus, and Julius Agricola, the latter Tacitus's father-in-law—enlarged the province to include Wales and northern England; Agricola even reached the Scottish highlands before Domitian recalled him.

Along the Rhine, weaknesses revealed by Civilis' revolt were repaired. Vespasian crossed the river in 74 and annexed the Agri Decumates, the triangle of land between the Rhine, Danube, and Main rivers. To consolidate the position, he and Domitian after him penetrated the Neckar River valley and Taunus mountains, and fortifications began to take shape to the east of the Rhine, a military boundary complete with strongpoints, watchtowers, and, later, a continuous rampart of earthworks and palisades. Once Saturninus's revolt in 89 had been suppressed, Domitian felt the situation along the Rhine sufficiently stable to warrant conversion of the military districts of Upper and Lower Germany into regular provinces and the transfer of some Rhineland troops to the Danube. To the north of this latter river, the Dacians had been organized into a strong kingdom, ruled by Decebalus and centring on modern Romania; in 85 they raided southward across the Danube, and in the next year they defeated the Roman punitive expedition. Domitian restored the situation in 88, but Saturninus's rebellion prevented him from following up his success. Domitian and Decebalus thereupon came to terms: Decebalus was to protect the lower

Danube against Sarmatian attack, and Domitian was to pay him an annual subsidy in recompense. The Danubian frontier, however, remained disturbed, and Domitian wisely strengthened its garrisons; by the end of his reign it contained nine legions, as against the Rhineland's six, and Pannonia was soon to become the military centre of gravity of the empire.

The Flavians also took measures to strengthen the eastern frontier. In Asia Minor, Vespasian created a large "armed" province by amalgamating Cappadocia, Lesser Armenia, and Galatia; and the whole area was provided with a network of military roads. South of Asia Minor, Judaea was converted into an "armed" province by getting legionary troops; and two client kingdoms—Commagene and Transjordan—were annexed and added to Syria. Furthermore, the legionary camps seem now to have been established right on the Euphrates at the principal river crossings. This display of military strength kept the empire and Parthia at peace for many years.

THE EARLY ANTONINE EMPERORS: NERVA AND TRAJAN

Marcus Cocceius Nerva, an elderly senator of some distinction, was the choice of Domitian's assassins for emperor; and the Senate promptly recognized him. The soldiers, however, did so much more reluctantly, and, because the year 69 had revealed that emperors no longer needed to be Roman aristocrats and could be chosen in places other than Rome, their attitude imposed caution.

Nerva, who ruled from 96 to 98, adopted a generally lavish and liberal policy, but it failed to win the soldiers over completely, and he proved unable to save all Domitian's murderers from their vengeance. Unrest subsided only when, overlooking kinsmen of his own, he adopted an outstanding soldier, Marcus Ulpius Trajanus, who was governor of Upper Germany, as his successor. Nerva himself died a few months later.

Trajan (ruled 98–117) was the first and perhaps the only emperor to be adopted by a predecessor totally unrelated to him by either birth or marriage. He was also the first in a series of "good" rulers who succeeded one another by adoption and for most of the second century provided the empire with internal harmony and careful government; they are collectively, if somewhat loosely, called the Antonine emperors. More significantly still, Trajan, a Spaniard, was also the first princeps to come from the provinces; with the greater number of provincials now in the Senate, the elevation of one of them, sooner or later, was practically inevitable. Throughout his reign, Trajan generally observed constitutional practices. Mindful of the susceptibilities of the Senate, he regularly consulted and reported to it. Modest in his bearing, he did not claim ostentatious honours such as frequent consulships or numerous imperial salutations, and he mixed easily with senators on terms of cordial friendship. This reestablished mutual respect between princeps and

Senate. Empire and liberty, in Tacitus's words, were reconciled, and the atmosphere of suspicion, intrigue, and terror surrounding the court in Domitian's day disappeared. Trajan endeared himself also to the populace at large with lavish building programs, gladiatorial games, and public distributions of money. Above all, he was popular with the armed forces; he was the soldier-emperor par excellence. Understandably, he received the title Optimus (Best), officially from 114 on (and unofficially for many years earlier).

Yet Trajan was a thoroughgoing autocrat who intervened without hesitation or scruple even in the senatorial sphere, whenever it seemed necessary. His aim was efficiency; his desire was to promote public welfare everywhere. He embellished Rome with splendid and substantial structures, and he showed his care for Italy by refurbishing and enlarging the harbours at Ostia, Centumcellae, and Ancona. He sent officials called *curatores* to Italian municipalities in financial difficulties and helped to rehabilitate them. He greatly expanded an ingenious charity scheme probably begun by Nerva: money was loaned to farmers on easy terms, and the low interest they paid went into a special fund for supporting indigent children. Nor did Trajan neglect Italy's highway network: he built a new road (Via Traiana) that soon replaced the Via Appia as the main thoroughfare between Beneventum and Brundisium.

Interest in Italy implied no neglect of the provinces. Curatores were also sent to them; to rescue Achaea and Bithynia, senatorial provinces, from threatened bankruptcy, Trajan made them both temporarily imperial, sending special commissioners of his own to them. His correspondence with his appointee in Bithynia, the younger Pliny, has survived and reveals how conscientiously the emperor responded on even the smallest details. At the same time, it reveals how limited was access to the central government and, consequently, how great a latitude for independent decisions must be left to the governors who lacked some special claim on the emperor's attention. Trajan's day was too short to hear every speech of every delegation from the provinces, every recommendation to bestow favour or grant promotion, and every appeal to himself as supreme judiciary. To assist him, he had a "bureaucracy" of only a few hundred in Rome and a few more hundred serving in various capacities in the provinces—to direct the lives of some 60 million people. Clearly, most government must in fact rest in the hands of local aristocracies.

In the military sphere, Trajan's reign proved a most dynamic one. He decided to strengthen the dangerous Danube frontier by converting Dacia into a salient of Roman territory north of the river in order to dismember the Sarmatian tribes and remove the risk of large, hostile combinations to a safer distance. Bringing to bear a force of 100,000 men, he conquered Decebalus in two hard-fought wars (101–102; 105–106) and annexed Dacia, settling it with people from neighbouring parts of the empire. On the eastern frontier he planned a similar operation, evidently in the conviction, shared by many eminent Romans both before and after him, that only conquest could solve the Parthian problem. Possibly, too, he wished to contain the menace of the Sarmatian Alani in the Caspian region. In a preliminary move, the Nabataean kingdom of Arabia Petraea was annexed in 105–106. Then, in 114, Trajan assembled another large army, incorporated the client kingdom of Armenia, and invaded Parthia.

After spectacular victories in 115 and 116, he created additional provinces (Northern Mesopotamia, Assyria) and reached the Persian Gulf. But he had merely overrun Mesopotamia; he had not consolidated it, and, as his army passed, revolts broke out in its rear. The Jews of the Diaspora and others seized their chance to rebel, and before the end of 116 much of the Middle East besides Parthia was in arms (Cyrene, Egypt, Cyprus, Anatolia). Trajan proceeded resolutely to restore the situation, but death found him still in the East.

Before his last illness he had not formally indicated his successor. But high honours and important posts had been accorded his nearest male relative, Publius Aelius Hadrianus, the governor of Syria; and, according to Trajan's widow, Hadrian had actually been adopted by Trajan on his deathbed. Accordingly, both Senate and soldiers recognized him. Trajan's posthumous deification was never in doubt.

HADRIAN AND THE OTHER ANTONINE EMPERORS

Hadrian (ruled 117–138), also a Spaniard, was an emperor of unusual versatility. Unlike Trajan, he was opposed to territorial expansion. Being himself in the East in 117, he renounced Trajan's conquests there immediately and contemplated evacuating Dacia as well. Furthermore, four of the consular generals particularly identified with Trajan's military ventures were arrested and executed "for conspiracy"; Hadrian claimed later that the Senate ordered their deaths against his wishes. The only heavy fighting during his generally peaceful reign occurred in Judaea—or Syria Palaestina, as it was thenceforth called—where Bar Kokhba led a furious, if futile, Jewish revolt (132–135) against Hadrian's conversion of Jerusalem into a Roman colony named Aelia Capitolina.

Instead of expansion by war, Hadrian sought carefully delimited but well-defended frontiers, with client states beyond them where possible. The frontiers themselves, when not natural barriers, were strongly fortified: in Britain, Hadrian's Wall, a complex of ditches, mounds, forts, and stone wall, stretched across the island from the Tyne to the Solway; Germany and Raetia had a limes (fortified boundary) running between Mainz on the Rhine and Regensburg on the Danube. Within the frontiers the army was kept at full strength, mostly by local recruiting of legionnaires and apparently of auxiliaries, too (so that Vespasian's system of having the latter serve far from their homelands gradually ceased). Moreover, the tendency for auxiliaries to be assimilated to legionaries continued; even the officers became less distinguishable, because equites now sometimes replaced senators in high posts in the legions. To keep his essentially sedentary army in constant readiness and at peak efficiency (no easy task), Hadrian carried out frequent personal inspections, spending about half his reign in the provinces (121–125; 128–134).

Hadrian also was responsible for significant developments on the civilian side. Under him, equites were no longer required to do military service as an essential step in their career, and many of them were employed in the imperial civil service, more even than under Domitian. By now the formative days of the civil service were over; its bureaucratic phase was beginning, and it offered those equites who had no military aspirations an attractive, purely civilian career. Formal titles now marked the different equestrian grades of dignity: a procurator was *vir egregius*; an ordinary prefect, *vir perfectissimus*; a praetorian prefect, *vir eminentissimus*, the latter title being obviously parallel to the designation *vir clarissimus* for a senator. Thenceforth, equites replaced freedmen in the imperial household and bureaus, and they even appeared in Hadrian's imperial council.

Hadrian also improved legal administration. He had his expert jurists codify the edictum perpetuum (the set of rules gradually elaborated by the praetors for the interpretation of the law). He also appointed four former consuls to serve as circuit judges in Italy. This brought Italy close to becoming a province; Hadrian's intent, however, was not to reduce the status of Italy but to make all parts of the empire important. For one part of his realm, he was exceptionally solicitous: he spent much time in Greece and lavishly embellished Athens.

Hadrian maintained good relations with but was never fully trusted by the Senate. His foreign policy seemed to be unheroic, his cosmopolitanism to be un-Roman, and his reforms to encroach on activities traditionally reserved for senators. Moreover, in his last two years he was sometimes capricious and tyrannous. Like Augustus, he had no son of his own and conducted a frustrating search for a successor. After executing his only male blood relative, his grandnephew, in 136, he adopted Lucius Ceionius Commodus, renaming him Lucius Aelius Caesar. The latter, however, died shortly afterward, whereupon Hadrian in 138 chose a wealthy but sonless senator, the 51-year-old Titus Aurelius Antoninus. Evidently intent on founding a dynasty, he made Antoninus, in his turn, adopt two youths—Marcus Aurelius (the nephew of Antoninus's wife) and Lucius Verus (the son of Aelius Caesar) 16 and 7 years old, respectively. When Hadrian died soon thereafter, Antoninus succeeded and induced a reluctant Senate to deify the deceased emperor. According to some, it was this act of filial piety that won for Antoninus his cognomen, Pius.

Antoninus Pius (ruled 138–161) epitomizes the Roman Empire at its cosmopolitan best. He himself was of Gallic origin; his wife was of Spanish origin. For most men his was a reign of quiet prosperity, and the empire under him deserves the praises lavished upon it by the contemporary writer Aelius Aristides. Unlike Hadrian, Antoninus traveled little; he remained in Italy, where in 148 he celebrated the 900th anniversary of Rome. Princeps and Senate were on excellent terms, and coins with the words *tranquillitas* and *concordia* on them in Antoninus's case mean what they say. Other of his coins not unreasonably proclaim *felicitas temporum* ("the happiness of the times"). Yet raids and rebellions in many of the borderlands (in Britain, Dacia, Mauretania, Egypt, Palaestina, and elsewhere) were danger symptoms, even though to the empire at large they seemed only faraway bad dreams, to use the expression of Aelius Aristides. Antoninus prudently pushed the Hadrianic frontiers forward in Dacia, the Rhineland, and Britain (where the Antonine Wall from the Firth of Forth to the River Clyde became the new boundary) and carefully groomed his heir apparent for his imperial responsibilities.

Marcus Aurelius (ruled 161–180) succeeded the deified Antoninus and more than honoured Hadrian's intentions by immediately co-opting Lucius Verus as his full co-emperor. Because Verus's competence was unproved, this excess of zeal

was imprudent. Fortunately, Verus left decision making to Marcus. Marcus's action was also dangerous for another reason; it represented a long step away from imperial unity and portended the ultimate division of the empire into Greek- and Latin-speaking halves. Nor was this the only foreboding development in Marcus's reign—formidable barbarian assaults were launched against the frontiers, anticipating those that were later to bring about the disintegration of the empire. Marcus himself was a stoic philosopher; his humanistic, if somewhat pessimistic, *Meditations* reveal how conscientiously he took his duties. Duty called him to war; he responded to the call and spent far more of his reign in the field than had any previous emperor.

At Marcus's very accession the Parthians turned aggressive, and he sent Verus to defend Roman interests (162). Verus greedily took credit for any victories but left serious fighting to Avidius Cassius and the army of Syria. Cassius succeeded in overrunning Mesopotamia and even took Ctesiphon, the Parthian capital; he was therefore able to conclude a peace that safeguarded Rome's eastern provinces and client kingdoms (166). In the process, however, his troops became infected with plague, and they carried it back with them to the west with calamitous results. The Danube frontier, already weakened by the dispatch of large detachments to the East, collapsed under barbarian assault. Pressed on from behind by Goths, Vandals, Lombards, and others, the Germanic Marcomanni and Quadi and the Sarmatian Iazyges poured over the river; the Germans actually crossed Raetia, Noricum, and Pannonia to raid northern Italy and besiege Aquileia. Marcus and Verus relieved the city shortly before Verus's death (169). Then, making Pannonia his pivot of maneuver, Marcus pushed the invaders back; by 175 they were again beyond the Danube. At that moment, however, a false report of Marcus's death prompted Avidius Cassius, by now in charge of all eastern provinces, to proclaim himself emperor. The news of this challenge undid Marcus's achievements along the Danube because it took him to the East and reopened the door to barbarian attacks. Fortunately, Cassius was soon murdered, and Marcus could return to central Europe (177). But he had barely restored the frontier again when he died at Vindobona (Vienna) in 180, bequeathing the empire to his son, the 19-year-old Commodus, who had actually been named co-emperor three years earlier.

Commodus (ruled 180–192), like Gaius and Nero, the youthful emperors before him, proved incompetent, conceited, and capricious. Fortunately, the frontiers remained intact, thanks to able provincial governors and to barbarian allies, who had been settled along the Danube with land grants and who gave military service in return. But Commodus abandoned Marcus's scheme for new trans-Danubian provinces, preferring to devote himself to sensual pleasures and especially to the excitements of the arena in Rome, where he posed as Hercules Romanus and forced the Senate to recognize his godhead officially. He left serious business to his favourites, whose ambitions and intrigues led to plots, treason trials, confiscations, and insensate murders. Commodus's assassination on the last day of 192 terminated a disastrous reign; thus the Antonines, like the Julio-Claudians, had come to an ignominious end. And there was a similar sequel. Commodus's damnatio memoriae, like Nero's, was followed by a year of four emperors.

THE EMPIRE IN THE SECOND CENTURY

The century and three-quarters after Augustus's death brought no fundamental changes to the principate, although so long a lapse of time naturally introduced modifications and shifts of emphasis. By Flavian and Antonine times the principate was accepted universally. For the provinces, a return to the republic was utterly unthinkable; for Rome and Italy, the year 69 served as a grim warning of the chaos to be expected if, in the absence of a princeps, the ambitions of a few powerful individuals obtained unfettered scope. A princeps was clearly a necessity, and people were even prepared to tolerate a bad one, although naturally they always hoped for a good one.

The princeps, moreover, did not have to be chosen any longer from the Julio-Claudians. The great achievement of the Flavians was to reconcile the soldiers and the upper classes everywhere to the idea that others were eligible. The Flavians' frequent tenure of consulship and censorship invested their family, although not of the highest nobility, with the outward trappings of prestige and the aristocratic appearance of an authentic imperial household. The deification of the first two Flavians contributed to the same end, and so did the disappearance of old republican families that might have outranked the reigning house (by 69 most descendants of the republican nobility had either died of natural causes or been exterminated by imperial persecution). After the Flavians, the newness of a man's senatorial dignity and the obscurity of his ultimate origin, whether it was Italian or otherwise, no longer forbade his possible elevation. Indeed, Domitian's successors and even Domitian himself in his last years did not need to enhance their own importance by repeated consulships. The Antonine emperors, like the Julio-Claudians, held the office infrequently. They did, however, continue the Flavian practice of emphasizing the loftiness of their families by deifying deceased relatives (Trajan deified his sister, his niece, and his father; Antoninus, his wife; and so forth).

TREND TO ABSOLUTE MONARCHY

Glorification of the reigning house, together with a document such as Vespasian's Lex de Imperio, helped to advertise the emperor's position; and under the Flavians and Antonines the principate became much more like an avowed monarchy. Proconsular *imperium* began to be reflected in the imperial titulary, and official documents started calling the emperor *dominus noster* ("our master").

The development of imperial lawmaking clearly illustrates the change. From the beginnings of the principate, the emperor had had the power to legislate, although no law is known that formally recognized his right to do so; by Antonine times, legal textbooks stated unequivocally that whatever the emperor ordered was legally binding. The early emperors usually made the Senate their mouthpiece and issued their laws in the form of senatorial decrees. In fact, by the second century, the emperor was openly replacing whatever other sources of written law had hitherto been permitted to function. After 100 the Assembly never met formally to pass a law, and the Senate often no longer bothered to couch its decrees in legal language, being content to repeat verbatim the speech with which the ruler had advocated the measure in question. After Hadrian, magistrates ceased modifying existing law by their legal interpretations because the praetors' *edictum perpetuum* had become a permanent code, which the emperor alone could alter.

By 200, learned jurists had lost the right they had enjoyed since the time of Augustus of giving authoritative rulings on disputed points (*responsa prudentium*). Meanwhile, the emperor more and more was legislating directly by means of edicts, judgments, mandates, and rescripts—collectively known as *constitutiones principum*. He usually issued such *constitutiones* only after consulting the "friends" (*amici Caesaris*) who composed his imperial council. But a *constitutio* was nevertheless a fiat. The road to the later dominate (after 284) lay open.

POLITICAL LIFE

Nevertheless, the autocratic aspect of the Flavian and Antonine regimes should not be overstressed. Augustus himself had been well aware that it was impossible to disguise permanently the supremacy that accumulation of powers gained piecemeal conferred; his deportment in his last years differed little from that of Vespasian, Titus, and the so-called five good emperors who followed them. Nor had other Julio-Claudians hesitated to parade their predominance—Claudius, by centralizing the imperial powers, reduced their apparent diversity to one all-embracing *imperium*; Gaius and Nero revealed the autocracy implicit in the principate with frank brutality.

What impresses perhaps as much as the undoubtedly autocratic behaviour of the Flavians and Antonines is the markedly civilian character of their reigns. They held supreme power, and some of them were distinguished soldiers; yet they were not military despots. For this the old republican tradition—whereby a state official might serve in both a civilian and a military capacity—was largely responsible. Matters, however, were open to change after Hadrian separated the two realms of service. Actually, the third century soon showed what it meant to have a princeps whose whole experience had been confined to camps and barracks.

As imperial powers became more concentrated, republican institutions decayed; the importance of imperial officials grew, while the authority of urban magistrates declined. Quaestorship, praetorship, and consulship (the last-named now reduced to a two-month sinecure) became mere stepping-stones to the great imperial posts that counted most in the life of the empire. Governors of imperial provinces and commanders of legions were Roman senators; but they were equally imperial appointees. Clearly, the emperor was the master of the Senate; and it was disingenuous for him to get impatient, as some emperors did, with the Senate's lack of initiative and reluctance to take firm decisions of its own. The emperor might not even consult the Senate much, preferring to rely on his imperial council, in which equestrian bureau chiefs over the course of the second century came to constitute an established element.

The Senate, however, at least until the reign of Commodus, was treated courteously by most Flavians and Antonines. They recognized its importance as a law-court, as the body that formally appointed a new emperor, and as a sounding board of informed opinion. Senators came increasingly from the provinces, and, although this meant preeminently the western provinces (the Greek-speaking

East being underrepresented), the Senate did reflect to some extent the views of the empire at large.

The equites, meanwhile, steadily acquired greater importance as imperial officials. In newly created posts they invariably became the incumbents, and in posts of long standing they replaced freedmen and *publicani*. During the second century equestrian procurators increased markedly in numbers as the direction of imperial business came to be more tidily subdivided. Four grades of service distinguished by salary were established. While the government assumed a more rational flow and outline, its total number of employees nevertheless remained quite tiny, compared with that of the fourth and later centuries.

ROME AND ITALY

By the second century the city of Rome had attracted freeborn migrants from all over the empire; it housed, additionally, large numbers of manumitted slaves. These newcomers were all assimilated and diluted the city's Italian flavour. The vast majority of them were poor, the handful of opulent imperial freedmen being entirely exceptional. But many were energetic, enterprising, and lucky, able to make their way in the world. Freedmen laboured under a social stigma, although some of them managed to become equites. Their sons, however, might overcome discrimination, and their grandsons were even eligible for membership in the Senate.

Inevitably, there was extensive trade and commerce (much of it in freedman hands) in so large a city, which was also the centre of imperial administration. There was little industry, however, and the urban poor had difficulty finding steady employment. Theirs was a precarious existence, dependent on the public grain dole and on the private charity of the wealthy. Large building programs gave Flavian and Antonine emperors the opportunity not only to repair the damage caused by fire and falling buildings (as stated, a frequent hazard among the densely packed and flimsily built accommodations for the urban plebs) but also to relieve widespread urban unemployment. They also made imperial Rome a city of grandeur. Augustus's building program had been vast but mostly concerned with repairing or rebuilding structures already existing, and his Julio-Claudian successors had built relatively little until the great fire made room for the megalomaniac marvels of Nero's last years. It was under the Flavians and Antonines that Rome obtained many of its most celebrated structures: the Colosseum, Palatine palaces, Trajan's Forum, the Pantheon, the Castel Sant' Angelo (Hadrian's mausoleum), the Temple of Antoninus and Faustina, Aurelius's Column, as well as the aqueducts whose arches spanned across Campagna to keep the city and its innumerable fountains supplied with water.

Italy was much less cosmopolitan and sophisticated and, according to literary tradition, much more sober and

The remains of Rome's famed Colosseum, built as part of a work project designed to stabilize the economy and help the city return to its former glory. Shutterstock.com

straitlaced than was Rome. It was the mistress of the empire, although the gap between it and the provinces was narrowing. Hadrian's policies especially helped to reduce its privileged position. His use of circuit judges was resented precisely because with them Italy resembled a province; actually, Italy badly needed them, and their abolition by Antoninus Pius was soon reversed by Marcus Aurelius. Also, in Aurelius's reign a provincial fate overtook Italy in the form of barbarian invasion; a few years later the country got its first legionary garrison under Septimius Severus.

The economic importance of Italy also declined. By the end of Augustus's reign, the ascendancy of its wine, oil, marble, and fine pottery in the markets of Gaul and Germany had already begun to yield to the competition of local production in the West; and, by Flavian times, Italy was actually importing heavily not only from Gaul (witness the crates of yet-unpacked Gallic bowls and plates caught in the destruction of Pompeii) but also from Spain. The latter province was especially represented by its extraordinarily popular condiment, *garum*; its olive oil, too, was a sizable item on Italian tables after AD 100, only to yield its primacy there, by the mid-second century, to oil from northern Africa. By then, Spanish, Gallic, and African farm products all outweighed Italian ones in Ostia and Rome. Against such tendencies, the emperors did what they could: Domitian, for example, protected Italian viticulture by restricting vine growing in the provinces; Trajan and his successors forced Roman senators to take an interest in the country, even though it was no longer the homeland of many of them, by investing a high proportion of their capital in Italian land (one-third under Trajan, one-quarter under Aurelius).

DEVELOPMENTS IN THE PROVINCES

The 18th-century historian Edward Gibbon's famous description of the second century as the period when men were happiest and most prosperous is not entirely false. Certainly, by then people had come to take for granted the unique greatness and invincibility of the empire. Even the ominous events of Aurelius's reign failed to shatter their conviction that the empire was impregnable, and the internal disturbances of the preceding reign had not given cause for much alarm. The credit for the empire's success lay less with what its rulers did and could do than with what they did not do: they did not interfere too much. The empire was a vast congeries of peoples and races with differing religions, customs, and languages, and the emperors were content to let them live their own lives. Imperial policy favoured a veneer of common culture transcending ethnic differences, but there was no deliberate denationalization.

Ambitious men striving for a career naturally found it helpful, if not necessary, to become Roman in bearing and conduct and perhaps even in language as well (although speakers of Greek often rose to exalted positions). But local self-government was the general rule, and neither Latin nor Roman ways were imposed on the communities composing the empire. The official attitude to religion illustrates this—in line with the absolutist trend, emperor worship was becoming slowly but progressively more theocratic (Domitian relished the title of god, Commodus demanded it). Yet this did not lead to the suppression of non-Roman or even outlandish cults, unless they were thought immoral (like Druidism, with its human sacrifice) or conducive to public disorder (like Christianity, with its uncompromising dismissal of all gods other than its own as mere demons, and wicked and hurtful ones at that).

While there is no indication that the central authorities consciously opposed the increase of governmental personnel, the number of government employees certainly grew very slowly. Thus the responsibilities of the magnates in provincial cities were correspondingly great. In parts of southern Spain or in the area south of the Black Sea, for example, where the extent of the territories dependent on cities stretched out over many scores of miles into the surrounding landscape, city senators had not only to collect taxes but also to build roads and carry out much rural police work. Within their cities, too, senators had to see to the collection of taxes and tolls. As a group, they had to oversee and assign the income from municipal lands or buildings rented out and from endowments established by generous citizens. They had to authorize the plans and financing of sometimes very elaborate civic structures—an aqueduct, an amphitheatre, or a temple to the imperial family—or of great annual festivals and fairs or of ongoing amenities serving the public baths (free oil for anointing oneself, heating, and upkeep) or the public markets. In the eastern provinces, they had to replenish from time to time the stock of small local bronze coins, and they had to insure that magistracies were effectively staffed, even though there usually was no salary of any sort to attract candidates. Magistrates and city senators generally had to pay handsomely for their election and thereafter make further handsome contributions, as need arose and so far as they could afford, toward the adornment of their community.

What attracted candidates in adequate numbers were most often three inducements: the feeling of community approval and praise, offered in the most public ways (described by writers of the time with striking psychological penetration); the enhancement of personal influence (meaning power) through the demonstration of great financial means; and finally, the social and political advancement that might follow on local prominence through attracting the attention of a governor or of the emperor himself. It was from the provincial elite that new Roman senators were made.

Cities, through their elite families, competed with each other across entire regions. City rivalries in northern Italy or western Anatolia happen to be especially well reported. Within individual cities, elite families were often in competition as well. In consequence, the standards of municipal beneficence rose, encouraged by a populace who on public occasions assembled in large numbers in the theatre, demanding yet more expenditure from their leaders. The emperors, who realized that the well-being of cities, the jewels of their realm, depended on such munificence, increasingly intervened to insure a continued flow of good things from the rich of a community to their fellow citizens. Legislation might, for example, specify the binding nature of electoral campaign promises or of formerly voluntary contributions connected with public service. As a consequence, in the second century consideration must for the first time be given to the local aristocrat unwilling to serve his city; the series of imperial pronouncements exerting compulsion on such a person to serve was to stretch far into the future, with increasing severity. Attempts to stabilize the benefits arising from ambitious rivalries thus had an oppressive aspect.

As to the lower orders, their voice is rarely heard in surviving sources, except in acclamation. So long as the rich voluntarily covered the bulk of local expenses and so long as they commanded the leisure and knowledge of the world to give to administration unsalaried, the poor could not fairly claim much of a right to determine the city's choices. Thus they acclaimed the candidacies of the rich and their gifts and otherwise gave vent to their wishes only by shouting in unison in the theatre or amphitheatre (in between spectacles) or through violent mob actions.

As noted above, the poor routinely solved the problems of daily life by appealing to someone of influence locally; this was true whether in Palestine, as indicated in the Talmud, or in Italy, as is evident from Pliny's correspondence. The higher one looked in society, the more it appeared crisscrossed and interconnected by ties of kinship or of past services exchanged. It was at these higher levels that answers to routine problems were to be sought. Appeal was not directed to one's peers, even though trade associations, cult groups of social equals, and burial insurance clubs with monthly meetings could be found in every town. Such groups served social, not political or economic, purposes, at least during the principate.

Accordingly, society was ordinarily described by contemporaries simply in terms of two classes: the upper and the lower, rich and poor, powerful and dependent, well known and nameless. The upper classes consisted of little more than 600 Roman senators, 25,000 equites, and 100,000 city senators; hence, a total amounting to 2 percent of the population.

This stratum, from the mid-second century defined in law as "the more honourable," *honestiores*, was minutely subdivided into degrees of dignity, the degrees being well advertised and jealously asserted; the entire stratum, however, was entitled to receive specially tender treatment in the courts. The remaining population was lumped together as "the more lowly," *humiliores*, subject to torture when giving witness in court; to beatings, not fines; and to execution (in increasingly savage forms of death) rather than exile for the most serious crimes. Yet because of the existing patterns of power, which directed the *humiliores* to turn for help to the upper stratum, the lower classes did not form a revolutionary mass but constituted a stable element.

The pyramidal structure of society suggested by the statistics given above is somewhat obscured by the reality and prominence of the urban scene. In the cities the harsh outlines of the distribution of wealth were moderated by a certain degree of social mobility. No class offers more success stories than that of freedmen. Especially in the West, freedmen are astonishingly prominent in the record of inscriptions and proverbial for what the upper classes called unprincipled enterprise and vulgar moneygrubbing. Artisans and tradespeople—lowly folk, in the eyes of someone like Cicero—in fact presented themselves with a certain dignity, even some financial ease. At the bottom, slaves were numerous, constituting perhaps one-tenth of the population in at least the larger towns outside of Italy and considerably more in Italy—as much as one-quarter in Rome.

In the cities many of them at least enjoyed security from starvation and had a good roof over their heads. When one turns to the rural scene, however, one encounters a far larger, harsher world. In the first place, nine-tenths of the empire's people lived on the land and from its yield. Where details of their lives emerge with any clarity, they most often tell of a changeless and bleak existence. The city looked down on the countryside with elaborate scorn, keeping the rural population at arm's length. Very often people in the country had their own language— such as Gallic, Syriac, Libyphoenician, or Coptic, which further isolated them—and their own religion, marriage customs, and forms of entertainment. In time, the very term "country dweller," *paganus*, set the rural population still further apart from the empire's Christianized urban population.

THE CREATION OF A UNIFIED CIVILIZATION

In the overall context of Western history, the degree to which the Mediterranean world during the period of the empire became one single system, one civilization, is a matter of the greatest importance. Clearly, one must distinguish between the life of the rural masses and that of the urban minority. The former retained many traits of a way of life predating not only Roman conquest but, in the East, the conquests of Alexander the Great centuries earlier. However, the device of organizing conquered territories under cities responsible for their surrounding territory proved as successful under the Romans as under the Greeks. The intent of both conquerors may have been limited to ensuring political control and the yield of tribute; however, in fact, they achieved much more: an approach to uniformity, at least in the cities.

URBAN CENTRES

The first thing to strike the traveler's eye, in any survey of the second-century empire, would have been the physical appearance of urban centres. Whatever the province, many of the same architectural forms could be observed: The suburbs tended to have aqueducts and racetracks and the cities a central grand market area surrounded by porticoes, temples, a records office, a council hall, a basilica for judicial hearings and public auctions, and a covered market hall of a characteristic shape for perishable foods (a macellum, as in Pompeii, in Perge on the southern coast of modern Turkey, or in North African Lepcis). There also would have been public baths with several separate halls for cold or hot bathing or exercise, a covered or open-air theatre, grand fountains, monumental arches, and honorific statues of local worthies by the dozens or even hundreds. Eastern centres would have gymnasia (occasionally Western ones as well) and Western

The hot room of the imperial baths at Trier, Ger. Fototeca Unione

cities would have amphitheatres (occasionally Eastern ones as well) for the imported institution of gladiatorial combats. Throughout the Western provinces, public buildings were likely to be arranged according to a single plan—more or less the same everywhere—in which a grid of right-angle streets was dominant, at least toward the central part of the city.

In the West, as opposed to the East, a great deal of urbanization remained to be done and was accomplished by the Romans. The grid plan, its particular mark, can be detected at the heart of places such as Turin, Banasa (Morocco), and Autun, all Augustan foundations, as well as in Nicopolis (Bulgaria), Budapest, and Silchester, all later ones. As noted above, orthogonal town planning was not a Roman invention, but the Romans introduced it to new regions and with a particular regularity of their own. Moreover, the grid of the central part of the city was matched, and sometimes extended on the same lines, by another grid laid across the surrounding territory. The process, referred to as centuriation,

The ancient Roman city of Thamugadi in northeastern Algeria, founded by Trajan in AD 100.
Fototeca Unione

typically made use of squares of 2,330 feet (710 metres) on a side, intended for land distribution to settlers and general purposes of inventory. Signs of it were first detected in northern Africa in the 1830s, through surviving crop marks and roads, and have since (especially through air photography) been traced in the environs of Trier and Homs (Syria) and large areas of northern Italy, Tunisia, and elsewhere. In the placing of cities and roads and property boundaries, the Romans of the empire therefore left a nearly indelible stamp of their organizing energies on the map of Europe; they also established the lives of conquered populations inside their own characteristic framework.

LATINIZATION

The special burst of energy in the Augustan colonizing spread abroad not only the visible elements of a ruling civilization but the invisible ones as well. Colonies and municipalities received Roman forms of government according to their charters, they were administered by Roman law in Latin, and they diffused these things throughout the general population within and around them. In frontier areas such lessons in an alien civilization were pressed home by garrison forces through their frequent contacts with their hosts and suppliers. By the second century considerable Latinization had occurred in the West. Modern Spanish, Portuguese, and French show that this was particularly true of the Iberian peninsula, which had been provincial soil ever since the Second Punic War, and of Gaul, where Latin enjoyed the advantage of some relationship to Celtic. In these regions, except in the less accessible rural or mountainous parts, even the lower orders adopted Latin. Today one can find in Romania the tongue that is the closest to its parent, Latin, even at so great a distance from its home. And Latin can be found not only in Romance languages; it has left its mark on languages such as Basque and German.

Inscriptions represent the most frequent testimony to linguistic allegiance; more than a quarter of a million survive in Latin from the period of the empire, the vast majority of them being funerary. The number of inscriptions per year increases slowly during the first century and a half AD, thereafter ascending in a steep line to a point in the second decade of the third and then falling off even more steeply. The curve is best explained as reflecting pride in "Romanness"—in possessing not only Latin but full citizenship as well and, thereby, admission to a group for whom commemoration of the deceased was a legal as well as a moral duty. Over the course of time, by individual gift from the emperors, by army service, and by election to magistracies or simply to the city senates of colonies and municipalities, a growing proportion of the empire's population had gained citizenship; moreover, their children were citizens, whose descendants in turn were Romans in the legal sense. By AD 212 this accelerating process had advanced so far that the emperor Caracalla could offer the gift of incorporation to the entirety of his subjects without much notice being taken of his generosity—it was already in the possession of most of the people who counted and whose reactions might be recorded. Once citizenship was universal, it ceased to constitute a distinction; thus the declaration of it through the custom of funerary commemoration rapidly passed out of favour.

LIMITS OF UNIFICATION

One great flaw in the picture of the empire as one single civilization by 212, triumphantly unified in culture as in its political form, has already been pointed out—what was achieved within the cities' walls did not extend with any completeness to the rural population, among whom local ways and native languages persisted. Peasants in fourth-century Syria spoke mostly Syriac, in Egypt mostly Coptic, in Africa often Punic or Libyphoenician, and in the Danube and northwestern provinces other native tongues.

There was still another great flaw: The empire was half Roman (or Latin), half Greek. The latter was hardly touched by the former except through what may be called official channels—that is, law, coinage, military presence, imperial cult, and the superposition of an alien structure of power and prestige, to which the elite of the Eastern provinces might aspire. On the other hand, the Roman half was steeped in Greek ways. Apuleius, for example, though born and reared in a small North African town of the second century, was sent to Athens to study rhetoric. On his return he could find not only an audience for his presentations in Greek but ordinary people in the marketplace able to read a letter in that language. In Rome the Christian community used Greek as its liturgical language well into the third century, and the crowds in the Circus Maximus could enjoy a pun in Greek. An aristocrat such as the emperor Marcus Aurelius could be expected to be as bilingual as was Cicero or Caesar before him or even, like the emperor Gallienus, help the Greek philosopher Plotinus found a sort of Institute for Advanced Studies in the Naples area.

Greece continued to supply a great deal of sculpture for Western buyers or even the teams of artisans needed for the decoration of public buildings in third-century northern Africa. By such various means the division between the two halves of the empire was for a time covered over.

CULT OF THE EMPERORS

Among the institutions most important in softening the edges of regional differences was the cult of the emperors. In one sense, it originated in the fourth century BC, when Alexander the Great first received veneration by titles and symbols and forms of address as if he were a superhuman being. Indeed, he must have seemed exactly that to contemporaries in Egypt, where the pharaohs had long been worshiped, and to peoples in the Middle East, for similar reasons of religious custom. Even the Greeks were quite used to the idea that beings who lived a human life of extraordinary accomplishment, as "heroes" in the full sense of the Greek word, would never die but be raised into some higher world; they believed this of heroes such as Achilles, Hercules, Pythagoras, and Dion of Syracuse in the mid-fourth century BC. Great Roman commanders, like Hellenistic rulers, had altars, festivals, and special honours voted to them by Greek cities from the start of the second century BC.

It was not so strange, then, that a freedman supporter of Caesar's erected a pillar over the ashes of the dead dictator in the Forum in April 44 BC and offered cult to him as a being now resident among the gods. Many citizens joined in. Within days Caesar's heir Octavian pressed for the declaration of Caesar as divine—which the Senate granted by its vote in 42. By 25 BC the city of Mytilene had organized annual cult acts honouring Augustus and communicated their forms and impulse to Tarraco in Spain as well as to other Eastern Greek cities. By 12 BC divine honours to Caesar and

Augustus's *genius* were established through the emperors' initiative both in the Gallic capital, Lugdunum, and in the neighbourhood chapels to the crossroads gods in Rome.

From these various points and models, emperor worship spread rapidly. Within a few generations, cities everywhere had built in its service new temples that dominated their forums or had assigned old temples to the joint service of a prior god and the imperial family. Such centres served as rallying points for the citizenry to express its devotion to Rome and the emperor. To speak for whole provinces, priests of the cult assembled during their year of office in central shrines, such as Lugdunum, as delegates of their cities, where they formulated for the emperor their complaints or their views on the incumbent governor's administration. Whether these priests were freedmen in urban neighbourhoods, municipal magnates in local temples, or still grander leaders of the provinces, they perceived the imperial cult as something of high prestige and invested it and Roman rule with glory.

The emotional and political unification of the empire was further promoted by submissive or flattering forms of reference or address, adopted even by the highest personages when speaking of the emperor, and by portraits of the emperors or their families with attendant written messages. Of these two most obvious means of propaganda, the first survives in the texts of many panegyrics delivered to the throne, rhetorical disquisitions on monarchy, and prefatory announcements accompanying the publication of government edicts. They established a tone in which it was proper to think of Roman rule and government. Portraits, the second means of propaganda, included painted ones on general display in cities, sculpted ones, especially in the early years of each reign, based on official models available in a few major cities (hundreds of these survive, including at least one in gold), and engraved ones on coins. Imperial coins offered a more rapidly changing exhibition of images than even postage stamps in the modern world. Because the dies soon wore out, many scores of issues had to be brought out each year, in gold, silver, and bronze. While the images ("types") and words ("legends") on them tended to repetition, there was much conscious inculcation of topical messages. For example, in the short and rocky reign of Galba in AD 69, one finds the legends "All's well that ends well" (*bonus eventus*), "Rome reborn," "Peace for Romans," and "Constitutional government restored" (*libertas restituta*, with iconographic reference to Brutus's coins of 43 BC) and superlative portraits of Galba himself. In other reigns, the legends, enriched with suitable symbolism, read "the soldiers loyal," "Italy well fed," and *fecunditas* of the royal family and its progeny. So far as it is possible to comprehend the mind of the empire's populace, there was no significant opposition to the government by the second century; instead, there prevailed a great deal of ready veneration for the principate as an institution.

THE ECONOMIC FACTOR

Economic factors, to the extent that they were favourable, played an obvious part in promoting both cultural and political unity. So far as acculturation was concerned, a limit to its achievement was clearly set by the amount of disposable capital among non-Romanized populations. The cost of such luxuries as schooling in Latin or frescoes on one's walls were high. But more and more people could afford them as the benefits of Roman occupation were spreading. The rising levels of prosperity did not, however, result from a special benevolence on the part of the conquerors, intent as they were (and often cruelly intent) on the pleasures and profits of physical mastery over the conquered. Rather, they can be explained, first, by the imposition of the Pax Romana, which gave urban centres surer access to the surrounding rural areas and rural producers access in turn to convenient, centralized markets; second, by the sheer attractiveness of imported articles, which intensified efforts to increase the power to buy them; third, by the economic stimulation afforded by taxes, which had to be paid on new earnings but which remained in the provinces where they were raised.

In the fourth place, prosperity also rose in the regions least Romanized. This can be explained by the fact that they tended to be heavily garrisoned and the soldiers spent their wages locally. So far as they could, they bought goods and services of a Roman sort and generally attracted concentrations of people likely to develop into cities of a Roman sort. The economic impact of army payrolls was all the greater because of the cash added to them from taxes raised in other, more developed provinces in the East. Much of the urbanization and enrichment of the western and northern provinces can be explained by these four factors.

The sources for studying the economy of the empire were insufficient until the mid-20th century. The archaeological sources were too scarce and heterogeneous to be of much help, and the written ones contained barely usable amounts of quantified data; economic analysis without quantification, however, is almost a contradiction in terms. Thus discussion was obliged to limit itself to rather general remarks about the obviously wide exchange of goods, the most famous points of production or sale of given articles, techniques of banking, or commercial law. This is still the case with regard to the Eastern half of the Mediterranean world, where excavation has made relatively little headway; but, for the West, archaeological data have greatly increased in recent decades in both quantity and intelligibility. As a result, a growing number of significant statements based on quantification can now be made. They are of special value because they bear on what was economically most important—namely, agriculture. Like any preindustrial economy, that of the empire derived the overwhelming bulk of its gross national product from food production. One would therefore like to know what regions in what periods produced what rough percentage of the chief comestibles—wine, oil, wheat, *garum*, or legumes. Thanks to techniques such as neutron activation analysis or X-ray fluorescence spectrometry, the contents of large samples of amphorae at certain market junctures can be identified, dated by shape of vessel, and occasionally ascribed to certain named producers of the vessel, and the information drawn into a graph; or, the numbers and find-spots of datable fine "china" (so-called Arretine ware or later equivalents) or ceramic oil lamps from named producers can be indicated on a map of, say, Spain or France. The yield of such data underlies statements made above regarding, for example, the supersession of Italy as producer of several essential agricultural products by the mid-first century ad, the concurrent transformation of Gaul from importer to exporter, and the emergence by the third century of northern Africa as a major exporter of certain very common articles. Information of this general nature provides some sense of the shift in prosperity in the Western provinces.

In the age of the Antonines, Rome's empire enjoyed an obvious and prosperous tranquility; modern consensus has even settled on about AD 160 as the peak of Roman civilization. Whatever measurement may be used in this identification, however, an economic one does not fit very well. Evidence, as it accumulates in more quantifiable form, does not seem to show any perceptible economic decline in the empire as a whole after roughly 160. Rather, Italy had probably suffered some decrease in disposable wealth in the earlier first century. Gaul's greatest city, Lugdunum, had begun to shrink toward the end of the second, and various other regions in the West suffered setbacks at various times, while all of Greece continued to be poor. Other regions, however, had more wealth to spend, and as is manifest in major urban projects of utility and beautification or in the larger rooms and increasingly expensive decoration of rural villas. Roman rule also brought extraordinary benefits to the economies of Numidia and Britain, to name its two most obvious successes.

To the extent the empire grew richer, modern observers are likely to look for an explanation in technology. As noted above, in Augustus's reign a new mode of glassblowing spread rapidly from Syria to other production centres; Syria in the third century was also the home of new and more complicated weave patterns. Such rather minor items, however, only show that technical improvements in industry were few and insignificant. The screw press for wine and olive oil was more efficient than the levered variety, but it was not widely adopted, even within Italy. Waterwheels for power, known in Anatolia in Augustus's reign, were little used; a few examples in Gaul belong only to the later empire. Similarly, the mechanical reaper was found only in Gaul of the fourth century. Perhaps the most significant advances were registered in the selective breeding of strains of grains and domestic animals: for example, the "Roman" sheep (which had originated in the Greek East) spread throughout Europe, banishing the inferior Iron Age species to a merited exile in the Outer Hebrides (the Soay sheep of St. Kilda island). What is vastly more significant, however, than these oddments of technological history is the minute subdivision of productive skills and their transmission from father to son in populations adequate to the demand—for iron ore from Noricum, most notably, or for glass and paper from Alexandria. Specialization in inherited skills produced a remarkably high level of proficiency, requiring only the security of the Pax Romana for the spreading of its products everywhere—transport itself being one of those skills.

The health of the economy no doubt helps to explain the political success of the empire, which was not disturbed by frequent revolts or endemic rural or urban unrest. On the other hand, there were limits in the economy, which expressed themselves through resistance to taxation. Tax levels settled at the enforceable maximum; but revenue fell far short of what one might expect, given the best estimates of the empire's gross national product. The basic problem was the tiny size of the imperial government and the resulting inefficiency of its processes. Moreover, it could not make good its inadequacies by borrowing in times of special need; Nero's need to harry his millionaire subjects with false charges of treason in order to pay for his incredibly expensive court and spendthrift impulses reflects the realities of raising revenue. So do the very cautious experiments of Augustus in setting army pay and army size. Ultimately, the military strength of the empire was insufficient—inadequate for emergencies—because of these realities.

THE ARMY

The army that enforced the Pax Romana had expanded little beyond the size envisaged for it by Augustus, despite the enlargement of the empire by Claudius, the Flavians, and Trajan. It reached 31 legions momentarily under Trajan, but it usually numbered 28 under the Flavians and Antonines until the onset of the frontier crisis in Aurelius's reign brought it to 30. Without raising pay rates to attract recruits more easily, a large force was seemingly beyond reach—which probably explains why Hadrian, and later Commodus, halted further expansion.

The army was used not to prop up a militarist government but to defend the frontiers. Shifts in enemy pressures, however, caused the legions to be distributed differently than in Julio-Claudian times. Under Antoninus Pius, the Danubian provinces (Pannonia, Moesia, Dacia) had 10, and the East (Anatolia, Syria, Palestine, Egypt) had 9, and both regions also had supporting naval flotillas; of the remaining 9 legions, Britain contained 3 and the Rhineland 4. Tacitus in his *Annals* (4.5) rates the auxiliary troops near the turn of the era as being about as numerous as the legionnaries. But they soon outnumbered them: that is, whereas legions contained somewhat more than 5,000 men each if they were at full strength and thus totaled roughly 150,000 in the mid-second century, the auxiliaries numbered 245,000—again, if at full strength. Recent estimates put the actual figure for the entire army at 375,000 to 400,000.

Two reasons, military and financial, explain the growing use of nonlegionnaries. Mustered in units mostly of 500, they were easier to move around and could be encouraged to maintain the special native skills of their inheritance—as slingers from the Balearic Islands or Crete, in camel corps from Numidia, or as light cavalry from Thrace. In addition, they could be recruited for lower wages than legionnaries. As regards recruitment for the legions, even that higher rate proved less and less attractive. Whereas legions in the early empire could be largely filled with men born in Italy and southern Gaul, by the second half of the first century most of the men had to be drawn from the provinces; after Trajan, they were largely natives of the frontier provinces. Young men from the inner parts of the empire, growing up in successive generations of continual peace, no longer looked on military service as a natural part of manhood, and the civilian economy appeared attractive compared

to the rewards at some frontier posting. Peace and prosperity thus combined to make the army less and less Roman, less and less of the centre, and more and more nearly barbarous.

The troops' loyalty did not suffer on that account. The men were no more ready to mutiny or to support a pretender around AD 200 than they had been in the early empire. However, experience especially in the year of the four emperors (AD 69) did suggest the desirability of splitting commands into smaller units, which, in turn, involved splitting up provinces, the number of which was constantly growing; by Hadrian's day subdivision began to anticipate the fragmentation later carried out by Diocletian.

CULTURAL LIFE

The literature of the empire is both abundant and competent, for which the emperors' encouragement and financing of libraries and higher education were perhaps in part responsible. The writers, however, with the possible exception of Christian apologists, were seldom excitingly original and creative. As Tacitus said, the great masters of literature had ceased to be. Perhaps Augustus's emphasis on tradition affected more than political ideals and practice. At any rate, men of letters, too, looked often backward. At the same time, they clearly reveal the success of the empire in spreading Greco-Roman culture, for the majority of them were natives of neither Italy nor Greece. Of the writers in Latin, the two

Senecas, Lucan, Martial, Columella, Hyginus, and Pomponius Mela came from Spain; Fronto, Apuleius, and probably Florus and Aulus Gellius, from Africa. Tacitus was perhaps from Gallia Narbonensis.

The Latin writers in general sought their models less in Greece than in Augustus's Golden Age, when Latin literature had reached maturity. Thus, the poets admired Virgil and imitated Ovid; lacking genuine inspiration, they substituted for it an erudite cleverness, the fruit of an education that stressed oratory of a striking but sterile kind. Authentic eloquence in Latin came to an end when, as Tacitus put it, the principate "pacified" oratory. Under the Flavians and Antonines, an artificial rhetoric, constantly straining after meretricious effects, replaced it. The epigrammatic aphorism (*sententia*) was especially cultivated; the epics of Lucan, Valerius Flaccus, Silius Italicus, and Statius are full of it, and it found a natural outlet in satirical writing, of which the Latin instinct for the mordant always ensured an abundance. In fact, Latin satire excelled: witness Martial's epigrams, Petronius's and Juvenal's pictures of the period, and Persius's more academic talent. For that matter, Tacitus's irony and pessimism were not far removed from satire.

In the East the official status of Greek and the favour it enjoyed from such emperors as Hadrian gave new life to Greek literature. It had something in common with its Latin counterpart in that it looked to the past but was chiefly written by authors who were not native to the birthplace of the language. The so-called Second Sophistic reverted to the atticism of an earlier day but often in a Roman spirit; its products from the Asian pens of Dio Chrysostom and Aelius Aristides are sometimes limpid and talented tours de force but rarely great literature. In Greek, too, the best work was in satire, the comic prose dialogues of the Syrian Lucian being the most noteworthy and original literary creations of the period. Among minor writers the charm of Arrian and Pausanias, Asians both, and above all of Plutarch abides (although Plutarch's talents were mediocre, and his moralizing was shallow, his biographies, like those of his Latin contemporary Suetonius, are full of information and interest).

Imperial encouragement of Greek culture and a conviction, no longer justified, of its artistic and intellectual superiority caused the East to resist Latinization. This attitude was bound to lead to a divided empire, and thoughtful observers must have noted it with misgivings. The split, however, was still far in the future. Meanwhile, there was a more immediate cause for disquiet. The plethora of summaries and anthologies that appeared implies a public progressively indifferent to reading whole works of literature for themselves. In other words, the outlook for letters was poor, and this had an unfortunate effect on the scientific literature of the age, which was in itself of first-class quality. Dioscorides on botany, Galen on medicine, and Ptolemy on mathematics, astronomy, and geography represent expert scholars expounding carefully, systematically, and lucidly the existing knowledge in their respective fields. But their very excellence proved fatal because, as the reading public dwindled, theirs remained standard works for far too long; their inevitable errors became enshrined, and their works acted as brakes on further progress.

Stoicism was the most flourishing philosophy of the age. In the East a sterile scholasticism diligently studied Plato and Aristotle, but Epictetus, the stoic from Anatolia, was the preeminent philosopher. In the West, stoicism permeates Seneca's work and much of Pliny's *Natural History*. Evidently, its advocacy of common morality appealed to the traditional Roman sense of decorum and duty, and its doctrine of a world directed by an all-embracing providence struck a responsive chord in the second-century emperors, though they deeply disapproved of its extremist offshoots, the cynics: Marcus Aurelius, as noted, was himself a stoic.

Imperial art, dealing above all with man and his achievements, excelled in portraits and commemoration of events; Roman sculpture and presumably Roman painting, also, owed much to Greek styles and techniques. It emerged, however, as its own distinctive type. The Augustan age had pointed the way that Roman art would go: Italian taste would be imposed on Hellenic models to produce something original. The reliefs of the Augustan Ara Pacis belong to Rome and Italy, no matter who actually carved them. By

Flavian times this Roman artistic instinct had asserted itself and with it the old Roman tendency toward lively and accurate pictorial representation. It can be seen from the reliefs illustrating the triumph over Judaea in the passageway of the Arch of Titus in the Roman Forum. The narrative description dear to Roman art found its best expression in the great spiral frieze on Trajan's Column, where the emperor can be seen among his soldiers at various times in the Dacian campaigns; the story of the war plays a most important part, although, like most imperial monuments, the column is meant to exalt the leader. Under Hadrian a reaction made sculpture less markedly Italian, as if to be in conformity with the slow decline of Italy toward quasi-provincial status. Also under Hadrian, the figure of the emperor was more prominent—bigger and more frontal than the other figures—as if to illustrate the growing monarchical tone of the principate. This tendency continued under the Antonines, when there was a magnificent flowering of sculpture on panels, columns, and sarcophagi; but its exuberance and splendour foreshadow the end of classical art.

The artistic currents that flowed in Rome were felt throughout the empire, the less developed areas being influenced most. In the West, provincial sculpture closely resembled Roman, although it sometimes showed variations, in Gaul especially, owing to local influences (the native element, however, is not always easy to identify). The Roman quality of portraits painted on Egyptian mummy cases shows that the Greek-speaking regions were also affected, although generally they maintained their own traditions. But by now the Greek East had become rather barren; much of its production was imitative rather than vitally creative. Greece proper contributed little, the centre of Hellenism having shifted to Anatolia, to places such as Aphrodisias, where there was a flourishing school of sculpture.

In at least one respect the East was heavily influenced by Rome. The use of concrete and cross vault enabled Roman architects and engineers to span wide areas. Their technological achievements included the covered vastness of the huge thermal establishments, the massive solidity of the amphitheatres, and the audacity of the soaring bridges and aqueducts. The East was greatly impressed. Admittedly, the agoras and gymnasiums in Greek towns are hardly Roman in aspect, but, for most structures of a practical utilitarian kind, the Greek debt to Rome was heavy. Sometimes Roman influence can be seen not only in the fundamental engineering of such buildings as market gateways, theatres, and amphitheatres but even in such decorative details as composite capitals as well. Roman features abound in exotic Petra, Palmyra, Gerasa, and Baalbek, and even in Athens itself.

CHAPTER 5

THE LATER ROMAN EMPIRE

After the assassination of Commodus on Dec. 31, AD 192, Helvius Pertinax, the prefect of the city, became emperor. In spite of his modest birth, he was well respected by the Senate, but he was without his own army. He was killed by the praetorians at the end of March 193, after a three-month reign.

THE DYNASTY OF THE SEVERI (AD 193–235)

The praetorians, after much corrupt bargaining, designated as emperor an old general, Didius Julianus, who had promised them the largest *donativum* (a donation given to each soldier on the emperor's accession). The action of the praetorians roused the ire of the provincial armies. The army of the Danube, which was the most powerful as well as the closest to Rome, appointed Septimius Severus as emperor in May 193.

SEPTIMIUS SEVERUS

Severus soon had to face two competitors, supported, like himself, by their own troops: Pescennius Niger, the legate of Syria, and Clodius Albinus, legate of Britain. After having temporarily neutralized Albinus by accepting him as Caesar (heir apparent), Septimius marched against Niger, whose troops, having come from Egypt and Syria, were already occupying Byzantium. The Danubian legions were victorious, and Niger was killed at the end of 194; Antioch and Byzantium were pillaged after a long siege. Septimius even invaded Mesopotamia, for the Parthians had supported Niger.

But this campaign was quickly interrupted. In the West, Albinus, disappointed at not being associated with the empire, proclaimed himself Augustus in 196 and invaded Gaul. He was supported by the troops, by the population, and even by the senators in Rome. In February 197 he was defeated and killed in a difficult battle near his capital of Lugdunum, which, in turn, was almost devastated. Septimius Severus remained the sole master of the empire, but the pillagings, executions, and confiscations left a painful memory.

A few months later, in the summer of 197, he launched a second Mesopotamian campaign, this time against the Parthian king Vologases IV, who had attacked the frontier outpost Nisibis conquered two years previously by the Romans. Septimius Severus was again victorious. Having arrived at the Parthian capitals (Seleucia and Ctesiphon), he was defeated near Hatra but in 198 obtained an advantageous peace: Rome retained a part of Mesopotamia, together with Nisibis, the new province being governed by an eques. After having inspected the East, the emperor returned to Rome in 202. He spent most of his time there until 208, when the incursions of Caledonian rebels called him to Britain, where he carried out a three-year campaign along Hadrian's

Septimius Severus converted the government of Rome into a military monarchy. Hulton Archive/Getty Images

Wall. He died at Eboracum (York) in February 211.

Septimius Severus belonged to a Romanized Tripolitan family that had only recently attained honours. He was born in Leptis Magna in North Africa and favoured his native land throughout his reign. He was married to Julia Domna of Emesa, a Syrian woman from an important priestly family, and was surrounded by Easterners. He had pursued a senatorial career and had proved himself a competent general, but he was above all a good administrator and a jurist. Disliking Romans, Italians, and senators, he deliberately relied on the faithful Danubian army that had brought him to power, and he always showed great concern for the provincials and the lower classes. Although he had sought to appropriate the popularity of the Antonines to his own advantage by proclaiming himself the son of Marcus Aurelius and by naming his own son Marcus Aurelius Antoninus, he in fact carried out a totally different policy—a brutal yet realistic policy that opened careers to new social classes. Indifferent to the prestige of the Senate, where he had a great many enemies, he favoured the equites.

The army thus became the seedbed of the equestrian order and was the object of all of his attentions. The ready forces were increased by the creation of three new legions commanded by equites, and one of these, the Second Parthica, was installed near Rome. Unlike Vespasian, who also owed his power to the army but who knew how to keep it in its proper place, Septimius Severus, aware of the urgency of external problems, established a sort of military monarchy. The praetorian cohorts doubled their ranks, and the dismissal of the old staff of Italian origin transformed the Praetorian Guard into an imperial guard, in which the elite of the Danube army were the most important element. The auxiliary troops were increased by the creation of 1,000-man units (infantry cohorts) and cavalry troops, sometimes outfitted with mail armour in the Parthian manner. The careers of noncommissioned officers emerging from the ranks now opened onto new horizons: centurions and noncommissioned grades could attain the tribunate and enter into the equestrian order. Thus, a simple Illyrian peasant might attain high posts: this was undoubtedly the most significant aspect of the "Severan revolution." This "democratization" was not necessarily a barbarization, for the provincial legions had long been Romanized. Their salaries were increased, and *donativa* were distributed more frequently; thenceforth, soldiers were fed at the expense of the provincials. Veterans received lands, mostly in Syria and Africa. The right of legitimate marriage, previously refused by Augustus, was granted to almost all of the soldiers, and the right to form *collegia* (private associations) was given to noncommissioned officers. Because more than a century had passed since the last raise in pay for the troops, despite a steady (if slow) rise in the level of prices, Severus increased the legionary's base rate from 300 to 500 *denarii*, with, no doubt, corresponding increases in other ranks. The reflection of this step in the content of precious metal in silver coinage recalls a point made earlier: the imperial revenues were constrained within the narrow limits of political and administrative reality.

The administrative accomplishments of Septimius Severus were of great importance: he clearly outlined the powers of the city prefect; he entrusted the praetorian prefecture to first-class jurists, such as Papinian; and he increased the number of procurators, who were recruited for financial posts from among Africans and Easterners and for government posts (*praesides*) from among Danubian officers. Italy lost its privileges and found itself subjected, like all the other provinces, to the new *annona* , a tax paid in kind, which assured the maintenance of the army and of the officials. The consequent increase in expenditures—for administration, for the salaries and the *donativa* of the soldiers, for the maintenance of the Roman plebs, and for construction—obliged the emperor to devalue the denarius in 194. But the confiscations increased his personal fortune, the *res privata*, which had been previously created by Antoninus.

Severus's social policy favoured both the provincial recruitment of senators (Easterners, Africans, and even Egyptians), causing a sharp decrease in the percentage of Italian senators, and the elevation of the equestrian order, which began to fill the prince's council with its jurists. The cities, which had been favoured by the Antonines, were more and more considered as administrative wheels in the service of the state: the richest *decuriones* (municipal councillors) were financially responsible for levying the taxes, and it was for this purpose that the towns of Egypt finally received a *boulē* (municipal senate).

The burden of taxes and forced government service was made weightier by numerous transport duties for the army and for the *annona* service and was regulated by the jurists through financial, personal, or mixed charges. The state was watchful to keep the *decuriones* in the service of their cities and to provide a control on their administration through the appointment of *curatores rei publicae*, or officials of the central government. The lower classes were, in principle, protected against the abuses of the rich, but in fact they were placed at the service of the state through the restrictions imposed on shipping and commercial corporations. Membership might entail forced contributions of capital or labour to such public necessities as the supply of food to Rome. The state became more and more a policeman, and the excesses of power of numerous grain merchants (*frumentarii*) weighed heavily on the little man.

Imperial power, without repudiating the ideological themes of the principate, rested in fact on the army and sought its legitimacy in heredity: the two sons of Septimius Severus, Caracalla and Geta, were first proclaimed Caesars, the former in 196, the latter in 198; later, they were directly associated with imperial power through bestowal of the title of Augustus, in 198 and 209, respectively. Thus, during the last three years of Septimius Severus's reign, the empire had three Augusti at its head.

CARACALLA

Caracalla, the eldest son of Septimius Severus, reigned from 211 to 217, after having assassinated his younger brother, Geta. He was a caricature of his father: violent, megalomaniacal, full of complexes, and, in addition, cruel and debauched. He retained the entourage of the equites and jurists who had governed with his father but enforced to an even greater degree his father's militaristic and egalitarian policy. He increased the wages of the army even further and, at the same time, began a costly building program that quickly depleted the fortune left him by his father. He forced the senators to pay heavy contributions, doubled the inheritance and emancipation taxes, and often required the *aurum coronarium* (a contribution in gold), thereby ruining the urban middle classes. To counter the effects of a general upward drift of prices and the larger and better-paid army of his own and his father's making, he created a new silver coin, the *antoninianus*. It was intended to replace the basic denarius at double its value, although containing only about one and a half times its worth in precious metal. The only historical source to suggest Caracalla's motive for his gift of universal citizenship, *Dio Cassius*, states that it was meant to increase

revenues by bringing new elements of the population under tax obligations formerly limited to Romans only.

Although little endowed with military qualities, Caracalla adopted as his patron Alexander the Great, whom he admired greatly, and embarked on an active external policy. He fought successfully against the Teutonic tribes of the upper Danube, among whom the Alamanni, as well as the Capri of the middle Danube, appeared for the first time; he often prudently mixed military operations with negotiation and gave important subsidies and money (in sound currency) to the barbarians, thus arousing much discontent. His ambition was to triumph in the East like his hero of old and, more recently, Trajan and his own father. He invaded Armenia and Adiabene and annexed Osroëne in northwest Mesopotamia, joining it to the part of Mesopotamia taken by Septimius Severus. In April 217, while pursuing his march on the Tigris, he was assassinated on the order of one of his praetorian prefects, Marcus Opellius Macrinus.

MACRINUS

Macrinus was accepted as emperor by the soldiers, who were unaware of the role he had played in the death of his predecessor. For the first time an eques had acceded to the empire after having been no more than a manager of financial affairs. The senators reluctantly accepted this member of the equestrian order, who, nevertheless, proved to be moderate and conciliatory; but the armies despised him as a mere civilian, and the ancient authors were hostile to him. His reign was brief, and little is known of him. He concluded an inglorious peace with the Parthians, which assured Mesopotamia to Rome through the payment of large sums of money. And to make himself popular, he canceled Caracalla's tax increases and reduced military expenditures. A plot against him was soon organized: two young grandnephews of Septimius Severus were persuaded by their mothers and especially by their grandmother, Julia Maesa, the sister of Julia Domna (who had recently died), to reach for imperial power. The eldest, Bassianus, was presented to the troops of Syria, who had been bought with gold, and was proclaimed in April 218. Shortly afterward, Macrinus was defeated and killed, as was his son (whom he had associated with him on the throne).

Elagabalus and Severus Alexander

The new emperor was presented as the son of Caracalla, whose name he took (Marcus Aurelius Antoninus). He is better known, however, under the name Elagabalus, the god whose high priest he was and whom he quickly and imprudently attempted to impose on the Romans, in spite of his grandmother's counsel of moderation. Fourteen years old, he caused himself to be detested by his heavy expenditures, his orgies, and the dissolute behaviour of his circle. The praetorians killed him in 222 and proclaimed as emperor his first cousin, Alexianus, who took the name of Severus Alexander.

Although well educated and full of good intentions, Severus Alexander showed some weakness of character by submitting to the counsel of his mother, Mamaea, and of his grandmother, Maesa. The *Scriptores historiae Augustae*, a collection of biographies of the emperors, attributes to him a complete program of reforms favourable to the Senate, but these reforms are not mentioned elsewhere. As in the time of Septimius Severus, his counselors were equites. Ulpian, the praetorian prefect, was the greatest jurist of this period, and the basic policies of the founder of the dynasty were carried on, but with less energy. This weakening of energy had disastrous results: in Persia, the Arsacids were replaced in 224 by the more ambitious Sāsānid dynasty, who hoped to recover the former possessions of the Achaemenids in the East. Their initial attacks were stopped in 232 by a campaign that was, however, poorly conducted by the emperor and that alienated the army as a result of its ineptitude. In Rome there were frequent disorders, and, as early as 223, Ulpian had been killed by the praetorians. While gathered on the Rhine to fight the Teutons, the soldiers once again revolted and killed Severus Alexander and his mother. A coarse and uneducated but energetic soldier, Maximinus the Thracian, succeeded him without difficulty in March 235. The Severan dynasty had come to an end.

RELIGIOUS AND CULTURAL LIFE IN THE THIRD CENTURY

On the right bank of the Tiber in Rome, in the least fashionable section of town among Lebanese and Jewish labourers, Elagabalus built an elegant temple to his ancestral god. He was no doubt in those precincts very well received when he presided personally at its inauguration. Yet the world that counted, the world of senators and centurions, reacted with indignation. Within the capital the ruler was expected to honour the gods of the capital, the ancient Roman ones. At the same time, it was deemed appropriate that he reverently recognize other gods, in their place. For this reason a biography presenting Severus Alexander for the reader's admiration records how scrupulously he offered worship on the Capitoline to Jupiter, while also having, in a chapel attached to his domestic quarters, the images of his *lares* (household gods), of the deified emperors of most beloved memory, and of such superhuman beings as the Greeks would have called "heroes," including Apollonius the holy man of Tyana, Christ, Abraham, and Orpheus. The furnishing of the chapel is described by a most dubious source. But if it is not history, it is at least revealing of ideals. A Roman ruler was to express not only the piety of the capital and its citizens but also that of all his people throughout his empire. Imperial religion was properly compounded of both Roman and non-Roman piety.

Official religion can hardly be said to have existed in the sense of being pressed on people by the state, but the statement needs qualification. The cults of Rome were certainly official in the city itself. They were supported out of the state treasury and by the devotion of the emperor, at least if he lived up to what everyone felt were his responsibilities. In the army, too, camps had shrines in which portraits of the emperor were displayed for veneration on certain days of the year. A third-century calendar has been found in an Eastern city that specifies for the garrison regiment the religious ceremonies to be carried out during the year, including a number of the oldest and most traditional ones in Rome. Many Western cities accorded special size and prominence to a temple in which Jupiter or the imperial family or both together were worshiped not by orders from on high, it is true, but spontaneously. The ubiquity of the imperial cult has already been emphasized. All these manifestations of piety gave some quality of "Romanness" to the religion of the empire.

On the other hand, the empire had been assembled from a great number of parts, whose peoples already had their own way of life fully matured. They were not about to surrender it nor, in fact, were they ever asked to do so by their conquerors. What characterized the religious life of the empire as a whole was the continued vitality of local cults in combination with a generally reverent awareness of one's neighbours' cults. The emperor, for example, might openly offer personal veneration to his favourite god, a god outside the traditional Roman circle, while also practicing a more conventional piety. When he was on his travels, he would offer cult at the chief shrines of all the localities he visited. What was expected of the emperor was expected of everyone: respectful toleration of all components in the religious amalgam. Of course, there were differences according to individual temperament and degree of education; approaches to religion might be literal or philosophical, fervent or relaxed. Rural society was more conservative than urban. But the whole can fairly be called an integrated system.

Just as the special power of the Greek gods had gained recognition among the Etruscans and, subsequently, among the Romans in remote centuries BC or as Serapis in Hellenistic times had come to be worshiped in scattered parts of the Ptolemies' realm—Macedonia and Ionia, for example—so at last the news of unfamiliar gods was carried by their worshipers to distant places in the Roman Empire where, too, they worked their wonders, attracted reverent attention, and received a pillared lodging, a priesthood, and daily offerings. The Pax Romana encouraged a great deal more than commerce in material objects. It made inevitable the exchange of ideas in a more richly woven and complex fabric than the Mediterranean world had ever seen, in which the Phrygian Cybele was at home also in Gaul and the Italian Silvanus in northern Africa.

Religious developments in the Eastern provinces during the centuries from Augustus to Severus Alexander followed a somewhat different course from those in the West. In the East the further jumbling together of already well-mixed traditions encouraged a tolerance that eroded their edges. It became possible to see predominant similarities in Selene, Artemis, and Isis, in Zeus, Iarhibol, Helios, and Serapis, or in Cybele, Ma, and Bellona. From recognition of basic similarities one might reason to a sort of monotheism, by the lights of which, for persons given to theology, local deities were no more than narrow expressions of greater truths. A juncture was then natural with Neoplatonism, the school of philosophy that later came to be held in high regard.

On the other hand, in Italy, the Danube provinces, and the Western provinces, religious change and development can be more easily seen in the immigration of worshippers of Easter deities. Those took root and became popular—none more so than Mithra, though Isis, Cybele, and Jupiter of Doliche were close behind. Apuleius in the closing chapters of his novel usually called *The Golden Ass* in English describes how a young man is brought from mere consciousness of Isis as a famous goddess with certain well-known rites and attributes, to a single-minded devotion to her. Aelius Aristides, a famous rhetorician of the time, recounts in his spiritual diary the development of a similar devotion in himself to Asclepius. Both the fictional and the factual account give a central place to benefits miraculously granted.

Isis, the Egyptian goddess of fertility, experienced a resurgence of popularity in the Western provinces during the third century. Hulton Archive/Getty Images

temples, and so forth—through which it is possible to trace the spread of foreign cults. Eastern cults, however, also introduced to the West complex liturgies, beliefs underlying beliefs that could be explained in especially dramatic ways to special *devotees* ("mysteries"), and much rich symbolism. Of no cult was this more true than Mithraism, known to the 20th century through excavation of the underground shrines that it preferred.

THE RISE OF CHRISTIANITY

During the first and second centuries, Christianity spread with relative slowness. The doctrines of Jesus, who was crucified about AD 30, first took root among the Jews of Palestine, where a large number of sects were proliferating—orthodox sects, such as the Sadducees and the Pharisees, as well as dissident and sometimes persecuted sects such as the Essenes, whose ascetic practices have been illuminated by the discovery of the Dead Sea Scrolls in the mid-20th century. At the end of Tiberius's reign, Christianity had spread to the gentiles as a result of the preaching of St. Paul in Anatolia and in Greece. At the same time, Christianity

It was by such means that piety was ordinarily warmed to a special fervour, whether or not that process should be called conversion.

In any case, it produced what are known as the testimonies—votive inscriptions, continued to make progress among the Jews of Jerusalem, Alexandria, and Syria and quickly reached even Osroëne and the Parthian towns of the Euphrates, where Jewish colonies were numerous. The Roman authorities at first had difficulty in distinguishing the "Christos" believers from the orthodox Jews, but the religion of the former, on leaving its original milieu, quickly became differentiated.

However, a familiar charge against the Jews, that they felt a hatred of mankind, continued to pursue the Christians. Their expectation of the end of the world aroused a suspicion that that was what they indeed desired; moreover, they were also suspect for their aloofness—they cut themselves off from family and community—and for their meetings, whose purpose was obscure. Their second-century spokesmen had to dispel the belief, often recorded, that they practiced magic involving cannibalism, indulged in sex orgies (incestuous to boot), and, the most common accusation of all, that they were atheists—people who denied the existence of the gods and rejected accepted cults. This last charge, which was, of course, exactly on the mark, must be set in the context of occasional episodes of mob violence against (non-Christian) atheists or doubters. Here the association of Christians with Jews, equally monotheistic, might have provided some protection for the Christians, but the Jews were faithful to a cult of the greatest antiquity and, moreover, had long made their peace with Caesar, Augustus, and their successors.

It was a peace that could not extend to people who had (it would be alleged) apostasized from their own Judaism. Christians did not participate in the Jewish revolt of 66–73, and, under the Flavians, Christianity completely severed itself from its origins.

At this time the East was the centre of the new religion, whose followers grew in numbers from Egypt to the Black Sea and were beginning to be noticed in Bithynia and in Greece. Christians seemed fairly numerous in Rome as early as the end of the first century. When the age of the Apostles ended, the age of the church began, with its bishops, presbyters, and deacons, with its catechism, preaching, and celebration of the Eucharist. In the second century, Christianity began to reach the intellectuals. Hellenistic culture offered educated Christians the resources of philosophical dialectic and of sophist rhetoric. The example of Philo of Alexandria had shown in the first century that it was possible to reconcile the Bible with the great Platonic ideas. By the second century the Christian "apologists" tried to show that Christianity was in harmony with Greco-Roman humanism and that it was intellectually, and above all morally, superior to paganism.

But the Christians did not succeed in convincing the authorities. The first persecution, that of Nero, was related to a devastating fire in the capital in 64, for which the Christians were blamed or, perhaps, only made the scapegoats. In any case, their position as bad people (*mali homines* of the sort a governor should try to suppress) had been established, and later suppressions could be justified by reference to "the Neronian practice." So far as criminal law was concerned, such a precedent had considerable authority, of the sort that Pliny, as governor, was looking for in his handling of the Christians of Bithynia-Pontus in 111. His master, the emperor Trajan, told him not to seek them out but to execute those who, being informed against, refused to abjure their religion.

Hadrian and other successors hewed to the same line thereafter. Thus, the persecutions remained localized and sporadic and were the result of private denunciations or of spontaneous popular protests. Under Marcus Aurelius, the difficulties of the times often caused the Christians, who refused to sacrifice to the state gods and to participate in the imperial cult, to be accused of provoking the wrath of the gods. Martyrs appeared in the East, in Rome, in Gaul, and in Africa. Commodus's reign was more favourable to them, perhaps because certain members of his circle, not a very edifying one in other respects, were Christians or Christian sympathizers.

This reprieve, however, was short-lived: Septimius Severus inaugurated the first systematic persecution. In 202 an edict forbade Christian (and Jewish) proselytism. Members of extremist sects were persecuted for preaching continence (which violated Augustus's laws against celibacy), for holding the state in contempt, and especially for refusing military service. Under Caracalla, the situation quieted, and the church continued to progress, favoured perhaps by the relative freedom that the law granted to funerary *collegia* (whence the first catacombs).

CULTURAL LIFE FROM THE ANTONINES TO CONSTANTINE

Latin literature enjoyed its "Silver Age" under the Antonines, with the majority of great authors, such as Tacitus, Juvenal, and Pliny the Younger, having begun their careers under Domitian. They had no heirs; after Tacitus, Roman history was reduced to biography. It was only in the fourth century that history began to flourish again, with Ammianus Marcellinus, a Greek writing in Latin. Satire, the Roman genre par excellence, came to an end with Juvenal; and Pliny the Younger, a diligent rhetorician but with a lesser degree of talent, had only the mediocre Fronto as a successor. More original was the aforementioned rhetorician, scholar, and picaresque novelist Apuleius of Madauros.

A Greek renaissance, however, took place during the second century. The Second Sophistic school reigned in every area: in rhetoric, history, philosophy, and even in the sciences. Schools of rhetoric and philosophy prospered in the East—in Smyrna, Ephesus, Pergamum, Rhodes, Alexandria, and even in Athens—protected and subsidized by the emperors, from Vespasian to Marcus Aurelius. The great sophists were Herodes Atticus, a multimillionaire from

Athens; Polemon; and Aelius Aristides, a valetudinarian devotee of Asclepius. Dio Cassius and Herodian were conscientious and useful historians (first half of the third century), as was later Dexippus the Athenian, whose work survives only in fragments.

Science was represented by the mathematician Nicomachus of Gerasa, medicine by Galen of Pergamum, and astronomy by the Alexandrian Ptolemy. Law remained the only Roman science, exemplified under the Antonines by Salvius Julianus and Gaius (the *Institutiones*) and rising to its zenith in the third century as a result of the works of three jurists: Papinian, Ulpian, and Modestinus. Philosophy, heavily influenced by rhetoric and ethics, was represented under Domitian and Trajan by Dio (or Chrysostom) of Prusa, who outlined the stoical doctrine of the ideal sovereign. The biographer Plutarch and Lucian of Samosata were more eclectic, especially Lucian, who resembled Voltaire in his caustic skepticism. Under Marcus Aurelius, one of Lucian's friends, Celsus, wrote the first serious criticism of Christianity, "The True Word," known through Origen's refutation of it in the third century. At this time philosophy leaned toward religious mysticism: under the Severans, Ammonius Saccas created the school of Alexandria, and his disciple Plotinus founded the Neo-platonist school, which was to fight bitterly against Christianity. After the apologists and, above all, Tertullian (*c.*

160–after 222), Christian thought deepened, and theology made its appearance. Clement and Origen (*c.* 185–*c.* 254), the greatest theologian of the time, were the luminaries of the church of Alexandria; the Roman church still wrote in Greek and was represented by the slightly old-fashioned Hippolytus; and the church of Africa had a powerful personality, St. Cyprian, bishop of Carthage.

The disappearance of the great lyric and poetic styles, the fossilizing of education as it came to be completely based on rhetoric (*paideia*), and the growing importance of philosophical and religious polemical literature among both pagans and Christians were the basic traits that, as early as the third century, foreshadowed the intellectual life of the late empire.

MILITARY ANARCHY AND THE DISINTEGRATION OF THE EMPIRE (235–270)

The period from the death of Severus Alexander to the time of Claudius II Gothicus was marked by usurpations and barbarian invasions. After Maximinus the Thracian, who bravely fought the Alemanni but showed great hostility toward the Senate and the educated elite, the Gordians rose to power as a result of a revolt by wealthy African landowners. A senatorial reaction first imposed civilian emperors, Pupienus and Balbinus together, and then named Gordian III, a youth backed by his father-in-law, the

The surrender of the emperor Valerian to the Persian king Shāpūr, rock relief, AD 260, in the province of Fārs, Iran. Roger-Viollet

praetorian prefect Timesitheus. Gordian III was murdered by the soldiers during a campaign against the Persians and was replaced, first by Philip the Arabian and then by Decius, both soldiers. Decius tried to restore Roman traditions and also persecuted the Christians, but he was killed by the Goths in 251 in a battle near the Black Sea. From 253 to 268 two Roman senators, Valerian and his son Gallienus, reigned. Valerian revived the persecution of the Christians, but he was captured by the Persians during a disastrous campaign and died in captivity (260).

His son then reigned alone, facing multiple invasions and several usurpations. He moved constantly between the Rhine and the Danube, achieving brilliant victories (Milan in 262, the Nestus in 267), but the Pannonian army raised several competitors against him (Ingenuus, Regalianus, Aureolus). Too busy to protect the Gauls against the Franks and the Alemanni and the East against the Persians, he had to tolerate the formation of the Gallic empire under the praetorian prefect Marcus Cassianius Postumus (259–268) and the Palmyrene kingdom of Odenathus (260–267). Some of his reforms were a foreshadowing of the future. The senators were practically excluded from the army, the equites received the majority of commands and of provincial governorships, and the composition of the army was modified by the creation of new army corps and especially of a strong cavalry, which was placed under the command of a single leader and charged with closing the breaches that the barbarians were opening along the frontiers.

Upon his father's death, Gallienus had put an end to the persecution of the Christians, preferring to fight the new religion through intellectual means; to that end, he favoured the ancient Greek cults (Demeter of Eleusis) and protected the Neoplatonist philosopher Plotinus. These initiatives increased the number of his enemies, particularly among the patriotic senators and the Pannonian generals. While Gallienus was in Milan besieging the usurper Aureolus, he was killed by his chiefs of staff, who proclaimed Claudius II (268), the first of the Illyrian emperors. The new emperor won a great victory against the Alemanni on the Garda lake and overwhelmed the Goths in Naissus (269) but died of the plague in 270. This fatal period brought to light one of the major defects of the empire: the lack of a legitimate principle of succession and the preponderant role of the army in politics. The structures that had created the strength of the principate were weakened, and the empire required deep reforms. Gallienus had felt their

necessity but had been too weak to impose them.

THE BARBARIAN INVASIONS

The Goths were Germans coming from what is now Sweden and were followed by the Vandals, the Burgundians, and the Gepidae. The aftereffect of their march to the southeast, toward the Black Sea, was to push the Marcomanni, the Quadi, and the Sarmatians onto the Roman *limes* in Marcus Aurelius's time. Their presence was brusquely revealed when they attacked the Greek towns on the Black Sea about 238. Timesitheus fought against them under Gordian III, and under Philip and Decius they besieged the towns of Moesia and Thrace, led by their kings, Ostrogotha and Kniva. Beginning in 253, the Crimean Goths and the Heruli appeared and dared to venture on the seas, ravaging the shores of the Black Sea and the Aegean as well as several Greek towns. In 267 Athens was taken and plundered despite a strong defense by the historian Dexippus.

After the victories of Gallienus on the Nestus and Claudius at Naissus (Nish), there was for a time less danger. But the countries of the middle Danube were still under pressure by the Marcomanni, Quadi, Iazyges, Sarmatians, and the Carpi of free Dacia, who were later joined by the Roxolani and the Vandals. In spite of stubborn resistance, Dacia was gradually overwhelmed, and it was abandoned by the Roman troops, though not evacuated officially. When Valerian was captured in

AD 259/260, the Pannonians were gravely threatened, and Regalianus, one of the usurpers proclaimed by the Pannonian legions, died fighting the invaders. The defense was concentrated around Sirmium and Siscia-Poetovio, the ancient fortresses that had been restored by Gallienus, and many cities were burned.

In the West the invasions were particularly violent. The Germans and the Gauls were driven back several times by the confederated Frankish tribes of the North Sea coast and by the Alemanni from the middle and upper Rhine. Gallienus fought bitterly, concentrating his defense around Mainz and Cologne, but the usurpations in Pannonia prevented him from obtaining any lasting results. In 259–260 the Alemanni came through the Agri Decumates (the territory around the Black Forest), which was now lost to the Romans. Some of the Alemanni headed for Italy across the Alpine passes; others attacked Gaul, devastating the entire eastern part of the country. Passing through the Rhône Valley, they eventually reached the Mediterranean, and some bands even continued into Spain. There they joined the Franks, many of whom had come by ship from the North Sea, after having plundered the western part of Gaul. Sailing up the estuaries of the great rivers, they had reached Spain and then, crossing the Strait of Gibraltar, had proceeded to Mauretania Tingitana. Outflanked, Gallienus entrusted Gaul and his young son Saloninus to Postumus, who then killed Saloninus and proclaimed himself emperor.

The several invasions had so frightened the people that the new emperor was readily accepted, even in Spain and Britain. He devoted himself first to the defense of the country and was finally considered a legitimate emperor, having established himself as a rival to Gallienus, who had tried in vain to eliminate him but finally had to tolerate him. Postumus governed with moderation, and, in good Roman fashion, minted excellent coins. He, too, was killed by his soldiers, but he had successors who lasted until 274.

DIFFICULTIES IN THE EAST

In the East the frontiers had been fixed by Hadrian at the Euphrates. But under Nero, the Romans had claimed control over the kings of Armenia, and under Caracalla they had annexed Osroëne and Upper Mesopotamia. The Parthian empire had been weak and often troubled, but the Sāsānids were more dangerous. In 241, Shāpūr I (Sapor), an ambitious organizer and statesman, mounted the throne. He united his empire by bringing the Iranian lords into line and by protecting the Zoroastrian religion. He also tolerated the Manichaeans and put an end to the persecutions of the Christians and Jews, thereby gaining the sympathy of these communities.

In 252, with a large army at his command, Shāpūr imposed Artavasdes on Armenia, attacked Mesopotamia, and took Nisibis. In 256 his advance troops entered Cappadocia and Syria and plundered Antioch, while Doura-Europus, on the middle Euphrates, was likewise falling to him. Valerian had rushed to its aid, but he could not remedy the situation; and in 259 or 260 he was imprisoned by Shāpūr during operations about which little is known. Mesopotamia was lost and Rome was pushed back to the Euphrates. Cappadocia, Cilicia, and Syria were again plundered, and a puppet emperor was appointed in Antioch. But these victories were transitory. In Osroëne, Edessa had shown resistance, a defense was organized in Cappadocia and Cilicia, and Odenathus, the prince of Palmyra, took Shāpūr by surprise and forced him back to Iran.

Having thus aided the Roman cause, Odenathus then began to act in his own interest. He continued the fight against the Persians and took the title "King of Kings." The Romans officially entrusted him with the defense of the East and conferred on him the governorship of several provinces; the "kingdom" of Palmyra thus extended from Cilicia to Arabia. He was murdered in 267 without ever having severed his ties with Gallienus. His widow Zenobia had her husband's titles granted to their son Vaballathus. Then in 270, taking advantage of the deaths of Gallienus and Claudius II, she invaded Egypt and a part of Anatolia. This invasion was followed by a rupture with Rome, and in 271 Vaballathus was proclaimed Imperator Caesar Augustus. The latent separatism of the Eastern provinces and, undoubtedly, some commercial advantages caused them to accept Palmyrene domination without difficulty, as they had, in the past,

supported Avidius Cassius and Pescennius Niger against the legitimate emperors. In 272 unity was restored by Aurelian, but Mesopotamia was lost, and the Euphrates became the new frontier of the empire.

ECONOMIC AND SOCIAL CRISIS

The invasions and the civil wars worked in combination to disrupt and weaken the empire over a span of half a century. Things were at their worst in the 260s, but the entire period from 235 to 284 brought the empire close to collapse. Many regions were laid waste (northern Gaul, Dacia, Moesia, Thrace, and numerous towns on the Aegean), many important cities had been pillaged or destroyed (Byzantium, Antioch, Olbia, Lugdunum), and northern Italy (Cisalpine Gaul) had been overrun by the Alemanni. During the crisis, the emperor either focused his forces on the defense of one point, inviting attack at another, or he left some embattled frontier altogether to its own devices; any commander who proved successful had the emperorship thrust upon him, on the very heels of his victories over the invaders. Counting several sons and brothers, more than 40 emperors thus established themselves for a reign of some sort, long or (more often) short.

The political destabilization fed on itself, but it also was responsible for heavy expenditure of life and treasure. To keep pace with the latter, successive emperors rapidly and radically reduced the percentage of precious metal in the standard silver coins to almost nothing so as to spread it over larger issues. What thus became a fiduciary currency held up not too badly until the 260s, when confidence collapsed and people rushed to turn the money they had into goods of real value. An incredible inflation got under way, lasting for decades.

The severity of damage done to the empire by the political and economic destabilization is not easily estimated since for this period the sources of every sort are extremely poor. Common sense would suggest that commerce was disrupted, taxes collected more harshly and unevenly, homes and harvests destroyed, the value of savings lost to inflation, and the economy in general badly shaken. A severe plague is reported that lasted for years in mid-century, producing terrible casualties. In some western areas, archaeology provides illustration of what one might expect. Cities in Gaul were walled, usually in much reduced circuits. Villas here and there throughout the Rhine and Danube provinces also were walled, and road systems were defended by lines of fortlets in northern Gaul and adjoining Germany. A few areas, such as Brittany, were abandoned or relapsed into pre-Roman primitiveness. Off the coasts of that peninsula and elsewhere, too, piracy reigned; on land, brigandage occurred on a large scale. The reentrant triangle of land between the upper Danube and upper Rhine had to be permanently abandoned to the barbarians around it in about 260.

The Pax Romana had then, in all these manifest ways, been seriously disrupted. On the other hand, in Egypt, where inflation is most amply documented, its harmful effects cannot be detected. The Egyptian economy showed no signs of collapse. Furthermore, some regions—most of Britain, for example—emerged from the half-century of crisis in a more prosperous condition than before. A summary of the effects of crisis can only underline one single fact that is almost self-evident: the wonders of civilization attained under the Antonines required an essentially political base. They required a strong, stable monarchy in command of a strong army. If either or both were seriously disturbed, the economy would suffer, along with the civilization's ease and brilliance. If, on the other hand, the political base could be restored, the health of the empire as a whole was not beyond recovery.

In the meantime, certain broad changes unconnected with the political and economic crisis were going forward in the third century. Civilians increasingly complained of harassment and extortion by troops stationed among them. Exaction of taxes intended for the army also became the target of more frequent complaint, and demands by soldiers to interfere in civilian government, foremost by those stationed in the capital, grew more insolent. The choice of emperor became more and more openly the prerogative of the military, not the Senate, and, in the 260s, senators were being largely displaced from high military commands. The equestrian rank, in which persons risen from military careers were often to be found, was the beneficiary of the new policy. In sum, the power of the military, high and low, was asserting itself against that of the civilians.

From this change, further, there flowed certain cultural consequences, for, continuing the tendencies detectable even in the first century, the army was increasingly recruited from the most backward areas, above all, from the Danubian provinces. Here, too—indeed, throughout the whole northern glacis of the empire—it had been state policy to allow entire tribes of barbarians to immigrate and to settle on vacant lands, where they dwelled, farmed, paid taxes, and offered their sons to the army. Such immigrants, in increasingly large numbers from the reign of Marcus Aurelius on, produced, with the rural population, a very non-Romanized mix. From the midst of just such people, Maximinus mounted to the throne in 235, and later, likewise, Galerius (Caesar from 293). It is quite appropriate aesthetically, from Aurelian on, that these later third-century rulers chose to present themselves to their subjects in their propaganda with stubbly chin, set jaw, and close-cropped hair on a bullet head.

THE RECOVERY OF THE EMPIRE AND THE ESTABLISHMENT OF THE DOMINATE (270–337)

After Claudius II's unexpected death, the empire was ruled from 270 to 284 by several "Illyrian" emperors, who were good generals and who tried in an energetic way to restore equilibrium. The most remarkable was Aurelian. He first gained hard-won victories over the Alemanni and the Juthungi, who had invaded the Alpine provinces and northern Italy. To cheer the inhabitants of Rome, who had succumbed to panic, he began construction of the famous rampart, Aurelian Wall. And while crossing the Danubian provinces, before marching against Palmyra, he decided on an orderly evacuation of Dacia, an undefendable region that had been occupied by the barbarians since the time of Gallienus. In the East, he defeated Zenobia's troops easily and occupied Palmyra in 272.

Shortly afterward, an uprising broke out in Egypt under the instigation of a rich merchant, who, like a great part of the population, was a partisan of the Palmyrene queen. In response, Aurelian undertook a second campaign, plundering Palmyra and subjugating Alexandria. These troubles, however, along with the devastation of the great caravan city, were to set back Roman trade seriously in the East. Later, rounding back on the Gallic empire of Postumus's successors, he easily defeated Tetricus, a peaceful man not very willing to fight, near Cabillonum. The unity of the empire was restored, and Aurelian celebrated a splendid triumph in Rome. He also reestablished discipline in the state, sternly quelled a riot of artisans in the mints of Rome, organized the

About two-thirds of the Aurelian Wall, built in the 3rd century AD to strengthen Rome's defenses against Germanic invaders, remains intact. Shutterstock.com

provisioning of the city by militarizing several corporations (the bakers, the pork merchants), and tried to stop the inflation by minting an antoninianus of sounder value. His religious policy was original. In order to strengthen the moral unity of the empire and his own power, he declared himself to be the protégé of the *Sol Invictus* (the Invincible Sun) and built a magnificent temple for this god with the Palmyrene spoils. Aurelian was also sometimes officially called *dominus et deus*: the principate had definitely been succeeded by the "dominate." In

275, he was murdered by certain officers who mistakenly believed that their lives were in danger.

For once, his successor, the aged senator Tacitus, was chosen by the Senate—at the army's request and on short notice; he reigned only for a few months. After him, Probus, another Illyrian general, inherited a fortified empire but had to fight hard in Gaul, where serious invasions occurred in 275-277. Thereafter, Probus devoted himself to economic restoration; he attempted to return abandoned farmland to cultivation and, with the aid of military labour, undertook works of improvement. To remedy the depopulation, he admitted to the empire, as had Aurelian, a great number of defeated Goths, Alemanni, and Franks and permitted them to settle on plots of land in Gaul and in the Danubian provinces. After the assassination of Probus in 282 by soldiers, Carus became emperor and immediately associated with himself his two sons, Carinus and Numerian. Carus and Numerian fought a victorious campaign against the Persians but died under unknown circumstances. Carinus, left behind in the West, was later defeated and killed by Diocletian, who was proclaimed emperor in November 284 by the army of the East.

DIOCLETIAN

Diocletian may be considered the real founder of the late empire, though the form of government he established—the tetrarchy, or four people sharing power simultaneously—was transitory. His reforms, however, lasted longer. Military exigencies, not the desire to apply a preconceived system, explain the successive nomination of Maximian as Caesar and later as Augustus in 286 and of Constantius and Galerius as Caesars in 293.

The tetrarchy was a collegium of emperors comprising two groups: at its head, two Augusti, older men who made the decisions; and, in a secondary position, two Caesars, younger, with a more executive role. All four were related either by adoption or by marriage, and all were Illyrians who had attained high commands after a long military career. Of the four, only Diocletian was a statesman. The unity of the empire was safeguarded, despite appearances, for there was no territorial partitioning. Each emperor received troops and a sector of operation: Maximian, Italy and Africa; Constantius, Gaul and Britain; Galerius, the Danubian countries; and Diocletian, the East.

Practically all governmental decisions were made by Diocletian, from whom the others had received their power. He legislated, designated consuls, and retained precedence. After 287 he declared his kinship with the god Jupiter (Jove), who Diocletian claimed was his special protector. Diocletian, together with his Caesar Galerius, formed the "Jovii" dynasty, whereas Maximian and Constantius, claiming descent from the mythical hero Hercules, formed the "Herculii." This "Epiphany of the Tetrarchs" served as the divine foundation of the regime. The ideological recourse to two traditional Roman divinities represented a break with the Orientalizing attempts of Elagabalus and Aurelian. Even though he honoured Mithra equally, Diocletian wanted to be seen as continuing the work of Augustus. In dividing power, Diocletian's aim was to avoid usurpations, or at least to stifle them quickly—as in the attempt of Carausius, chief of the army of Britain, who was killed (293), as was his successor, Allectus (296), after a landing by Constantius.

The deification of the imperial function, marked by elaborate rituals, tended to set the emperors above the rest of mankind. But it was still necessary to avoid future rivalries and to assure the tetrarchy a legitimate and regular succession. Some time between 300 and 303 Diocletian found an original solution. After the anniversary of their 20-year reign the two Augusti abdicated (Maximian quite unwillingly), and on the same day (May 1, 305) the two Caesars became Augusti. Two new Caesars were chosen, Severus and Maximinus Daia, both friends of Galerius, whose strong personality dominated Constantius. In repudiating the principle of natural heredity (Maximian and Constantius each had an adult son), Diocletian took a great risk: absolute divine monarchy, which Diocletian largely established, implies the hereditary transmission of power, and the future was soon to demonstrate the attachment of the troops and even of the population to the hereditary principle.

In order to create a more efficient unity between subjects and administrators, Diocletian multiplied the number of provinces; even Italy was divided into a dozen small units of the provincial type. Rome, moreover, was no longer the effective capital of the empire, each emperor having his own residence in the part of the empire over which he ruled (Trier, Milan, Sirmium, Nicomedia). Although a few provinces were still governed by senators (proconsuls or consuls), the majority were given to equestrian *praesides*, usually without any military power but with responsibility for the entirety of civil

administration (justice, police, finances, and taxes). The cities lost their autonomy, and the curiales administered and collected the taxes under the governor's direct control. The breaking up of the provinces was compensated for by their regrouping into a dozen dioceses, under equestrian vicars who were responsible to the emperor alone. The two praetorian prefects had less military power but played an important role in legislative, judicial, and above all, financial matters: the administration of the *annona*, which had become the basis of the fiscal system, in fact gave them management of the entire economy. Within the central administration the number of offices increased, their managers being civilians who carried out their functions as a regular career. All officials were enrolled in the *militia*, whose hierarchy was to be outlined during the fourth century.

Great efforts were devoted to strengthening the borders, and the *limes* were outfitted with fortresses (*castella*) and small forts (*burgi*), notably in Syria. The army's strength was increased to 60 legions (but with reduced personnel); and, in principle, each border province received a garrison of two legions, complemented by subsidiary troops. Adopting one of Gallienus's ideas, Diocletian created an embryonic tactical army under the direct orders of the emperor whose escort (*comitatus*) it formed. The troops were most often commanded by *duces* and *praepositi* rather than by provincial governors and were mainly recruited from among the sons of soldiers and from barbarians who enlisted individually or by whole tribes. In addition, the landowners had to provide either recruits or a corresponding sum of money.

All of these reforms were instituted gradually, during defensive wars whose success demonstrated the regime's efficiency. Constantius put down Carausius's attempted usurpation and fought the Alemanni fiercely near Basel; Maximian first hunted down the Bagaudae (gangs of fugitive peasant brigands) in Gaul, then fought the Moorish tribes in Africa, in 296–298, triumphing at Carthage; and on the Danube, Diocletian, and later Galerius, conquered the Bastarnae, the Iazyges, and the Carpi, deporting them in large numbers to the provinces. In the East, however, the opposition of the Persians, led by the enterprising Narses, extended from Egypt to Armenia. The Persians incited uprisings by both the Blemmyes nomads in southern Egypt and the Saracens of the Syrian desert and made use of anti-Roman propaganda by the Manichaeans and Jews. Diocletian succeeded in putting down the revolt in Egypt and fortified the south against the Blemmyes. But in 297, Narses, the heir to Shāpūr's ambitions, precipitated a war by taking Armenia, Osroëne, and part of Syria. After an initial defeat, Galerius won a great victory over Narses, and in 298 the peace of Nisibis reinstated a Roman protégé in Armenia and gave the empire a part of Upper Mesopotamia that extended even beyond the Tigris. Peace was thus assured for some decades.

The wars, the reforms, and the increase in the number of officials were costly, and inflation reduced the resources of the state. The *annona*, set up by Septimius Severus, had proved imperfect, and Diocletian now reformed it through the *jugatio-capitatio* system: henceforth, the land tax, paid in kind by all landowners, would be calculated by the assessment of fiscal units based on extent and quality of land, type of crops grown, number of settlers and cattle, and amount of equipment. The fiscal valuation of each piece of property, estimated in *juga* and *capita* (interchangeable terms whose use varied by region and period of time), required a number of declarations and censuses similar to those practiced long before in Egypt. Each year, the government established the rate of tax per fiscal unit; and every 15 years, beginning in 312, taxes were reassessed. This complicated system was not carried out uniformly in every region. Nevertheless, it resulted in an improved accounting of the empire's resources and a certain progress in fiscal equity, thus making the administration's heavy demands less unbearable.

In addition, Diocletian wished to reorganize the coinage and stabilize inflation. He thus minted improved sterling coins and fixed their value in relation to a gold standard. Nevertheless, inflation again became disturbing by the end of the century, and Diocletian proclaimed his well-known *Edictum de Maximis Pretiis*, fixing price ceilings for foodstuffs and for goods and services, which could not be exceeded under pain of death. The edict had indifferent results and was scarcely applied, but the inscriptions revealing it have great economic interest.

Diocletian's reforms adumbrated the principal features of late Roman society—a society defined in all parts that could be useful to the state by laws fixing status and, through status, responsibility. The persons owning grain mills in Rome were (to anticipate developments that continued to unfold throughout the next two or three generations) responsible for the delivery of flour for the dole and could not bequeath or withdraw any part of their capital from their enterprise. Several other labour groups were similarly restricted, such as owners of seagoing vessels that served the supply of Rome, bargees in the Tiber, Ostian grain handlers, distributors of olive oil and pork for the dole, bath managers, and limeburners. A ban on moving to some other home or job along with production quotas were placed on people in trades serving state factories that made imperial court and army garments, cavalry equipment, and arms. Diocletian built a number of such factories, some in his capital Nicomedia, others in cities close to the groups whose needs they served. The laws imposing these obligations affected only labour groups serving the army and the capital (or capitals, plural, after the promotion of Constantinople); and, to identify them, induce them to serve, and hold them in their useful work, emperors as early as Claudius had offered privileges and

imposed controls. Diocletian, however, greatly increased the weight and complexity of all these obligations.

Diocletian also changed the administrative districts in Egypt, in keeping with the model found elsewhere, by designating in each a central city to take responsibility for the whole. The last anomalous province was thus brought into line with the others. Everywhere, the imperial government continued to count on the members of the municipal senate to serve it, above all in tax collection but also in the supply of recruits, in rural police work, billeting for troops, or road building. As had been the case for centuries, they had to have a minimum of landed property to serve as surety for the performance of their administrative duties as well as to submit to nomination as senator, if it was so determined by the Senate. There had never been any one law to that effect, but by Diocletian's time the emperor had at his command a body of long-established custom and numerous imperial decisions that served just as well. Local elites were thus hereditary, compulsory agents of his purpose, exactly like the Tiber bargees.

Two other groups were frozen into their roles in the same fashion: soldiers and farmers. The sons of soldiers were required to take up their fathers' occupation (a law to that effect was in operation at least by 313); and the natural tendency of tenant farmers (*coloni*) to renew their lease on land that they, and perhaps their fathers and grandfathers, had worked was confirmed by imperial decisions—to such effect that, in 332, Constantine could speak of tenants on his Sardinian estates as bound to the acres they cultivated. This is the earliest explicit pronouncement on what is called the "colonate." Soon the institution was extended beyond imperial estates to tie certain categories of tenants to private estates as well. The emperors wanted to ensure tax revenue and, for that, a stable rural labour supply.

The empire, as it is seen in abundant legislation for the period of Diocletian and beyond into the fifth century, has been called a "military dictatorship" or even a sort of totalitarian prison, in which every inhabitant had his own cell and his own shackles. This may well have been the rulers' intent. By their lights, such a system was needed to repair the weaknesses revealed in the third-century crisis. The principle of hereditary obligations was not, after all, so very strange, set against the natural tendencies of the economy and the practices that had developed in earlier, easier times. Yet Diocletian's intentions could not be fully realized, given the limits on governmental effectiveness.

After a period of initial indifference toward the Christians, Diocletian ended his reign by unleashing against them, in 303, the last and most violent of their persecutions. It was urged on him by his Caesar Galerius and prolonged in the East for a decade (until 311) by Galerius as Augustus and by other emperors. As in earlier persecutions, the initiative arose at the heart of government; some emperors, as outraged by the Christians as many private citizens, considered it their duty to maintain harmony with the gods, the *pax deorum*, by which alone the empire flourished. Accordingly, Decius and Valerian in the 250s had dealt severely with the Christians, requiring them to demonstrate their apostasy by offering sacrifice at the local temples, and for the first time had directly struck the church's clergy and property. There were scores of Christians who preferred death, though the great majority complied or hid themselves. Within a matter of months after he had begun his attacks, however, Decius had died (251), and the bloody phase of Valerian's attacks also lasted only months (259/260). His son Gallienus had issued an edict of tolerance, and Aurelian was even appealed to by the church of Antioch to settle an internal dispute.

Christianity had now become open and established, thanks to the power of its God so often, it seemed, manifested in miraculous acts and to the firmness with which converts were secured in a new life and community. The older slanders—cannibalism and incest—that had troubled the Apologists in the second century no longer commanded credence. A measure of respectability had been won, along with recruits from the upper classes and gifts of land and money. By the end of the third century Christians actually predominated in some of the smaller Eastern towns or districts, and they were well represented in Italy, Gaul, and Africa around Carthage. All told, they numbered perhaps as many as 5 million out of the empire's total population of 60 million. Occasional meetings on disputed matters might bring together dozens of bishops, and it was this institution or phenomenon that the Great Persecutions sought to defeat.

The progress of a religion that could not accept the religious basis of the tetrarchy and certain of whose members were imprudent and provocative, as in the incidents at Nicomedia (where a church was built across from Diocletian's palace), finally aroused Galerius's fanaticism. In 303–304 several edicts, each increasingly stringent, ordered the destruction of the churches, the seizure of sacred books, the imprisonment of the clergy, and a sentence of death for all those who refused to sacrifice to the Roman gods. In the East, where Galerius was imposing his ideas more and more on the aging Diocletian, the persecution was extremely violent, especially in Egypt, Palestine, and the Danubian regions. In Italy, Maximian, zealous at the beginning, quickly tired, and in Gaul, Constantius merely destroyed a few churches without carrying reprisals any further. Nevertheless, Christianity could no longer be eradicated, for the people of the empire and even some officials no longer felt the blind hatred for Christians that had typified previous centuries.

STRUGGLE FOR POWER

The first tetrarchy had ended on May 1, 305; the second did not last long. After Constantius died at Eboracum in 306, the armies of Britain and Gaul, without observing the rules of the tetrarchic system, had hastened to proclaim Constantine, the young son of Constantius, as Augustus. Young Maxentius, the son of Maximian (who had never wanted to retire), thereupon had himself proclaimed in Rome, recalled his father into service, and got rid of Severus. Thus, in 307–308 there was great confusion. Seven emperors had, or pretended to have, the title of Augustus: Maximian, Galerius, Constantine, Maxentius, Maximinus Daia, Licinius (who had been promoted Augustus in 308 by Galerius against Constantine), and, in Africa, the usurper Domitius Alexander.

This situation was clarified by successive eliminations. In 310, after numerous intrigues, old Maximian was killed by his son-in-law Constantine, and in the following year Alexander was slain by one of Maxentius's praetorian prefects. In 311 Galerius died of illness a few days after having admitted the failure of his persecutions by proclaiming an edict of tolerance. There remained, in the West, Constantine and Maxentius and in the East, Licinius and Maximinus Daia. Constantine, the best general, invaded Italy with a strong army of faithful Gauls and defeated Maxentius near the Milvian Bridge, not far from Rome. While attempting to escape, Maxentius drowned. Constantine then made an agreement with Licinius, and the two rallied the Eastern Christians to their side by guaranteeing them religious tolerance in the Edict of Milan (313). This left Maximinus

Daia, now isolated and regarded as a persecutor, in a weak position; attacked by Licinius near Adrianople, he fell ill and died soon afterward, in 313. This left the empire with two leaders, Constantine and Licinius, allied in outward appearances and now brothers-in-law as a result of Licinius's marriage to Constantine's sister.

THE REIGN OF CONSTANTINE

Constantine and Licinius soon disputed among themselves for the empire. Constantine attacked his adversary for the first time in 316, taking the dioceses of Pannonia and Moesia from him. A truce between them lasted 10 years. In 316 Diocletian died in Salona, which he had never felt a desire to leave despite the collapse of his political creation. Constantine and Licinius then reverted to the principles of heredity, designating three potential Caesars from among their respective sons, all still infants, with the intention of securing their dynasties (two sons of Constantine and one of Licinius). The dynastic concept, however, required the existence of only a single emperor, who imposed his own descendance. Although Constantine favoured the Christians, Licinius resumed the persecutions, and in 324 war erupted once again. Licinius, defeated first at Adrianople and then in Anatolia, was obliged to surrender and, together with his son, was executed. Next, Constantine's third son, Constantius, was in turn named Caesar, as his two elder brothers, Crispus and Constantine the Younger, had been

some time before. The second Flavian dynasty was thus founded, and Constantine let it be believed that his father, Flavius Constantius (Chlorus), was descended from Claudius Gothicus.

Constantine's conversion to Christianity had a far-reaching effect. Like his father, he had originally been a votary of the Sun. Worshiping at the Grand Temple of the Sun in the Vosges Mountains of Gaul, he had had his first vision, albeit a pagan one. During his campaign against Maxentius, he had had a second vision—a lighted cross in the sky—after which he had painted on his men's shields a figure that was perhaps Christ's monogram (although he probably had Christ confused with the Sun in his manifestation as *summa divinitas* ["the highest divinity"]). After his victory he declared himself Christian. His conversion remains somewhat mysterious and his contemporaries—Lactantius and Eusebius of Caesarea—are scarcely enlightening and even rather contradictory on the subject. But it was doubtless a sincere conversion, for Constantine had a religious turn of mind. He was also progressive and greatly influenced by the capable bishops who surrounded him from the very beginning.

Until 320–322 solar symbols appeared on Constantine's monuments and coins, and he was never a great theologian. Yet his favourable policy toward the Christians never faltered. Christianity was still a minority religion in the empire, especially in the West and in the countryside (and consequently within his own army), thus excluding the possibility of any political calculation on his part. But it was enthusiastically welcomed in the East, and thanks to Constantine the new religion triumphed more rapidly; his official support led to the conversion of numerous pagans, although with doubtful sincerity because they were indifferent in their moral conviction.

The church, so recently persecuted, was now suddenly showered with favours: the construction of magnificent churches (Rome, Constantinople), donations and grants, exemptions from decurial duties for the clergy, juridical competences for the bishops, and exceptional promotions for Christian officials. Pagans were not persecuted, however, and Constantine retained the title of *pontifex maximus*. But he spoke of the pagan gods with contempt and forbade certain types of worship, principally nocturnal sacrifices. In 331 he ordered an inventory of pagan property, despoiled the temples of their treasure, and finally destroyed a few Eastern sanctuaries on the pretext of immorality.

The churches were soon to feel the burden of imperial solicitude: the "secular arm" (i.e., the government) was placed at the service of a fluctuating orthodoxy, for the emperor was impressionable to arguments of various coteries and became quite lost in theological subtleties. In 314 the Council of Arles had tried in vain to stop the Donatist schism (a nationalistic heretical movement questioning the worthiness of certain church officials) that arose in Africa after

Diocletian's persecutions. The Arian heresy raised even more difficulties. Arius, an Alexandrian priest and disciple of Lucian of Antioch, questioned the dogma of the Trinity and of the godhead of Christ, and his asceticism, as well as the sharpness of his dialectics, brought him many followers. He was convicted several times, but the disorders continued.

Constantine, solicited by both sides and untroubled by doctrinal nuances that were, moreover, foreign to most believers in the West, wished to institute a universal creed. With this in mind he convened the general Council of Nicaea, or Nicene Council, in 325. He condemned Arius and declared, in spite of the Easterners, that Jesus was "of one substance" with God the Father. Nevertheless, the heresy continued to exist, for Constantine changed his mind several times; he was influenced by Arian or semi-Arian bishops and was even baptized on his deathbed, in 337, by one of them, Eusebius of Nicomedia.

Between 325 and 337 Constantine effected important reforms, continuing Diocletian's work. The division between the *limitanei* border troops and the tactical troops (*comitatenses* and imperial guard) led by *magistri militum* was clarified, and military careers became independent of civil careers. At the same time, however, he lodged an increasing number of troops in or next to cities, a process whose objective was ease and economy of supply. However, training and discipline were harder to enforce because of it, and the men hung about in idleness.

It was also under Constantine that a barbarian commander in the Roman army attained a historical significance. He was Crocus the Alaman, who led the movement among the troops that resulted in Constantine's seizure of the rank of Augustus in 306 immediately after his father Constantius's death. A similar figure was the great commander Bonitus, a Frank, in the years 316–324. Constantine credited his victories against Maxentius in 311–312 principally to his barbarian troops, who were honoured on the triumphal Arch of Constantine in Rome. In opposition to him, Licinius mustered drafts of Goths to strengthen his army. Goths were also brought in by Constantine, to the number of 40,000, it is said, to help defend Constantinople in the latter part of his reign, and the palace guard was thenceforward composed mostly of Germans, from among whom a great many high army commands were filled. Dependence on immigrants or first-generation barbarians in war was to increase steadily, at a time when conventional Roman troops were losing military value.

Constantine raised many equestrians to senatorial rank, having in his earlier reign the still rapidly increasing ranks of the civil service to fill—it was at least 50 times the size of the civil service under Caracalla—and having in his later reign a second senate to fill, in Constantinople. A rapid inflation in titles of honour also took place. As a result of these several changes, the equestrian order ceased to have meaning, and a new nobility of imperial service developed. Constantine gave first rank in the central administration to the palace quaestor, the *magister officiorum*, and the counts of finance (*comes sacrarum largitionum, comes rei privatae*). The diocesan vicars were made responsible to the praetorian prefects, whose number was increased and whose jurisdictions were now vast territories: the prefectures of Gaul, Italy, Illyricum, and the East. The unification of political power brought with it a corresponding decentralization of administration.

In order to reorganize finances and currency, Constantine minted two new coins: the silver *miliarensis* and, most important, the gold *solidus*, whose stability was to make it the Byzantine Empire's basic currency. And by plundering Licinius's treasury and despoiling the pagan temples, he was able to restore the finances of the state. Even so, he still had to create class taxes: the *gleba* for senators, and the *chrysargyre*, which was levied in gold and silver on merchants and craftsmen in the towns.

Constantine's immortality, however, rests on his founding of Constantinople. This "New Rome," established in 324 on the site of Byzantium and dedicated in 330, rapidly increased in population as a result of favours granted to immigrants. A large number of churches were also built there, even though former temples were not destroyed; and the city became the administrative capital of the empire, receiving a senate and proconsul. This choice of site was due not to religious considerations, as has been suggested, but rather to reasons that were both strategic (its proximity to the Danube and Euphrates frontiers) and

After Emperor Constantine personally embraced Christianity, the empire itself evolved into a Christian state. Shutterstock.com

economic (the importance of the straits and of the junction between the great continental road, which went from Boulogne to the Black Sea, and the eastern commercial routes, passing through Anatolia to Antioch and Alexandria). Constantine died on May 22, 337.

THE ROMAN EMPIRE UNDER THE FOURTH-CENTURY SUCCESSORS OF CONSTANTINE

After some months of confusion, Constantine's three surviving sons (Crispus, the eldest son, had been executed in mysterious circumstances in 326), supported by the armies faithful to their father's memory, divided the empire among themselves and had all the other members of their family killed. Constantine II kept the West, Constantius the East, and Constans, the youngest brother, received the central prefecture (Italy, Africa, and Illyricum). In 340 Constantine II tried to take this away from Constans but was killed. For the next 10 years there was peace between the two remaining brothers, and Constans won acceptance for a religious policy favourable to the Nicaeans, whose leader, Athanasius, had received a triumph in Alexandria. In 350 a mutiny broke out in Autun. Constans fled but was killed in Lugdunum by Magnentius, a usurper who was recognized in Gaul, Africa, and Italy. Constantius went out to engage Magnentius, and the Battle of Mursa (351) left the two strongest armies of the empire—those of Gaul and of the Danube—massacred, thus compromising the empire's defense. Magnentius retreated after his defeat and finally committed suicide in 353.

Thenceforth, Constantius reigned alone as Augustus, aided by a meddlesome bureaucracy in which mission deputies (*agentes in rebus*), informers, and spies played an important role. He named two Caesars in succession, his two young surviving cousins, Gallus in the East and Julian in Gaul. Constantius eventually had to get rid of Gallus, who proved incompetent and cruel and soon terrorized Antioch. Julian, however, was a magnificent success, a fact that aroused Constantius's jealousy and led to Julian's usurpation; for the latter was proclaimed Augustus, in spite of Constantius's opposition, at Lutetia in 361. Civil war was averted when Constantius died in November 361, leaving the empire to Julian, the last ruler of the Constantinian family.

At the time of his death in 337, Constantine had been preparing to go to war against the Persians. This legacy weighed heavily on the shoulders of Constantius, a military incompetent when compared to the energetic Sāsānian king Shāpūr II. Nearly every year the Persians attacked and pillaged Roman territory; the Mesopotamian towns were besieged, and Nisibis alone resisted. There was a lull between 350 and 357, while Shāpūr was detained by troubles in the eastern regions of his own kingdom. The war resumed, however, and Mesopotamia was partly lost when the emperor had to leave in order to fight Julian.

Constantius had fought Shāpūr conscientiously, but his generals were mediocre, except for Urisicinus, and he himself was clumsy. In the meantime, the Rhine and Danube were threatened frequently, because the troops had been withdrawn from there and sent to the East. Constantius, moreover, had made a mistake in sending Chnodomar, the Alemannic king, against Magnentius in 351, for his tribes had gone on to ravage Gaul. Julian, however, soon revealed himself to be a great military leader by winning several well-fought campaigns between 356 and 361, most notably at Strasbourg in 357, and by restoring approximately 70 plundered villages. His abandonment, in AD 358, of the district of Toxandria, roughly equivalent to modern Belgium, to its barbarian squatters, on condition of their defending it against other invaders, was no doubt a realistic decision. Constantius defeated the Quadi and the Goths on the Danube in 359, but court intrigues, Magnentius's usurpation, and the interminable war against the Persians allowed the barbarians to wreak great havoc.

Constantius was primarily interested in religious affairs. His interventions created a "caesaro-papism" that was unfavourable to the church, for after the Battle of Mursa the emperor had become violently Arian. The Christological problem had moved to the forefront. In 360 Constantius obtained a new creed by force from the Council of Constantinople, which, rejecting the notion of "substance" as too risky, declared only that the Son was like the Father and thus left the problem unresolved. Pagans as well as orthodox Nicaeans (Homoousians) and extremist Arians (Anomoeans) were persecuted, for in 356–357 several edicts proscribed magic, divination, and sacrifices and ordered that the temples be closed. But when Constantius visited Rome in 357, he was so struck by its pagan grandeur that he apparently suspended the application of these measures.

THE REIGN OF JULIAN

Julian, who had been spared because of his tender age from the family butchering in 337, had been brought up far from the court and was undoubtedly intended for the priesthood. Nevertheless, he had been allowed to take courses in rhetoric and philosophy at Ephesus and, later, at Athens. He developed a fondness for Hellenic literature, and he secretly apostatized around 351. When he became sole emperor at the end of 361, Julian proclaimed his pagan faith, ordered the restitution of the temples seized under Constantius, and freed all the bishops who had been banished by the Arians, so as to weaken Christianity through the resumption of doctrinal disputes.

The religion he himself espoused was compounded of traditional non-Christian elements of piety and theology, such as might have been found in any fairly intellectual person in the preceding centuries, along with elements of Neoplatonism developed by Porphyry and Iamblichus of two or three generations earlier, and, finally, much of the organization and social ethic of the church. From Neoplatonism he learned the techniques of direct communication with the gods (theurgy) through prayer and invocation. From the church he adopted, as the church itself had adopted from the empire's civil organization, a hierarchy of powers: provincial, metropolitan, urban, with himself as supreme pontiff. His deep love of traditional higher culture, moreover, provoked his war on Christian intellectuals and teachers who, he protested, had no right to Homer or Plato. Many Christians both before and later concurred with him, being themselves troubled by the relationship between Christianity and inherited literature and thought, steeped as both were in pagan beliefs.

In the latter part of his 18-month reign, Julian forbade Christians from teaching, began the rebuilding of the Temple at Jerusalem, restored many pagan shrines, and displayed an exaggerated piety. Whereas Constantine (and his sons to a lesser degree) had introduced a huge number of coreligionists into the upper ranks of the army and government, achieving a rough parity between the members of the two religions, Julian began to reverse the process. Within a short while Julian was successful enough in his undertaking to have aroused the fear and hatred of the Christians, who for a long time thought of him as the Antichrist.

In the political realm, Julian wished to return to the liberal principate of the Antonines—to a time before the reforms of Diocletian and Constantine, whom he detested. He put an end to the terrorism of Constantius's eunuchs and *agentes in rebus* and reduced the personnel and expenditures of the court, while he himself lived like an ascetic. In the provinces he lightened the financial burden on individuals by reducing the *capitatio*, and on cities, by reducing the *aurum coronarium* and restoring the municipal properties confiscated by Constantius. On the other hand, he increased the number of curiales by reinstating numerous clerks in an attempt to return the ancient lustre to municipal life. Thus, he earned the gratitude of pagan intellectuals, who were enamoured of the past of free Greece; and Ammianus made him the central hero of his history.

Taking up Trajan's dream, Julian wished to defeat Persia definitively by engaging the empire's forces in an offensive war that would facilitate a national reconciliation around the gods of paganism. But his army was weak—corrupted perhaps by large numbers of hostile Christians. After a brilliant beginning, he was defeated near Ctesiphon and had to retrace his steps painfully; he was killed in an obscure encounter on June 26, 363.

Julian's successor, Jovian, chosen by the army's general staff, was a Christian, but not a fanatic. He negotiated a peace with Shāpūr, by which Rome lost a good part of Galerian's conquests of 298 (including Nisibis, which had not surrendered) and abandoned Armenia. He also restored tolerance in religious affairs, for he neither espoused any of the heresies nor persecuted pagans. In February 364 he died accidentally.

THE REIGN OF VALENTINIAN AND VALENS

Once again the general staff unanimously chose a Pannonian officer—Valentinian, an energetic patriot and, like Jovian, a moderate Christian. But Valentinian had to yield to the rivalry of the armies by dividing authority. Taking the West for himself, he entrusted the East to his brother Valens, an inexperienced man whom he raised to the rank of Augustus. For the first time the two parts of the empire were truly separate, except for the selection of consuls, in which Valentinian had precedence.

Although he served the state with dedication, Valentinian could be brutal, choleric, and authoritarian. His foreign policy was excellent. All the while he was fighting barbarians (the Alemanni in Gaul, the Sarmatians and Quadi in Pannonia) and putting down revolts in Britain and Africa (notably that of the Berber Firmus) with the aid of his top general, Theodosius the Elder, he was taking care to improve the army's equipment and to protect Gaul by creating a brilliant fortification. His domestic measures favoured the curiales and the lower classes: from then on, taxes would be collected exclusively by officials. The protection of the poor was entrusted to "defenders of the plebs," chosen from among retired high officials (*honorati*).

Nevertheless, the needs of state obliged him to accentuate social immobility, to reinforce corporation discipline and official hierarchization, and to demand taxes ruthlessly. At first he was benevolent to the Senate of Rome, supervised the provisioning of the city, and legislated in favour of its university, the nursery of officials (law of 370). But beginning in 369, under the influence of Maximin, the prefect of Gaul, he initiated a period of terror, which struck the great senatorial families. Meanwhile, religious peace reigned in the West, tolerance was proclaimed, and after some difficulty, Rome found a great pope in Damasus, who, beginning in 373, actively supported the new bishop of Milan, St. Ambrose, an ardent defender of orthodoxy.

In the East, Valens, who was incapable and suspicious, had fallen under the influence of legists, such as the praetorian prefect Modestus. The beginning of Valens' reign was shadowed by the attempted usurpation of Procopius (365–366), a pagan relative of Julian's who failed and was killed by the army, which remained faithful to Valens. Modestus instituted harsh persecutions in Antioch of the educated pagan elite. Valens was a fanatic Arian, who exiled even moderate Nicaean bishops and granted to Arians favours that aroused violent reactions from the orthodox, whose power had increased in the East. Valens' policies made the East prey to violent religious passions.

On the Danube, Valens fought the Visigoths and made a treaty with their king, Athanaric, in 369; but in 375 the Ostrogoths and the Greutingi appeared on the frontiers, pushed from their home in southern Russia by the powerful Huns. In 376 Valens authorized the starving masses to enter Thrace; but, being exploited and mistreated by the officials, they soon turned to uncontrollable pillaging. Their numbers continually increased by the addition of new bands, until finally they threatened Constantinople itself. Valens sent for aid from the West, but without waiting for it to arrive he joined battle and was killed in the Adrianople disaster of 378, which to some critics foreshadowed the approaching fall of the Roman Empire.

The Goths, who were also stirring up Thrace and Macedonia, could no longer be driven out. The provinces subject to their pillaging soon included Pannonia farther up the Danube, where Gratian agreed with a cluster of three tribal armies to settle them as a unit under their own chiefs on vacant lands (380). By a far more significant arrangement of the same sort two years later, Theodosius assigned to the Goths a large area of Thrace along the Danube as, in effect, their own kingdom. There they enjoyed autonomy as well as a handsome subsidy from the emperor, exactly as tribes beyond the empire had done in previous treaties. They were expected to respond to calls on their manpower if the Roman army needed supplementing, as it routinely did. Although the Goths considered this treaty ended with Theodosius's death and resumed their lawless wanderings for a while, it nevertheless represented the model for subsequent ones, again struck with the Goths under their king Alaric (from 395) and with later barbarian tribes. The capture of the empire had begun.

THE REIGN OF GRATIAN AND THEODOSIUS I

Following Valentinian's sudden death in 375, the West was governed by his son Gratian, then 16 years old, who had been given the title of Augustus as early as 367. The Pannonian army, rife with intrigue, quickly proclaimed Gratian's half-brother, Valentinian II, only four years old. The latter received Illyricum under his older brother's guardianship, and this arrangement satisfied everybody. Valentinian's advisers were executed; Maximian was sacrificed to the spite of the Senate and Theodosius the Elder became the victim of personal jealousies. Gratian announced a liberal principate, supported in Gaul by the wealthy family of the Bordeaux poet Ausonius and in Rome by the Symmachi and the Nicomachi Flaviani, representatives of the pagan aristocracy. His generals defeated the Alemanni and the Goths on the Danube but arrived too late to save Valens.

On Jan. 19, 379, before the army, Gratian proclaimed Theodosius, the son of the recently executed general, as Eastern emperor. Theodosius was chosen for his military ability and for his orthodoxy (Gratian, extremely pious, had come under the influence of Damasus and Ambrose). The East was enlarged by the dioceses of Dacia and Macedonia, taken from Valentinian II. Gratian and Theodosius agreed to admit the Goths into the empire, and Gratian applied the policy also to the Salian Franks in Germany. Theodosius soon dominated his weak colleague and entered the battle for the triumph of orthodoxy. In 380 the Arians were relieved of their churches in Constantinople, and in 381 the Nicaean faith was universally imposed by a council whose canons established the authority of the metropolitan bishops over their dioceses and gave the bishop of the capital a primacy similar to that of the bishop of Rome.

In ecclesiastical affairs, the separation between East and West was codified. The Westerners bowed to this policy, satisfied with the triumph of orthodoxy. Gratian then permitted Ambrose and Damasus to deal harshly with the Arians, with the support of the state. Paganism also was hounded: following Theodosius's lead, Gratian refused the chief priesthood, removed the altar of Victory from the hall of the Roman Senate, and deprived the pagan priests and the Vestal Virgins of their subsidies and privileges. The pagan senators were outraged, but their protests were futile because Gratian was watched over by Ambrose.

This militantly orthodox policy aroused the displeasure of the pagans and of the Western Arians: thus, when Gratian left Trier for Milan, the army of Gaul and Britain proclaimed its leader, Maximus, in 383. He conquered Gaul without difficulty, and Gratian was killed in Lyons. Maximus, who, like Theodosius, was Spanish and extremely orthodox, was recognized by the latter. In the meantime, the third Augustus, Valentinian II, had taken refuge in Milan after suffering defeat in Pannonia. He was effectively under the domination of his mother, Justina, an Arian who sought support for her son among the Arians and pagans of Rome and even among the African Donatists (a Christian heresy). In 388 Maximus, after arriving in Italy, first expelled Valentinian and then prepared to attack Theodosius. The latter, accepting the inevitability of war, strengthened his resolve and gained several victories. Maximus was killed at Aquileia in 388, and thenceforth Theodosius ruled both West and East; he was represented in the East by his son Arcadius, an Augustus since 383. Valentinian II was sent to Trier, accompanied by the Frankish general Arbogast to control him.

After a few years' respite, during the prefectureships of Nicomachus Flavianus in Rome and Tatian in the East, paganism waged its last fight: Theodosius, influenced by Ambrose, who had dared to inflict public penance on him in 390 after the massacre at Thessalonica, had determined to eliminate the pagans completely. After a few hostile clashes, the law of Nov. 8, 392, proscribed the pagan religion. Then Arbogast, after Valentinian II's death in 392 under shadowy circumstances, proclaimed as emperor the rhetorician Eugenius. When Theodosius refused to recognize him, Eugenius was thrown into the arms of the pagans of Rome. But this last "pagan reaction" was short-lived. In 394, with his victory at the Frigidus (modern Vipacco) River, between Aquileia and Emona, Theodosius put an end to the hopes of Eugenius and his followers. His intention was to place his son Honorius, proclaimed Augustus in 393, over the West, while returning his eldest son, Arcadius, to the East. But Theodosius's sudden death in January 395 precipitated the division of the empire.

Theodosius had successfully dealt with the danger of the Goths, although not without taking risks, and had both established a dynasty and imposed the strictest orthodoxy. A compromise peace with the Persians had given Rome, in 387, a small section of Armenia, where he had founded Theodosiopolis (Erzurum). He had survived two pretenders in the West. These military successes were, however, won with armies in which barbarians were in the majority, which was not a good sign. The barbarian presence is reflected in the names of his commanding officers, including such Franks as Richomer, Merovech, and Arbogast, and the half-Vandal Stilicho, who through his marriage to Serena, Theodosius's niece, had entered the imperial family.

SOCIAL AND ECONOMIC CONDITIONS

During the fourth century the emperor's power was theoretically absolute, the traditions of the principate having given way to the necessities of defense.

The emperor was both heir to the Hellenistic *basileus* (absolute king) and the anointed of the deity. Pagans and Christians alike considered him "emperor by the grace of God," which, strictly speaking, rendered the imperial cult unnecessary. Indeed, he hardly needed the ceremonies and parade of god-awfulness with which Diocletian and his successors were surrounded. Yet imperial authority had actually lost much of its effectiveness due to the growth and nature of late Roman government. Its ranks can be estimated at more than 30,000 men—perhaps an insignificant number compared with that of modern governments but gigantic when set against the total of only a few hundred a century earlier. The problem, however, lay not in numbers but in the assumption, held throughout both bureaucracy and army, that a position of power ex officio entitled the holder to a rake-off of some sort, to be extracted both from the citizenry with whom he came in contact and from fellow members of the service in ranks below his own.

This ethos was not new, but during the principate it had been restrained by higher officers and officials, who operated according to a different, essentially aristocratic, code expressed in patron-dependent relations and mutuality. Its currency was not money but favours and services. Such a code was swept away by the rapid increase in the size of government in the later third century and the rise to high civil and military posts by men recruited from the ranks rather than from the upper classes. As they had bought their own promotions or appointments, so they expected to recoup their expenses (and more besides) by such means as selling exemptions and extortion. The more intrusive and demanding the military tax collection or the state's control of the rosters of city senates, the more profit there was for a pervasively corrupt administration. Those close to the emperor could, for a price, generally screen him from knowledge of what was going on. Constantine, for example, complained quite in vain—and the complaint was endlessly repeated by his successors—that the city senates were being "emptied of persons obligated to them by birth, who yet are asking for a government post by petition to the emperor, running off to the legions or various civil offices." Such posts could easily be bought. A great deal of imperial planning was thus vitiated by sale. Many of the profiteers started life in the urban upper classes, but, as nouveaux riches, they joined the older landed nobility after a term in the emperor's service.

In a few areas where measurement is possible, one can see that a process of consolidation of landownership had been going on for a long time, bringing the rural population increasingly into dependence on the larger property holders. Diocletian's new system of property assessment accelerated this process. It was more thorough and thus exposed the poor and ignorant to exploitation by local officialdom. In response, they sought the protection of some influential man to ward off unfair assessments, selling their land to him and becoming his tenants. In areas disturbed by lawlessness, a large landowner offered them safety as well. The strength of rural magnates in their formidable, even fortified, dwellings, with a dependent peasantry of 100 or even 1,000 around them made much trouble for tax collectors, and landowners thus became the target of many laws. Consolidation of ownership, however, was not apparent in northern Africa, and the reverse process has been established for a carefully researched area of Syria.

Regional differences cannot be disregarded. They were responsible for guiding the development of the later empire along quite varied paths. The archaeological data, which reflect these developments most clearly, register such changes as the degree of wealth in public buildings and the use and elegance of carved sarcophagi or of mosaics in private houses. Broadly speaking, a decline is noticeable throughout the European provinces; it tends to affect the cities earlier than the rural areas and is detectable sometimes by 350, generally by 375. In the Danube provinces, the evidence fits neatly with political history following the Battle of Adrianople in 378, after which their condition was continually disturbed by the Visigothic immigrants.

There is, however, no such obvious explanation for areas such as Spain or central Gaul. Italy of the third and fourth centuries was not perceptibly worse off than before, though wealth in the Po region was more concentrated in the cities north of the river. Northern Africa seems to have maintained nearly the same level of prosperity as in earlier centuries, if proper weight is given to ecclesiastical building after Constantine. For Egypt, no clear picture emerges, but all the other Eastern provinces enjoyed in the later empire the same level of economic well-being as before or a still higher one, with more disposable wealth and an increasing population. These conditions continued into the fifth century.

The vast differences between the European and the Eastern provinces are best explained by the shifting focus of imperial energies. It can be traced in the locus of heaviest military recruitment, in the lower Danube, as the third century progressed; in the consequent concentration of military expenditure there; and in the siting of the emperors' residence as it was moved from Rome to Milan in the 260s, then to the lower Danube later in the third century (where much fighting occurred), and subsequently to Nicomedia (Diocletian's capital). None of the Tetrarchs chose Rome—its days as the imperial centre were over—and when, from among various Eastern cities he considered, Constantine decided on Byzantium as his permanent residence, he simply made permanent a very long-term development.

Meanwhile the Rhine frontier and the upper Danube were repeatedly overrun.

As can be inferred from the signs of fortification in Pannonia, Gaul, Britain, and Spain, internal policing was neglected. Commercial intercourse, which had been the key to raising the economy and the level of urbanization, became less safe and easy. Villas turned into self-sufficient

Mosaic from the Villa Romana del Casale. Archaeologists have noted a decline in such household and public building refinements in the later days of the empire. DEA/G.Dagli Orti/Getty Images

villages, and the smaller towns also reverted to villages. Only the larger towns, such as Bordeaux, Arles, or Cartagena, maintained their vitality.

Although there was considerable inflation (culminating under Theodosius), in spite of a deflationary fiscal policy, commercial transactions ignored barter and were based instead on currency throughout the empire at the end of the century. The economy was partially under state direction, which was applied to agriculture through bias toward the settler system on imperial estates and to industry through the requisitioning of corporations (artisans, merchants, carriers) and the creation of state workshops (especially for manufacturing military goods). Opinions differ on the intensity of trade, but there was certainly clear progress in comparison with that of the third century.

THE REMNANTS OF PAGAN CULTURE

The spread of Christianity in no way harmed the flourishing of pagan literature. Instruction in the universities (Rome, Milan, Carthage, Bordeaux, Athens, Constantinople, Antioch, and Alexandria) was still based on rhetoric, and literature received the support of senatorial circles, especially in Rome (for example, those of the Symmachi and the Nicomachi Flaviani). Latin literature was represented by Symmachus and the poet Ausonius. The last great historian of Rome was Ammianus Marcellinus, a Greek who wrote in Latin for the Roman aristocracy; of his *Res gestae*, the most completely preserved part describes the period from 353 to 378. The works of Sextus Aurelius Victor and Eutropius, who ably abridged earlier historical works, are fairly accurate and more reliable than the *Scriptores historiae Augustae*, a collection of imperial biographies of unequal value, undoubtedly composed under Theodosius but for an unknown purpose. Erudition was greatly prized in aristocratic circles, which, enamoured of the past, studied and commented on the classic authors (Virgil) or the ancestral rites (the *Saturnalia* of Macrobius). Greek literature is represented by the works of philosophers or sophists: Themistius, a political theoretician who advocated absolutism; Himerius of Prusias; and above all Libanius of Antioch, whose correspondence and political discourses from the Theodosian period bear witness to his perspicacity and, often, to his courage.

THE CHRISTIAN CHURCH

In the last decade of the fourth century the harsh laws against the perpetuation of the old pieties promulgated by Theodosius gave impetus and justification to waves of icon and temple destruction, especially in the East. It is, nonetheless, likely that a majority of the population was still non-Christian in 400, although less so in the cities and in the East and more so in rural and mountainous areas and the West. Efforts by the church to reach them were intermittent and lacked energy. Bishops generally expected rural magnates to do their job for them; and the church leadership was, in any case, of a social class that viewed the peasantry from a great distance and wanted to keep it that way. Except by such unusual figures as Martin of Tours or Marcellus of Apamea, little effort was made to convert people who were hard to reach. As always in antiquity, it was in the cities where changes occurred—with the exception of monasticism.

Only in the reign of Constantine, and about simultaneously in Egypt and Palestine, had monasticism, a religious movement whose followers lived as hermits and pursued a life of extreme asceticism, become more than the little-regarded choice of rare zealots. Near Gaza and in the desert along the eastern side of Jerusalem a number of tiny clusters of cells had been made from caves and taken as residence by ascetics, from whose fame and example that way of life later spread to many other corners of the Levant. The bishop of Jerusalem, Cyril, by mid-century could speak of "regiments of monks." But it was in the desert on both sides of the Nile that similar ascetic experiments of much greater importance were made, by the hero of the movement, St. Anthony, and others. True monasticism, tempered only by weekly communal worship and organizing, established itself on Anthony's model and under his inspiration in the first decade of the fourth century. It took root above all in the desert of Scete, just west of the base of the Nile delta.

Coenobitism, joint life in enclosed communities, was the model preferred by St. Pachomius around 330, vigorously directed and diffused by him until mid-century, when both he and Anthony died. Basil of Caesarea was to establish monastic communities in Cappadocia under the influence of what he saw in Egypt on his visit there in the year of Anthony's death; and Athanasius was shortly to write a biography of that saint of enormous influence and to carry word of his life to Italy and Gaul during his own exile there. The biography was soon translated into Latin and inspired a scattering of experiments in asceticism or coenobitism in the West—in Vercellae in Italy, for example, by 330, and at Tours in the 370s under Martin's direction. Tours became the first monastery in the West comparable to those in the East, but development subsequently was slow compared to the 10,000 or more monasteries founded in Egypt by AD 400.

The most distinct and well-reported phenomenon during the century after the conversion of Constantine was the continued religious rioting and harrying in the cities, both in all the major ones and in dozens of minor ones. The death toll exceeded the toll among Christians at the hands of pagans in earlier persecutions. It was rarely of Jews or

St. Jerome in His Study *by Albrecht Dürer. St. Jerome was a central figure in the rise of Christian literature in late Rome.* Rafa Rivas/AFP/Getty Images

pagans at the hands of Christians or of Christians at the hands of pagans, but ordinarily of Christians at each others' hands in the course of sectarian strife. For a time, no one sect enjoyed a majority among Homoousians, Arians, Donatists, Meletians, and many others. Bishoprics were fiercely contested and appeals often made to armed coercion. The emperors had assumed the right to interfere and often did so. But under Theodosius, Pope Damasus and St. Ambrose reacted. The state was to restrict itself to furnishing the "secular arm," while the church, in the name of evangelical ethics, claimed the right to judge the emperors, a policy that had grave implications for the future. The "caesaro-papism" of Constantius later gained adherents under the Byzantine emperors. In the meantime, the Goths had been converted to Arianism by Ulfilas during the period of Constantius and Valens, thus presaging conflicts that were to come after the great invasions. Orthodox missionaries had converted Osroëne, Armenia, and even some countries on the Red Sea.

The Christian literature of the fourth century is remarkable. Its first representative is Eusebius of Caesarea, a friend and panegyrist of Constantine and a church historian whose creation of a "political theology" sealed the union between the Christian emperor and the church. St. Athanasius wrote apologetic works and a life of St. Anthony. Also prominent were the great Cappadocians: St. Basil of Caesarea, St. Gregory of Nazianzus, St. Gregory of Nyssa, and St. John Chrysostom of Antioch, the greatest preacher of his time. The Westerners, too, had great scholars and brilliant writers: St. Hilary of Poitiers, enemy of the Arians and of Constantius; St. Ambrose, administrator and pastor, whose excessive authority was imposed on Gratian and even on Theodosius; and St. Jerome, a desert monk and confessor of upper-class Roman ladies. St. Jerome was a formidable polemicist who knew Greek and Hebrew and made the first faithful translation of the Old and New Testaments (the Vulgate) as well as of a chronicle of world history, which was a translation and continuation of the work of Eusebius. Finally, St. Augustine, the bishop of Hippo, was a great pastor, a vigorous controversialist, a sensitive and passionate writer (the *Confessions*), and the powerful theologian of *The City of God*. The century that developed these great minds cannot be considered decadent.

THE ECLIPSE OF THE ROMAN EMPIRE IN THE WEST (C. 395–500) AND THE GERMAN MIGRATIONS

After the death of Theodosius, the Western empire was governed by young Honorius. Stilicho, an experienced statesman and general, was charged with assisting him and maintaining unity with the East, which had been entrusted to Arcadius. The Eastern leaders soon rejected Stilicho's tutelage. An anti-barbarian reaction had developed in Constantinople, which impeded the objectives of the half-Vandal Stilicho. He wanted to intervene on several occasions in the internal affairs at Constantinople but was prevented from doing so by a threat from the Visigoth chieftain Alaric, whom he checked at Pollentia in 402, then by the Ostrogoth Radagaisus's raid in 406, and finally by the great invasion of the Gauls in 407. The following year he hoped to restore unity by installing a new emperor in Constantinople, Theodosius II, the son of Arcadius, who had died prematurely; but he succumbed to a political and military plot in August 408. The division of the two *partes imperii* was now a permanent one.

Honorius, seated in Ravenna, a city easier to defend than Milan, had only incompetent courtiers surrounding him, themselves animated by a violent hatred of the barbarians. Alaric soon reappeared, at the head of his Visigoths, demanding land and money. Tired of the Romans' double-dealing, he descended on Rome itself. The city was taken and pillaged for three days, thus putting an end to an era of Western history (August 410). An Arian, Alaric spared the churches. He died shortly thereafter in the south; his successor, Athaulf, left the peninsula to march against the Gauls.

Fleeing from the terrifying advance of the Huns, on Dec. 31, 406, the Vandals, Suebi, and Alani, immediately followed by the Burgundians and bands of Alemanni, crossed the frozen Rhine and swept through Gaul, effortlessly throwing back the federated Franks and Alemanni from the frontiers. Between 409 and 415 a great many of these barbarians arrived in Spain and settled in Lusitania (Suebi) and in Baetica (Vandals, whence the name Andalusia). As soon as Gaul had become slightly more peaceful, Athaulf's Visigoths arrived, establishing themselves in Narbonensis and Aquitania. After recognizing them as "federates," Honorius asked them to go to Spain to fight the Vandals.

Meanwhile, the Roman general Constantius eliminated several usurpers in Gaul, confined the Goths in Aquitania, and reorganized the administration (the Gallic assembly of 418). But he was unable to expel the Franks, the Alemanni, and the Burgundians, who had occupied the northern part of the country, nor to eliminate the brigandage of the Bagaudae. He was associated with the empire and was proclaimed Augustus in 421, but he died shortly afterward. His son, Valentinian III, succeeded Honorius in 423 and reigned until 455.

THE BEGINNING OF GERMANIC HEGEMONY IN THE WEST

During the first half of the fifth century, the barbarians gradually installed themselves, in spite of the efforts of the Roman General Aetius, at the head of a small army of mercenaries and of Huns. Aetius took back Arles and Narbonne from the Visigoths in 436, either pushed back the Salian and Ripuarian Franks beyond the Rhine or incorporated them as federates, settled the defeated Burgundians in Sapaudia (Savoy), and established the Alani in

Orléans. The other provinces were lost: Britain, having been abandoned in 407 and already invaded by the Picts and Scots, fell to the Angles, Saxons, and Jutes; a great Suebi kingdom, officially federated but in fact independent, was organized in Spain after the departure of the Vandals, and it allied itself to the Visigoths of Theodoric I, who were settled in the country around the Garonne.

In 428 the Vandal Gaiseric led his people (80,000 persons, including 15,000 warriors) to Africa. St. Augustine died in 430 in besieged Hippo, Carthage fell in 435, and in 442 a treaty gave Gaiseric the rich provinces of Byzacena and Numidia. From there he was able to starve Rome, threaten Sicily, and close off the western basin of the Mediterranean to the Byzantines.

Shortly afterward, in 450, Attila's Huns invaded the West—first Gaul, where, after having been kept out of Paris, they were defeated by Aetius on the Campus Mauriacus (near Troyes), then Italy, which they evacuated soon after having received tribute from the pope, St. Leo. Attila died shortly afterward; and this invasion, which indeed left more legendary memories than actual ruins, had shown that a solidarity had been created between the Gallo-Romans and their barbarian occupiers, for the Franks, the Alemanni, and even Theodoric's Visigoths had come to Aetius's aid.

After the death of Aetius, in 454, and of Valentinian III, in 455, the West became the stake in the intrigues of the German chiefs Ricimer, Orestes, and Odoacer, who maintained real power through puppet emperors. In 457–461 the energetic Majorian reestablished imperial authority in southern Gaul until he was defeated by Gaiseric and assassinated shortly afterward. Finally, in 476, Odoacer deposed the last emperor, Romulus Augustulus, had himself proclaimed king in the barbaric fashion, and governed Italy with moderation, being de jure under the emperor of the East. The end of the Roman Empire of the West passed almost unperceived.

BARBARIAN KINGDOMS

Several barbarian kingdoms were then set up: in Africa, Gaiseric's kingdom of the Vandals; in Spain and in Gaul as far as the Loire, the Visigothic kingdom; and farther to the north, the kingdoms of the Salian Franks and the Alemanni. The barbarians were everywhere a small minority. They established themselves on the great estates and divided the land to the benefit of the federates without doing much harm to the lower classes or disturbing the economy. The old inhabitants lived under Roman law, while the barbarians kept their own "personality of laws," of which the best-known is the judicial composition, the Wergild. Romans and barbarians coexisted but uneasily. Among the obstacles to reconciliation were differences in mores; social and political institutions (personal monarchies, fidelity of man to man), language (although Latin was still used in administration), and, above all, religion. The

Arianism of the barbarians permitted the Roman Catholic bishops to retain their hold over their flocks. The only persecution, however, was under the Vandals, whose domination was the harshest.

Two great kingdoms marked the end of the fifth century. In Gaul, Clovis, the king of the Salian Franks (reigned 481/482–511), expelled Syagrius, the last Roman, from Soissons, took Alsace and the Palatinate from the Alemanni (496), and killed Alaric II, king of the Visigoths, at Vouillé (507). His conversion to Catholicism assured him the support of the bishops, and Frankish domination was established in Gaul. At the same time, Theodoric, king of the Ostrogoths, reigned in Italy. He had been charged by the emperor Zeno to take back Italy from Odoacer in 488, and in 494 he had himself proclaimed king at Ravenna. His Goths, few in number, were established in the north. Elsewhere he preserved the old imperial administration, with senators as prefects. Externally, he kept Clovis from reaching the Mediterranean and extended his state up to the valley of the Rhône. Theodoric died in 526. Ten years later Justinian charged his general Belisarius with the reconquest of Italy, a costly, devastating, and temporary operation that lasted from 535 to 540.

ANALYSIS OF THE DECLINE AND FALL

The causes of the fall of the empire have been sought in a great many directions and with a great deal of interest, even urgency, among historians of the West, for it has been natural for them to see or seek parallels between Rome's fate and that of their own times. In any choice of explanations there is likely to be a hidden sense of priorities determining the definition of "civilization," or specifically the civilization of "Rome" or of "the classical world." If, for example, classical civilization is identified with the literature of the ancients at what one conceives to be its best, then "the end" of this civilization has to be set at some point of decline and explanations for its coming to be sought in the preexisting conditions. If not on literature but on political domination, then some other point in time must be chosen and explained in terms of what seems to have led up to it.

There have been endless variations on this search, and there will continue to be more, no doubt, since it is agreed that literature did, in fact, diminish in quality, as did jurisprudence, although at a different date, and oratory, and vigorous political debate in the capital, and powerfully innovative philosophy, and sculpture, and civic patriotism, and the willingness to die for one's country. "Civilization" turns out to be not one single entity but a web of many strands, each of its own length.

Perhaps the view attracting the most adherents, however, has focused on the ability of the empire to maintain its political and military integrity—that being the strand apparently most central and significant—and the juncture at which that ability is most dramatically challenged and found wanting—the period of "the barbarian invasions," meaning 407 and roughly the ensuing decade. If this juncture in turn is examined and the antecedents of the empire's weakness sought in internal developments, they can only be found in the government. Belief in and obedience to the monarch was not lacking, nor military technology at least matching that of the invaders, nor a population large enough to field a large force, nor the force itself (on paper, at least), nor the economic potential adequate to the arming of it.

Particular defeats described by contemporaries in reasonable detail are almost uniformly attributable to the rottenness of government, rendering soldiers undisciplined, untrained, frequently on indefinite leave, and without good morale or proper equipment. Soldiers were unpaid because of various abuses in the collection and delivery of supplies and money from taxpayers, and they were distracted from their proper duties by their own and their officers' extortionate habits in contact with their civilian hosts. For the same basic reason—that is, abuse of power wielded through service in the army or bureaucracy—the administration of the cities no longer enjoyed the efforts of the urban elites, who by 407 had long since fled from active service to some exempt government post or title.

For the same reason, finally, corrective measures needed against these systemic weaknesses could not be developed by enlightened men at the centre because they were screened from the truth of things, were at the mercy of incompetent or venal agents, or were unable to maintain themselves in power against the plotters around them. The details of all these charges that can be made against late Roman government are writ large in the great collection of imperial edicts published in 438, the Theodosian Code, as well as in the works of roughly contemporary writers from East and West, such as Synesius, Augustine, Libanius, Themistius, Chrysostom, Symmachus, Bishop Maximus of Turin, and, above all, Ammianus Marcellinus. An empire that could not deliver to a point of need all the defensive force it still possessed could not well stand against the enemy outside.

Appendix A: Table of Roman Emperors from 27 BC through AD 476

Roman Emperors	
Augustus (Augustus Caesar)	27 BC–AD 14
Tiberius (Tiberius Caesar Augustus)	14–37
Caligula (Gaius Caesar Germanicus)	37–41
Claudius (Tiberius Claudius Caesar Augustus Germanicus)	41–54
Nero (Nero Claudius Caesar Augustus Germanicus)	54–68
Galba (Servius Galba Caesar Augustus)	68–69
Otho (Marcus Otho Caesar Augustus)	69
Vitellius (Aulus Vitellius)	69
Vespasian (Caesar Vespasianus Augustus)	69–79
Titus (Titus Vespasianus Augustus)	79–81
Domitian (Caesar Domitianus Augustus)	81–96
Nerva (Nerva Caesar Augustus)	96–98
Trajan (Caesar Divi Nervae Filius Nerva Traianus Optimus Augustus)	98–117
Hadrian (Caesar Traianus Hadrianus Augustus)	117–138
Antoninus Pius (Caesar Titus Aelius Hadrianus Antoninus Augustus Pius)	138–161
Marcus Aurelius (Caesar Marcus Aurelius Antoninus Augustus)	161–180
Lucius Verus (Lucius Aurelius Verus)	161–169
Commodus (Caesar Marcus Aurelius Commodus Antoninus Augustus)	177–192
Pertinax (Publius Helvius Pertinax)	193
Didius Severus Julianus (Marcus Didius Severus Julianus)	193
Septimius Severus (Lucius Septimius Severus Pertinax)	193–211
Caracalla (Marcus Aurelius Severus Antoninus Augustus)	198–217
Septimius Geta (Publius Septimius Geta)	209–212
Macrinus (Caesar Marcus Opellius Severus Macrinus Augustus)	217–218

Roman Emperors	
Elagabalus (Caesar Marcus Aurelius Antoninus Augustus)	218–222
Alexander Severus (Marcus Aurelius Severus Alexander)	222–235
Maximinus (Gaius Julius Verus Maximinus)	235–238
Gordian I (Marcus Antonius Gordianus Sempronianus Romanus)	238
Gordian II (Marcus Antonius Gordianus Sempronianus Romanus Africanus)	238
Pupienus Maximus (Marcus Clodius Pupienus Maximus)	238
Balbinus (Decius Caelius Calvinus Balbinus)	238
Gordian III (Marcus Antonius Gordianus)	238–244
Philip (Marcus Julius Philippus)	244–249
Decius (Gaius Messius Quintus Trianus Decius)	249–251
Hostilian (Gaius Valens Hostilianus Messius Quintus)	251
Gallus (Gaius Vibius Trebonianus Gallus)	251–253
Aemilian (Marcus Aemilius Aemilianus)	253
Valerian (Publius Licinius Valerianus)	253–260
Gallienus (Publius Licinius Egnatius Gallienus)	253–268
Claudius (II) Gothicus (Marcus Aurelius Claudius Gothicus)	268–270
Quintillus (Marcus Aurelius Claudius Quintillus)	269–270
Aurelian (Lucius Domitius Aurelianus)	270–275
Tacitus (Marcus Claudius Tacitus)	275–276
Florian (Marcus Annius Florianus)	276
Probus (Marcus Aurelius Probus)	276–282
Carus (Marcus Aurelius Carus)	282–283
Carinus (Marcus Aurelius Carinus)	283–285
Numerian (Marcus Aurelius Numerius Numerianus)	283–284
Diocletian (Gaius Aurelius Valerius Diocletianus) *East only*	284–305
Maximian (Marcus Aurelius Valerius Maximianus) *West only*	286–305 306–308
Galerius (Gaius Galerius Valerius Maximianus) *East only*	305–311
Constantius I Chlorus (Marcus Flavius Valerius Constantius) *West only*	305–306

ROMAN EMPERORS	
Severus (Flavius Valerius Severus) *West only*	306–307
Maxentius (Marcus Aurelius Valerius Maxentius) *West only*	306–312
Licinius (Valerius Licinianus Licinius) *East only*	308–324
Constantine I (Flavius Valerius Constantinus)	312–337
Constantine II (Flavius Claudius Constantinus)	337–340
Constans I (Flavius Julius Constans)	337–350
Constantius II (Flavius Julius Constantius)	337–361
Magnentius (Flavius Magnus Magnentius)	350–353
Julian (Flavius Claudius Julianus)	361–363
Jovian (Flavius Jovianus)	363–364
Valentinian I (Flavius Valentinianus) *West only*	364–375
Valens (Flavius Valens) *East only*	364–378
Procopius *East only*	365–366
Gratian (Flavius Gratianus Augustus) *West only*	375–383
Valentinian II (Flavius Valentinianus) *West only*	375–392
Theodosius I (Flavius Theodosius)	379–395
Arcadius (Flavius Arcadius) *East only*	395–408
Honorius (Flavius Honorius) *West only*	395–423
Theodosius II *East only*	408–450
Constantius III *West only*	421
Valentinian III (Flavius Placidius Valentinianus) *West only*	425–455
Marcian (Marcianus) *East only*	450–457
Petronius Maximus (Flavius Ancius Petronius Maximus) *West only*	455
Avitus (Flavius Maccilius Eparchius Avitus) *West only*	455–456
Leo I (Leo Thrax Magnus) *East only*	457–474
Majorian (Julius Valerius Majorianus) *West only*	457–461
Libius Severus (Libius Severianus Severus) *West only*	461–467
Anthemius (Procopius Anthemius) *West only*	467–472
Olybrius (Anicius Olybrius) *West only*	472
Glycerius *West only*	473–474

ROMAN EMPERORS	
Julius Nepos *West only*	474–475
Leo II *East only*	474
Zeno *East only*	474–491
Romulus Augustulus (Flavius Momyllus Romulus Augustulus) *West only*	475–476

APPENDIX B: ANCIENT ITALIC PEOPLES

The following is a select list of the peoples—diverse in origin, language, traditions, and territorial extension—who inhabited pre-Roman Italy, a region heavily influenced by neighbouring Greece, with its well-defined national characteristics, expansive vigour, and aesthetic and intellectual maturity. Italy attained a unified ethnolinguistic, political, and cultural physiognomy only after the Roman conquest, yet its most ancient peoples remain anchored in the names of the regions of Roman Italy—Latium, Campania, Apulia, Bruttium, Lucania, Samnium, Picenum, Umbria, Etruria, Venetia, and Liguria.

AEQUIANS

The Aequians (Aequi) originally inhabited the region watered by the tributaries of the Avens River (modern Velino River). Long hostile to Rome, they became especially menacing in the fifth century BC, advancing to the Alban Hills. Although repulsed by the Romans in 431, the Aequians were not completely subdued by Rome until the end of the Second Samnite War (304 BC), when they received *civitas sine suffragio* ("citizenship without voting rights"). The establishment of the Latin colony of Carsioli (302 BC) and the extension of the Via Valeria through the territory of the Aequians aided the rapid Romanization of that people. The Volscians (see page 212) were their constant allies.

APULIANS

The Apulians (Apuli) inhabited the southeastern extremity of the Italian peninsula. The ancients often called this group of tribes Iapyges (and their territory Iapygia, in which "Apulia" [modern Puglia] may be recognized).

The territory of Apulia included the Salentinians and Messapians peoples in the Salentine Peninsula (Calabria) and the Peucetians (Peucetii) and Daunians (Dauni) farther north. Ancient tradition insists upon an overseas origin for these tribes, held to be Cretan or Illyrian. Sometimes the designations Iapyges and Messapians are used interchangeably. The Iapygian or, more commonly, Messapic language is known from a considerable series of public funerary, votive, monetary, and other inscriptions written in the Greek alphabet and found in the Apulian area, especially in the Salentine Peninsula, from words reported by the ancient writers, and from toponomastic (local place-name) data. Messapic is without doubt an Indo-European language, distinct from Latin and from the Umbro-Sabellic dialects, with Balkan and central

European analogies. This confirms the overseas provenance of the Iapyges from the Balkans, the more so because there existed in Illyria a tribe called the Iapodes and because a people known as the Iapuzkus lived farther north, on the Adriatic coast of Italy. Rather than a true immigration, however, there was a gradual prehistoric penetration of trans-Adriatic elements. The expansion of the Iapyges must have brought them to Lucania and even to what is now Calabria, as would be deduced from traditional and archaeological indications.

The Apulian civilization, which was considerably influenced by that of the nearby Greek colonies, developed from the ninth to the third century BC. In the most ancient period there were pit graves, sometimes in large stone tumuli. In the Siponto area, near what is now Manfredonia, the graves were accompanied by anthropomorphic stelae with geometric bas-reliefs. Geometrically painted ceramics in linear motifs persisted to the threshold of the Hellenistic Age. Later graves took the form of large trunks and of catacombs with paintings on the sides. Burial was the disposition exclusively used.

Beginning in Archaic times, large cities developed, linked to each other by bonds of confederation. These included Herdonea (now Ordona), Canusium (Canosa di Puglia), Rubi (Ruvo di Puglia), Gnathia, Brundisium (Brindisi), Uria (Oria), Lupiae (Lecce), Rudiae, and Manduria. They preserved their independence, tenaciously defended against the Greeks, until the age of the Roman conquest.

AURUNCIANS

The Auruncians (Aurunci, or Ausones) were an ancient tribe of Campania. They were exterminated by the Romans in 314 BC as the culmination of 50 years of Roman military campaigns against them. They occupied a strip of coast situated between the Volturnus and Liris (Volturno and Liri) rivers in what is now the province of Caserta, with their capital at Suessa Aurunca (modern Sessa Aurunca). No written record of their language survives, but the frequency of the use of the "-co" suffix in that part of the coast suggests that the Auruncians spoke Volscian, the same Italic dialect as their northern neighbours, the Volscians. The name Ausones, the Greek form from which the Latin Aurunci was derived, was applied by the Greeks to various Italic tribes, but the name came to denote in particular the tribe that the great Roman historian Livy called Aurunci. The name was later applied to all Italians, and Ausonia became a poetic term, in Greek and Latin, for Italy.

BRUTTIANS

This group inhabited what is now southwestern Italy, occupying an area coextensive with modern Calabria, an area sometimes referred to as the "toe of the boot." This area was separated from Lucania (corresponding to modern Basilicata) on the north, and it was to the whole or to a part of this peninsula that the name Italia was first applied.

In alliance with the Lucanians, the Bruttians (Bruttii) made war on the Greek colonies of the coast and seized on Vibo in 356 BC. Though for a time overcome by the Greeks who were aided by Alexander of Epirus and Agathocles, tyrant of Syracuse, they reasserted their mastery of the town from about the beginning of the third century BC and held it until it became a Latin colony at the end of the same century.

At this time the Bruttians were speaking Oscan as well as Greek, and two of three Oscan inscriptions in a Greek alphabet still testify to the language spoken in Vibo in the third century BC. Despite their use of the Oscan language, the Bruttians were not actually akin to the Samnite tribe of the Lucanians, who also spoke Oscan. The name Bruttii was used by the Lucanians to mean "runaway slaves," but it is considerably more likely that this signification was attached to the tribal name of the Bruttians from the historical fact that they had been conquered and expelled by the Samnite invaders.

The Bruttians were at the height of their power during the third century BC. Their chief towns were Consentia (modern Cosenza), Petelia (near Strongoli), and Clampetia (Amantea). To this period (about the time of the Pyrrhic War) is assigned the series of coins they struck, and they appear to have retained the right of coinage even after their final subjugation by the Romans. The influence of Hellenism over the Bruttians can be seen in finds in tombs and their use of the Greek language in addition to their own. The mountainous country, ill suited for agricultural purposes, was well adapted for these hardy warriors, whose training was Spartan in its simplicity and severity.

The Bruttians first confronted the Romans during the war with Pyrrhus, to whom they sent auxiliaries. After his defeat, they submitted and were deprived of half their territory in the Sila forest, which was declared state property. In the war with Hannibal, they were among the first to declare in his favour after the battle of Cannae, and it was in their country that Hannibal held his ground during the last stage of the war (at Castrum Hannibalis on the Gulf of Scylacium). The Bruttians entirely lost their freedom at the end of the Hannibalic war; in 194 BC colonies of Roman citizens were founded at Tempsa and Croton, and a colony with Latin rights at Hipponium called thereafter Vibo Valentia. In 132 BC the great inland road from Capua through Vibo and Consentia to Rhegium (Reggio di Calabria) was built, but neither in the Social War nor in the rising of Spartacus, who held out a long time in the Sila (71 BC), do the Bruttians play a further part as a distinct group.

ETRUSCANS

The Etruscans (Etrusci) were an ancient people of Etruria (between the Tiber and

Arno rivers west and south of the Apennines), whose urban civilization reached its height in the sixth century BC. Many features of Etruscan culture were adopted by the Romans.

The origin of the Etruscans has been a subject of debate since antiquity. The Greek historian Herodotus, for example, argued that the Etruscans descended from a people who invaded Etruria from Anatolia (what is now Turkey) before 800 BC and established themselves over the native Iron Age inhabitants of the region, whereas Dionysius of Halicarnassus, also a Greek historian, believed that the Etruscans were of local Italian origin. Both theories, as well as a third 19th-century theory, have turned out to be problematic, and today scholarly discussion has shifted its focus from the discussion of provenance to that of the formation of the Etruscan people.

In any event, by the middle of the seventh century BC the chief Etruscan towns had been founded. Before reaching the Arno River in the north and incorporating all Tuscany in their dominion, the Etruscans embarked upon a series of conquests initially probably not coordinated but undertaken by individual cities. The pressing motive for expansion was that by the middle of this century the Greeks not only had obtained a grip on Corsica and expanded their hold on Sicily and southern Italy but also had settled on the Ligurian coast (northwestern Italy) and in southern France.

Etruscan expansion to the south and east was confined at the line of the Tiber River by the strong Italic Umbrian people settled beyond it on the south and the Picenes on the east. To the northeast no such united power opposed their expansion, since the Apennine mountains in Aemilia (modern Emilia) and Tuscany were held by scattered Italic tribes. Through these the Etruscans were able, in the middle of the sixth century, to push into the Po River valley.

As capital of this northward region they established the old Villanovan centre at Bologna (the Etruscan city of Felsina) and on the banks of the Reno founded Marzabotto. On the Adriatic coast to the east, Ravenna, Ariminum (modern Rimini), and Spina traded with Istra (modern Istria) and the Greek Dalmatian colonies. From the Po valley, contacts were made with the central European La Tène cultures. Etruscan conquests in the northeast extended to include what are now the modern cities of Piacenza, Modena, Parma, and Mantua. To the south they were drawn into Latium and Campania from the end of the seventh century, and in the sixth century they had a decisive impact on the history of Rome, where the Etruscan dynasty of the Tarquins is said to have ruled from 616 to 510/509 BC. It is possible that the Roman Tarquins were connected with a family called Tarchu, which is known from inscriptions.

Rome before the Etruscan advent was a small conglomeration of villages. It was under the new masters that, according to tradition, the first public works such as the walls of the Capitoline hill and the Cloaca Maxima (a sewer) were constructed. Considerable evidence of the Etruscan period in Rome's history has come to light in the region of the Capitol. That there were rich tombs in Rome itself cannot be doubted—tombs similar to those in the Latin town of Praeneste (modern Palestrina).

Meanwhile, by the beginning of the sixth century the Etruscans had included Faesulae (modern Fiesole) and Volaterrae (modern Volterra) in their northern limits and at the same time began to push southward into Campania. Capua became the chief Etruscan foundation in this region and Nola a second; a necropolis has been found in the Salerno region and Etruscan objects in low levels at Herculaneum and Pompeii. The coastal region was still, however, in Greek hands. When the Etruscans attacked the Greek foundation of Cumae in 524 BC, their advance was finally checked by their defeat at the hands of Aristodemus of that city.

The rivalry between Greek trade in the western Mediterranean and that carried on between the Etruscans and Carthage had already come to a head at the battle of Alalia in 535 BC, a battle which the Greeks claimed to have won but which so upset them that they determined to abandon Corsica to Etruscan and Carthaginian influence.

In the last quarter of the sixth century, when Etruscan power was at its height from the Po to Salerno, small settlements of Etruscans might have been planted beyond these limits. At Spoletium (modern Spoleto) in the north and Fossombrone in Liguria their power was not, however, to last long; Cumae felt the first of sharp waves of resistance coming from Greeks, Samnites, Romans, and Gauls. In 509 BC the Etruscans were chased from Rome, as reflected in the story of the expulsion of Tarquinius Superbus, the intervention of Lars Porsena of Clusium, and the Latin victory over Aruns Porsena's son at Aricia. When Latium was lost, relations between Etruria and its Campanian possessions were broken with disastrous effect. A series of piecemeal feuds between Etruscan cities and Rome led to the incorporation of the former into the Roman sphere—first the nearby town of Veii in 396 BC, after which Capena, Sutri, and Nepet (modern Nepi) fell in turn, thus beginning the end of the first of many unsuccessful attempts at unifying Italy.

Nevertheless, the Etruscans had established a thriving commercial and agricultural civilization. Characteristic of their artistic achievements are the wall frescoes and realistic terra-cotta portraits found in their tombs. Their religion employed elaborately organized cults and rituals, including the extensive practice of divination.

HERNICIANS

The territory of the Hernicians (Hernici) was in Latium between the Fucine Lake (modern Fucino) and the Trerus (modern Sacco) River, bounded by the Volscians on the south and by the Aequians and the

Marsians on the north. In 486 BC they were still strong enough to conclude a treaty with the Romans on equal terms. They broke away from Rome in 362–358. In 306 their chief town, Anagnia (modern Anagni), was taken by the Romans and deprived of its independence and their league was broken up. By 195 their territory was not distinguished from Latium and they were regarded as Latins, both politically and in language. Their original language is unknown.

LATINS

The Latins (Latini) inhabited Latium in west-central Italy. Originally this territory was limited to a region around the Alban Hills, but by about 500 BC it extended south of the Tiber River as far as the promontory of Mount Circeo. It was bounded on the northwest by Etruria, on the southeast by Campania, on the east by Samnium, and on the northeast by the territory of the Sabines, Aequians, and Marsians.

The Latins were sprung from those Indo-European tribes that, during the second millennium BC, came to settle in the Italian peninsula. By the first centuries of the first millennium BC, the Latins had developed as a separate people, originally established on the mass of the Alban Hills, which was isolated and easy to defend. The Latin tribes that settled there were influenced both by the civilization of the Iron Age of southern Italy and by the Villanovan civilization of southern Etruria. The Latins cremated their dead and deposited their ashes in urns of Villanovan type—a biconical, or two-storied, form covered with a bowl—as well as in hut-shaped urns that were faithful imitations of the huts of the living. The decoration of these funerary containers is of a simple geometric type, similar to that engraved on bronze objects found in these tombs, such as razors, spindles, weapons, and brooches. The material used for the tombs in the Alban Hills resembles the material found in contemporary tombs in Rome but is occasionally rougher and coarser in appearance.

In approximately 600 BC, when the Etruscans occupied Latium and settled in Rome, the influence of Etruscan civilization and art made itself felt as much in the other Latin towns as in Rome itself. But Rome soon became a large city, similar to the powerful cities of southern Etruria, and it took precedence over its neighbours. According to the annalistic tradition, it was a specifically Roman uprising that drove the Etruscans from Rome in 509. In fact it was a coalition of Latins and Greeks that led to the Etruscans' withdrawal from Latium in 475 BC.

After the departure of the Etruscans the fortunes of Latium changed; it became impoverished. Rome lost its pre-eminence over the neighbouring cities and took a long time to recover it. Throughout the fifth century BC the Latin League imposed its policy on Rome. Every year the delegates of the Latin cities elected a dictator who commanded a federal army, which included Roman troops. In this league Tusculum seemed to exercise the leadership that Rome had held in the Etruscan period. The territory of Rome did not extend beyond the sixth mile from the city.

The Latin people were threatened by the proximity of turbulent peoples: the Volscians, who dwelt in Antium, and the Aequians, who ruled Praeneste and Tibur. The legendary story of Coriolanus shows how, in the early fifth century BC, Rome began to extend its territory toward the south by fighting on the side of Ardea and Aricia against the Volscians. At the end of the fifth century Roman colonies were established in the Monti Lepini. In the fourth century BC Rome began to take precedence among the sister cities of Latium, weakened by their dissensions. In 358 BC, however, Rome and the Latin confederacy concluded a treaty of alliance on a basis of equality. They nominated in turn the dictator of the league. But the strength of Rome grew, and it established two tribes in Volscian territory. In 340 war broke out between Rome and the Latins. It ended in 338 in the defeat of the Latins and the dissolution of their league. The Latin cities were given political statutes that limited or abolished their autonomy. Thereafter Roman hegemony in Latium was an accomplished fact, and the life of the Latin country was soon modeled on that of the city.

LIGURIANS

The Ligurians (Ligures) constituted a collection of ancient peoples who inhabited the northwestern Mediterranean coast from the mouth of the Ebro River in Spain to the mouth of the Arno River in Italy in the first millennium BC.

No ancient texts speak of Ligurians in southern Gaul as nations or attribute definite ethnic characteristics to them. They were apparently an indigenous collection of Neolithic peoples living in village settlements in remote places, and it was probably to loose political groupings of these people that ancient authors attached the name. Such authors as the Greek geographer and historian Strabo and Greek historian Diodorus Siculus described them as a rough and strong people whose piracy the Romans deplored. These views, however, appear in late texts and refer to the Celticized Ligurians (Celtoligures) between the Rhône and Arno rivers. Strabo declared that they were a different race from the Gauls or Celts, and Diodorus mentioned that they lived in villages and made a difficult living from the rocky, mountainous soil. In any event, their reputed boldness caused them to be in great demand as mercenaries. They served the Carthaginian commander Hamilcar in 480 BC and the Sicilian Greek colonies in the time of Agathocles and openly sided with Carthage in the Second Punic War (218–201 BC). Steps were not taken for their final reduction by Rome until 180 BC, when 40,000 Ligurians were deported to Samnium and settled near Beneventum (Benevento).

The name Ligurian, or Ligures, has been used by modern archaeologists to designate a stratum of Neolithic remains in the region from northeastern Spain to northwestern Italy.

MARSIANS

The Marsians (Marsi) inhabited the eastern shore of Lake Fucinus (now drained) in the modern province of L'Aquila. In 304 BC they and their allies, the Vestinians, Paelignians, and Marrucinians, made an alliance with Rome that lasted until the Social War, sometimes called the Marsic War (90–89 BC). This war ended when the allies were finally given Roman citizenship.

The earliest pure Latin inscriptions of the Marsians are dated to about 150 BC, whereas the earliest inscriptions in the local dialect date from about 300 to 150 BC. The Marsians were among those who worshipped Angitia, a goddess of healing, and, because they practiced a medicine based on superstition, their country was held by the Romans to be the home of witchcraft. The name of the tribe is derived from the god Mars.

MESSAPIANS

The Messapians (Messapii) lived in the southeastern part of the Italian peninsula (Calabria and Apulia) and with the closely related Apulians they probably penetrated Italy from the other side of the Adriatic Sea about 1000 BC. They spoke Messapic (Messapian), an Indo-European language. (Messapic inscriptions date from the sixth to the first century BC. The language is believed to be related to the extinct Illyrian languages that were spoken on the east side of the Adriatic.) They frequently fought the Greeks of the nearby Spartan colony of Tarentum (modern Taranto), but they supported Tarentum and Pyrrhus of Epirus in their wars against Rome (280–275 BC). In 266 the Messapians were conquered by Rome, and they rarely appeared in history after that.

PICENES

The Early Iron Age inhabitants of the Adriatic coast of Italy from Rimini to the Sangro River were known as Picenes (Piceni, or Picentes). Men and women dressed in wool; men wore armour, weapons, and ornaments of bronze or iron; women had numerous fibulae, torques, bracelets, girdles, and ornamental pendants. They had two main centres, one at Novilara in the north, and another around Belmonte and Fermo farther south. The Picenes traded with the Greeks as early as the seventh century BC, but there is little evidence of trade with Etruria, except at the inland site of Fabriano. The evidence suggests that Picenes were warlike, with little artistic ability of their own, but wealthy enough to sustain a flourishing trade. In 268 BC their territory was annexed by Rome.

SABINES

The Sabines (Sabini) were located in the mountainous country east of the Tiber River. They were known for their religious practices and beliefs, and several Roman institutions were said to have derived from them. The story recounted by the Greek biographer and author Plutarch that Romulus, the founder of Rome, invited the Sabines to a feast and then carried off (raped) their women, is legendary. Though there was a considerable Sabine infiltration into Rome, the view that the Sabines conquered the city in the first half of the fifth century BC is improbable; rather, the Romans had many skirmishes with the Sabines before their victory in 449. Nothing is known thereafter until in 290 the Sabines were conquered and granted *civitas sine suffragio*; in 268 they received full Roman citizenship.

The Sabines probably spoke Oscan. No inscription has survived of their dialect, but a large number of single words are attributed to them by Latin writers. The tradition that the Sabines were the parent stock of the Samnite tribes is probably correct.

SAMNITES

The Samnites were a collection of warlike tribes inhabiting the mountainous centre of southern Italy. These tribes, who spoke Oscan and were probably an offshoot of the Sabines, apparently referred to themselves not as Samnite but by the Oscan form of the word, which appears in Latin as Sabine.

Four cantons formed a Samnite confederation: Hirpini, Caudini, Caraceni,

and Pentri. The league probably had no federal assembly, but a war leader could be chosen to lead a campaign. Although allied with Rome against the Gauls in 354 BC, the Samnites were soon involved in a series of three wars (343–341, 327–304, and 298–290) against the Romans. Despite a spectacular victory over the Romans at the Battle of the Caudine Forks (321), where a Roman army was forced to march under the yoke, the Samnites were eventually subjugated. The Romans surrounded Samnite land with colonies and then split it with colonies at Beneventum (268) and Aesernia (263).

Although reduced and depopulated, the Samnites later helped Pyrrhus and Hannibal against Rome. They also fought from 90 BC in the Social War and later in the civil war against Lucius Cornelius Sulla, who defeated them at the Battle of the Colline Gate (82 BC).

The longest and most important inscription of the Samnite dialect is the small bronze Tabula Agnonensis, which is engraved in full Oscan alphabet. In June 2004, archaeologists in Pompeii discovered the remains of a wall from a temple built by Samnites.

SICANS

According to ancient Greek writers, the Sicans (Sicani) were the aboriginal inhabitants of central Sicily, as distinguished from the Sicels (Siculi) of eastern Sicily and the Elymi of western Sicily. Archaeologically there is no substantial difference between Sicans and Sicels in historical times; but the Greek historian Thucydides believed the Sicans to be Iberians from Spain who were driven by the invading Sicels into the central parts of the island.

SICELS

Sicels (Siculi) were an ancient people that occupied the eastern part of Sicily. Old tales related that they once lived in central Italy but were driven out and finally crossed to Sicily, leaving remnants behind—e.g., at Locri. They are hard to identify archaeologically, although some words of their Indo-European language are known. Phases of the Italic Apennine culture have been identified on the Eolie (Aeolian) Islands off the northeast coast of Sicily and in northeastern Sicily, which may indicate emigration from Italy during the late Bronze Age. The Sicels lived in independent towns; thus, they were easily displaced by the Greek colonists who migrated to Sicily, and they did not react en masse until the 450s BC under Ducetius. Their most important gods were the Palici, protectors of agriculture and sailors; Adranus, perhaps the father of the Palici; and the goddess Hybla, or Hyblaea.

UMBRIANS

The Umbrians (Umbri) were an Etruscan people who gradually concentrated in Umbria (in what is now central Italy) in response to Etruscan and Gallic pressure. By about 400 BC the inhabitants of this area spoke an Indo-European dialect closely related to Oscan (Umbrian). It is best known from the ritual texts called the Iguvine Tables. The Umbrians never fought any important wars against the Romans; in the Social War (90–89 BC), for instance, they joined the rebel allies tardily and were among the first to make peace with Rome. Ancient authors described the Umbrians as closely resembling their Etruscan enemies in their habits, and the Umbrian alphabet was undoubtedly of Etruscan origin.

VENETIANS

An ancient people of northeastern Italy, the Venetians (Veneti) arrived about 1000 BC and occupied country stretching south to the Po and west to the neighbourhood of Verona. They left more than 400 inscriptions from the last four centuries BC, some in the Latin alphabet, others in a native script.

The chief Venetic settlement was Este (later the Roman colony of Ateste), which was also the cult centre of their important divinity Reitia, possibly a goddess of childbirth. The horses bred in Venetia were famous in the Greek world, and there was other commerce both with Greek lands and with the Alps and northern Europe, including some control of the amber route from the Baltic. The Venetians were friendly to Rome throughout and assisted Rome against the Gauls, especially in the war of 225 BC. The colony of Aquileia, founded in 181 BC, protected Venetia from raids by its mountain neighbours, and a century of peace and Romanization followed, though probably much land was bought up by Roman settlers. The towns were given Latin rights in 89 BC and full citizen status in 49 BC.

VESTINIANS

The Vestinians (Vestini) were an ancient Sabine tribe, which occupied the eastern and northern bank of the Aternus (modern Aterno) River in central Italy. They entered into the Roman alliance in 302 BC and remained loyal until they joined the Social War (90–89 BC), by which they won Roman citizenship.

The Vestinian local dialect, belonging to the Northern Oscan group, probably survived until this time. The oldest known Latin inscriptions of the district are not earlier than 100 BC, and they indicate that the Latin first spoken by the Vestinians was not that of Rome but that of their neighbours, the Marsians and the Aequians.

VOLSCIANS

The people known as Volscians (Volsci) were prominent in the history of Roman expansion during the fifth century BC.

They belonged to the Osco-Sabellian group of tribes and lived (c. 600 BC) in the valley of the upper Liris River. Later events, however, drove them first westward and then south to the fertile land of southern Latium.

Knowledge of the Volscians depends largely upon Roman accounts of their mutual wars. To increase their pressure against Rome and the Latins, the Volscians allied themselves with the Aequians. Rome and the Latins in turn joined in alliance with the Hernicians, who lived between the Aequians and the Volscians. For about 200 years campaigns dragged on intermittently between these opponents. The Volscians are said to have made peace with Rome in 396 but profited by Rome's weakness after the Gauls sacked the city in 390 to renew their warfare. In the course of these struggles the Romans established several colonies in the fifth and fourth centuries to stem the advance of the Volscians. In 340 the Volscians joined the Latin revolt but were defeated (338), and they had finally submitted to Rome by 304. Thereafter they became Romanized so quickly and completely that it is difficult to ascertain their original culture. Their language is known from an inscription (early third century) from Velitrae.

GLOSSARY

aedile A magistrate of ancient Rome who originally had charge of the temple and cult of Ceres.

anachronistic A person or thing that is chronologically out of place, especially as it pertains to one item from a former age that is incongruous in the present.

annalistic Relating to the writing of historical events.

aphorism A concise expression of doctrine or principle or any generally accepted truth conveyed in a pithy, memorable statement.

apostasy The renunciation of religious faith.

ascetic One who practices strict self-denial as a measure of personal or spiritual discipline.

capricious Impulsive and unpredictable.

censor In ancient Rome, a magistrate whose original function of registering citizens and their property was expanded to include supervision of senatorial rolls and moral conduct.

collegium A group in which each member has approximately equal power and authority.

deification To glorify as if a god; to make someone or something an object of worship.

demagogue A leader who makes use of popular prejudices or false claims in order to gain power; in ancient times, one who championed the cause of the common people.

didrachm Ancient Greek currency.

ethos The distinguishing character, sentiment, moral nature, or guiding beliefs of a person, group, or institution.

exigency A state of affairs that makes urgent demands.

hegemony A preponderant influence or authority over others.

homogeneity The quality of being of uniform structure or composition throughout; having equal parts that are similar or the same.

imperium The supreme executive power in the Roman state, involving both military and judicial authority.

manumission Formal emancipation from slavery.

megalomaniacal Having delusions of personal omnipotence.

meretricious Tawdrily and falsely attractive.

oligarchy Government by the few, especially despotic power exercised by a small and privileged group for corrupt or selfish purposes.

panegyric Eulogistic oration or laudatory discourse that originally was a speech delivered at an ancient Greek general assembly (*panegyris*), such as the Olympic and Panathenaic festivals.

philhellenism Admiration for Greece and the Greeks.

polemicist One who stages an aggressive attack or refutation of another's opinions or principles.

pomerium A sacred, open space located just inside the wall surrounding the four hills of early ancient Rome.

praetor A judicial officer who had broad authority in cases of equity, was responsible for the production of the public games, and, in the absence of consuls, exercised extensive authority in the government.

sacrosanct Treated as if holy.

sarcophagus A stone coffin.

stoicism The belief that the goal of all inquiry is to provide a mode of conduct characterized by tranquillity of mind and certainty of moral worth; when capitalized, a school of thought that flourished in Greek and Roman antiquity.

tetrarchy A collegium of emperors comprising two groups: two Augusti, older men who made the decisions, and two younger Caesars with a more executive role

tribune Any of various military and civil officials in ancient Rome.

triumvir One of three officers that mutually share the same administrative role.

usurpation To seize or hold office or powers by force or without right.

BIBLIOGRAPHY

GENERAL WORKS

A wealth of information on ancient Roman civilization is provided by the volumes in *The Cambridge Ancient History* (1923–), some in newer 2nd and 3rd editions; by N.G.L. Hammond and H.H. Scullard (eds.), *The Oxford Classical Dictionary*, 2nd ed. (1970, reprinted 1984); and by John Boardman, Jasper Griffin, and Oswyn Murray (eds.), *The Oxford History of the Classical World* (1986). Michael Grant and Rachel Kitzinger (eds.), *Civilization of the Ancient Mediterranean: Greece and Rome*, 3 vol. (1988), discusses the geography, inhabitants, arts, language, religion, politics, technology, and economy of the area from the early 1st millennium BC to the late 5th century AD. Broad coverage of the physical and cultural settings and of archaeological discoveries is also provided by Tim Cornell and John Matthews, *Atlas of the Roman World* (1982); and Nicholas G.L. Hammond (ed.), *Atlas of the Greek and Roman World in Antiquity* (1981). Overviews of the histories of Roman civilization include M. Cary and H.H. Scullard, *A History of Rome Down to the Reign of Constantine*, 3rd ed. (1975); and Michael Vickers, *The Roman World* (1977, reissued 1989). Many ancient historical sources are available in *The Loeb Classical Library* series, with original text and parallel English translation; in the series *Translated Documents of Greece and Rome*; and in Naphtali Lewis and Meyer Reinhold (eds.), *Roman Civilization: Selected Readings*, 3rd ed., 2 vol. (1990).

ROME FROM ITS ORIGINS TO 264 BC

Archaeological evidence on early Rome is discussed and analyzed by Raymond Bloch, *The Origins of Rome*, rev. ed. (1963; originally published in French, 1946); T.J. Cornell, "Rome and Latium Vetus," *Archaeological Reports*, 26:71–88 (1979–80); and Robert Drews, "The Coming of the City to Central Italy," *American Journal of Ancient History*, 6:133–165 (1981). The archaeology of early Italy in general is covered in David Trump, *Central and Southern Italy Before Rome* (1966). Livy's work on early Rome is carefully annotated and commented on in part by R.M. Ogilvie, *A Commentary on Livy, Books 1–5* (1965, reissued 1984). A good survey of Livy's annalistic predecessors is E. Badian, "The Early Historians," in T.A. Dorey (ed.), *Latin Historians* (1966), pp. 1–38. The single best modern treatment of the regal period and the early republic is Jacques Heurgon, *The Rise of Rome to 264 B.C.* (1973; originally published in French, 1969). A complete chronological listing of all known magistrates of the Roman Republic with full ancient citations can be found in T. Robert S. Broughton, *The*

Magistrates of the Roman Republic, 2 vol. and a supplement (1951–60, reprinted 1984–86). A collection and modern analysis of ancient sources concerning Rome's economic development is Tenney Frank (ed.), *An Economic Survey of Ancient Rome*, 6 vol. (1933–40, reprinted 1975). The legal evidence from early Rome is treated by Alan Watson, *Rome of the XII Tables: Persons and Property* (1975).

The evolution of Rome's foundation myth is discussed by E.J. Bickerman, "Origines Gentium," *Classical Philology*, 47(2):65–81 (April 1952). Bickerman treats a number of important methodological questions on early Rome in "Some Reflections on Early Roman History," *Rivista di Filologia e di Istruzione Classica*, 97:393–408 (1969). Richard I. Ridley, "Fastenkritik: A Stocktaking," *Athenaeum*, 58(3–4):264–298 (1980), surveys various modern views on the reliability of the consular *fasti*. The single best treatment of the Roman ruling class is Matthias Gelzer, *The Roman Nobility* (1969; originally published in German, 1912). The Roman assemblies and voting procedures are thoroughly examined by George Willis Botsford, *The Roman Assemblies from Their Origin to the End of the Republic* (1909, reprinted 1968); and Lily Ross Taylor, *Roman Voting Assemblies from the Hannibalic War to the Dictatorship of Caesar* (1966). Taylor has also carefully studied the origin and development of the 35 urban and rural voting tribes in *The Voting Districts of the Roman Republic* (1960). E. Stuart Staveley, "Forschungsbericht: The

Constitution of the Roman Republic 1940–1954," *Historia*, 5:74–122 (1956), surveys modern scholarship on a number of important constitutional problems of early Roman history. Staveley has discussed the problem of the distinction between patricians and plebians in "The Nature and Aims of the Patriciate," *Historia*, 32:24–57 (1983). A collection of essays by different scholars addressing this same problem is Kurt A. Raaflaub (ed.), *Social Struggles in Archaic Rome: New Perspectives on the Conflict of the Orders* (1986), which contains an excellent bibliography on early Rome. A detailed and novel approach to the problem of patricians and plebeians is Richard E. Mitchell, *Patricians and Plebeians: The Origin of the Roman State* (1990). The single best treatment of the military tribunes with consular power and related questions is Kurt von Fritz, "The Reorganization of the Roman Government in 366 B.C. and the So-called Licinio-Sextian Laws," *Historia*, 1:3–44 (1950).

The best modern discussion of Roman imperialism is William V. Harris, *War and Imperialism in Republican Rome, 327–70 B.C.* (1979). Harris's *Rome in Etruria and Umbria* (1971), examines Rome's relations with those two regions. Other informative works on Roman expansion include R.M. Errington, *The Dawn of Empire: Rome's Rise to World Power* (1971); Erich S. Gruen, *The Hellenistic World and the Coming of Rome*, 2 vol. (1984); and E. Badian, *Foreign Clientelae, 264–70 B.C.* (1958). E.T. Salmon, *Roman Colonization Under the*

Republic (1969), surveys the methods, aims, and consequences of Roman colonization.

THE MIDDLE REPUBLIC (264–133 BC)

H.H. Scullard, *A History of the Roman World: 753-146 BC*, 4th ed. (1980), provides a reliable narrative. Gaetano de Sanctis, *Storia dei Romani*, 4 vol. (1907–65), is more detailed. The standard reference work on Polybius is F.W. Walbank, *A Historical Commentary on Polybius*, 3 vol. (1957–79). On the wars with Carthage, Ulrich Kahrstedt, *Geschichte der Karthager von 218-146* (1913, reprinted 1975), provides source criticism. Military aspects of this period are presented in Johannes Kromayer and Georg Veith, *Antike Schlachtfelder*, vol. 3 in 2 parts (1912); Johannes Kromayer and Georg Veith (eds.), *Schlachten-Atlas zur antiken Kriegsgeschichte*, 5 parts (1922–29); J.H. Thiel, *A History of Roman Sea-power Before the Second Punic War* (1954), and *Studies on the History of Roman Sea-power in Republican Times* (1946); J.F. Lazenby, *Hannibal's War: A Military History of the Second Punic War* (1978); and H.H. Scullard, *Scipio Africanus: Soldier and Politician* (1970). Stéphane Gsell, *Histoire ancienne de l'Afrique du Nord*, 3rd ed., 8 vol. (1928); and B.H. Warmington, *Carthage*, rev. ed. (1969), deal with Carthage. Works on the provinces include David Magie, *Roman Rule in Asia Minor to the End of the Third Century After Christ*, 2 vol. (1950, reissued 1988); G.H. Stevenson, *Roman Provincial Administration till the Age of the Antonines* (1939, reprinted 1975); and C.H.V. Sutherland, *The Romans in Spain, 217 B.C.-A.D. 117* (1939, reprinted 1982).

THE TRANSFORMATION OF ROME AND ITALY DURING THE MIDDLE REPUBLIC

Citizenship, constitution, and politics are discussed in Theodor Mommsen, *Römisches Staatsrecht*, 3rd ed., 3 vol. in 5 (1887–88, reprinted 1969); A.N. Sherwin-White, *The Roman Citizenship*, 2nd ed. (1973, reissued 1987); and C. Nicolet, *The World of the Citizen in Republican Rome* (1980; originally published in French, 1976). Arnold J. Toynbee, *Hannibal's Legacy: The Hannibalic War's Effects on Roman Life*, 2 vols. (1965); P.A. Brunt, *Italian Manpower, 225 B.C.-A.D. 14* (1971, reprinted 1987); and Keith Hopkins, *Conquerors and Slaves* (1977), explore the social and economic consequences of Rome's victories. P.A. Brunt, *Social Conflicts in the Roman Republic* (1971, reissued 1986), presents an excellent brief account. Many important aspects of second-century politics and culture are covered in Alan E. Astin, *Scipio Aemilianus* (1967).

THE LATE REPUBLIC (133–31 BC)

The best outline in English for the late republic is the first half of H.H. Scullard, *From the Gracchi to Nero*, 5th ed. (1982), with excellent notes and bibliography. The classic reference work is W. Drumann, *Geschichte Roms in seinem Übergange von der republikanischen zur monarchischen Verfassung*, 2nd ed. edited by P. Groebe, 6 vol. (1899–1929), giving biographies (with full source material) of all prominent figures of the period, arranged by families. Classic interpretations of the fall of the republic are Ronald Syme, *The Roman Revolution* (1939, reissued 1987); P.A. Brunt, *The Fall of the Roman Republic and Related Essays* (1988); Lily Ross Taylor, *Party Politics in the Age of Caesar* (1949, reissued 1975); Erich S. Gruen, *The Last Generation of the Roman Republic* (1974); and Matthias Gelzer, *Caesar: Politician and Statesman* (1968; originally published in German, 1940). The army and expansion are analyzed in Emilio Gabba, *Republican Rome, the Army, and the Allies* (1976; originally published in Italian, 1973); and E. Badian, *Roman Imperialism in the Late Republic*, 2nd ed. (1968). Aspects of public and social life are dealt with in T.P. Wiseman, *New Men in the Roman Senate, 139 B.C.–A.D. 14* (1971); Israël Shatzman, *Senatorial Wealth and Roman Politics* (1975); Susan Treggiari, *Roman Freedmen During the Late Republic* (1969); A.W. Lintott, *Violence in Republican Rome* (1968); and E. Badian, *Publicans and Sinners: Private Enterprise in the Service of the Roman Republic* (1972, reissued 1983). On cultural development, the standard work is Elizabeth Rawson, *Intellectual Life in the Late Roman Republic* (1985); it may be supplemented by J.H.W.G. Liebeschuetz, *Continuity and Change in Roman Religion* (1979); Bruce W. Frier, *The Rise of the Roman Jurists* (1985); and George Kennedy, *The Art of Rhetoric in the Roman World, 300 B.C.–A.D. 300* (1972).

THE EARLY ROMAN EMPIRE (31 BC–AD 193)

Colin Wells, *The Roman Empire* (1984), is an intelligent short history up through the Severi. The history is carried further by Michael Grant, *The Climax of Rome: The Final Achievements of the Ancient World, A.D. 161–337* (1968). Donald Earl, *The Age of Augustus* (1968, reissued 1980), is useful in providing a little more depth. As to governmental institutions, Fergus Millar, *The Emperor in the Roman World, 31 BC–AD 337* (1977), offers a monumentally detailed study of the ruler in his capacity as civil governor up through Constantine; and Richard J.A. Talbert, *The Senate of Imperial Rome* (1984), describes the role and actions of the ruler's partner. On provincial government, as well as much else, Fergus Millar (ed.), *The Roman Empire and Its Neighbours*, 2nd ed. (1981; originally published in German, 1966), is informative and readable. Commentary on the economy is supplied by Kevin Greene, *The Archaeology of the Roman Economy* (1986). Géza Alföldy, *The Social History of Rome* (1985), on the structure of society; and Ramsay MacMullen, *Roman Social Relations, 50 B.C. to A.D. 284* (1974), on the feelings uniting or dividing groups or strata, are complementary works.

Provincial history broadly interpreted may be sampled in Sheppard Frere, *Britannia: A History of Roman Britain*, 3rd ed. rev. (1987); Paul MacKendrick, *The North African Stones Speak* (1980); and A.H.M. Jones, *The Greek City from Alexander to Justinian* (1940, reissued 1979), still useful, since archaeology has little touched the eastern end of the Mediterranean world. Bernard Andreae, *The Art of Rome* (1977; originally published in German, 1973), a large, luxuriously illustrated work with an equally rich scholarly text; and Niels Hannestad, *Roman Art and Imperial Policy* (1986; originally published in Danish, 1976), deal with their material in quite different ways: the former is conventionally art-historical, the latter uses his material to illuminate its context. Architecture is best approached through W.L. MacDonald, *The Architecture of the Roman Empire*, rev. ed., 2 vol. (1982–86), a well-written, imaginative account; and through such specialized studies as John Percival, *The Roman Villa: An Historical Introduction* (1976, reissued 1988). Philippe Ariès and Georges Duby (eds.), *A History of Private Life*, vol. 1, *From Pagan Rome to Byzantium*, ed. by Paul Veyne (1987; originally published in French, 1985), is a social history in an old-fashioned sense by a master of the most up-to-date approaches. The importance of emperor worship is well argued in the detailed work by Duncan Fishwick, *The Imperial Cult in the Latin West*, vol. 1 in 2 vol. (1987); and, with more interpretation

and for the other half of the empire, by S.R.F. Price, *Rituals and Power: The Roman Imperial Cult in Asia Minor* (1984). Ramsay MacMullen, *Paganism in the Roman Empire* (1981), provides a comprehensive view. Military history is made accessible through G.R. Watson, *The Roman Soldier* (1969, reissued 1985). An explication of a major aspect of culture may be found in the latter half of a work by a notable historian, H.I. Marrou, *A History of Education in Antiquity* (1956, reprinted 1982; originally published in French, 1948). Albin Lesky, *A History of Greek Literature* (1966; originally published in German, 2nd ed., 1963), may be paired with H.J. Rose, *A Handbook of Latin Literature, from the Earliest Times to the Death of St. Augustine*, 3rd ed. (1966); and with the more elegant study by Gordon Williams, *Change and Decline: Roman Literature in the Early Empire* (1978). On the church, W.H.C. Frend, *The Rise of Christianity* (1984), is readable and comprehensive up through the 6th century.

THE LATER ROMAN EMPIRE

André Piganiol, *L'Empire chrétien (325-395)*, 2nd ed. updated by André Chastagnol (1972), offers an exceptionally rich and informative narrative among modern works. Diana Bowder, *The Age of Constantine and Julian* (1978), is good on those two reigns. A.H.M. Jones, *The Later Roman Empire, 284-602: A Social Economic and*

Administrative Survey, 2 vol. (1964, reprinted 1986), is extraordinarily clear and detailed on these topics. On a major development, monasticism, Derwas J. Chitty, *The Desert a City: An Introduction to the Study of Egyptian and Palestinian Monasticism Under the Christian Empire* (1966, reissued 1977), is highly readable. Ramsay MacMullen, *Corruption and the Decline of Rome* (1988), includes an up-to-date survey of evidence for decline, and also argues a thesis. Herwig Wolfram, *History of the Goths* (1988; originally published in German, 2nd ed., 1980), is a superb study of a crucial player in the 4th to 6th centuries. Walter Goffart, *Barbarians and Romans, A.D. 418–584: The Techniques of Accommodation* (1980), carries the account further.

INDEX

A

Achaean League, 50, 51, 52–53
aedile, 59, 60
Aelian and Fufian law, 61
Aemilia, Via, 75
Aeneas, 20, 62
Aequi, 33, 34
Africa, 17, 40, 41, 42, 45, 46, 47–48, 56, 57, 63, 72, 82, 83, 84, 85, 90, 97, 111, 112, 115, 136, 140, 142, 143, 144, 147, 150, 155, 160, 163, 164, 172, 174, 176, 177, 179, 181, 182, 184, 189, 195
Agrippa, Marcus Vipsanius, 105, 110, 116, 121
Albinus, Clodius, 153, 154
Alexander the Great, 140, 144, 157
amicitia, 76
Antiochus III, 49, 50
Antonine emperors, 127–132, 133, 134, 135, 147, 148, 150, 151, 155, 164, 169, 184
Antoninus Pius, 130–131, 133, 136, 156
Antony, Mark, 97, 99, 100, 104, 116
Apamea, Treaty of, 50
Appia, Via, 36, 74, 128
Armenia, 93, 116, 123, 127, 129, 157, 167, 174, 184, 187, 193
Asia, 17, 50, 53, 57, 81, 85–86, 87, 88, 91, 93, 98, 111, 116, 123, 127
Attila, 195
auctoritas, 86, 92, 107
Augustan military, 113–115
Augustine, Saint, 193, 195, 197
Augustus (Octavian), 20, 99–100, 103, 104–107, 108, 109, 110, 111, 112, 113, 115, 116, 117, 118, 120–121, 122, 125, 130, 132, 133, 134, 135, 136, 144, 145, 147, 148, 149, 150, 155, 162, 184
Aurelian, 170–171, 172
auxiliaries, 113, 114, 126, 129, 130, 149, 155

B

Bacchic worship, 66
Balbinus, 164
barbarian invasions, 166–167, 169, 185–186, 193–197
Britain, 116, 122, 123, 126, 129, 131, 147, 149, 153, 154, 167, 169, 172, 177, 184, 187, 190, 195
Brutus, Marcus Junius, 98, 99, 100, 145

C

Caesar, Julius, 27, 52, 83, 84, 93, 94–98, 99, 101, 102, 104, 106, 112, 113, 120, 121, 144, 162
Caesar, Lucius, 87
calendar, history of, 18, 32, 98
Caligula (Gaius Caesar), 122
Campania, 35–36, 43, 44, 45, 67, 69, 76, 88, 89
Capua, 35, 44, 45, 46, 74
Caracalla, 143, 156, 157, 158, 180
Carneades, 63
Carthage, 33, 35, 37, 38, 39–41, 42, 43, 44, 45–48, 53, 55–56, 77, 78, 81, 195
Cassian law, 61
Cassius, Avidius, 131, 132
Cassius Longinus, Gaius, 98, 99, 100
Catiline, 94
Cato the Censor, 52, 54, 63, 64, 65, 69, 70, 102
Catullus, 103
Catulus, Quintus, 83, 90
censor, 27, 31, 58, 64, 71, 86, 89, 92, 101, 107, 122, 125, 126, 133
centuriate assembly, 26, 27–28, 31, 32, 34, 49, 59, 105, 133
Christianity, 122–123, 137, 140, 144, 149, 161–163, 164, 165, 166, 167, 176–177, 178, 179, 183–184, 186, 187, 188, 190, 191–193, 196
Cicero, Marcus Tullius, 77, 92, 93, 94, 96, 98, 99, 100–101, 102, 139, 144

Cimbri people, 83, 86
Cinna, Lucius, 88, 89, 90
Civil War, 84, 97–98
Claudian law of 218, 69
Claudius I, 109, 116, 122, 125, 134, 148
Claudius II, 164, 166, 170
Cleopatra, 97, 100, 104
clientela, 93
Clodia, Via, 74
Clodius, Publius, 96, 97
Clovis, 196
Commodus, 132, 134, 137, 148, 153, 163
Constantine, 177–181, 182, 183, 189, 192, 193
Constantinople, 175, 179, 180, 183, 185, 186, 190, 193, 194
Constantius, 172, 173, 174, 177, 181–183, 193
constitutions principum, 134
consulship, 26, 30, 31, 34, 59, 60, 82, 83, 85, 88, 89, 92, 94, 95, 96, 97, 105, 106, 107, 108, 111, 126, 134
Corinth, 53, 77
Council of Nicaea, 179
Crassus, Marcus, 91–92, 93, 94, 95, 96, 98, 116
Critolaus, 63
Crocus the Alaman, 180
cursus honorum, 59, 60

D

damnatio memoriae, 124, 132
Danube region, 17, 116, 124, 125, 126–127, 128, 129, 131, 132, 143, 148, 153, 155, 157, 160, 165, 166, 169, 170, 172, 174, 177, 180, 182, 185, 186, 189
De Agricultura, 64, 69, 102
Decebalus, 126
Decius, 165
Demetrius, 50–51
dictator, history of office of, 26–27
Didian law, 64
Diocletian, 149, 172–177, 179, 184, 188
Diogenes, 63

divorce, 74
dominate, establishment of the, 171
Domitian, 125–127, 128, 130, 133, 137, 163, 164
Drusus, Marcus Livius, 87, 88, 89
Duilius, Gaius, 40

E

early republic of Rome, 24–38
early Roman empire, 104–152
edictum perpetuum, 130, 133
Egypt, 52, 97, 100, 104, 105, 109, 111, 115, 124, 129, 131, 143, 144, 148, 153, 156, 162, 168, 169, 170, 174, 175, 177, 189, 191, 192
Elagabulus, 158, 159, 172
emperor worship, 98, 112, 113, 120, 125, 129, 130, 131, 133, 137, 144–146, 159, 171, 172, 188
Ennius, Quintus, 62–63
equestrian order (equites), 81, 82, 83, 85, 87, 89, 93, 108, 109, 110, 111, 114, 115, 118, 122, 126, 130, 135, 139, 154, 155, 156, 157, 158, 166, 170, 173, 180
Esquiline Hill, 23
Etruria, 34–35, 37, 43, 45, 67, 74, 76, 87, 160
Etruscan people, 18, 23, 24, 33, 34, 36

F

Fabius Maximus, Quintus, 43, 44
Fabius Pictor, Quintus, 19, 20, 62
Fannian law, 64
farming, 67, 68–70
fasces, 18, 57
fetial, 34
Fidenae, 34, 35
Flaccus, Marcus Fulvius, 81, 82
Flaminia, Via, 74
Flamininus, Titus Quinctius, 49, 50, 59, 62
Flavian emperors, 124–127, 132, 133, 134, 135, 148, 150, 162
free marriage, 73–74

G

Gabinian law, 61
Galba, 124
Galerius, 170, 172, 173, 174, 176, 177
Gallienus, 165–166, 167, 170, 173
Gallus, Aelius, 115
Gaul, 18, 42, 45, 72, 75, 85, 90, 93, 95, 96, 97,
    100, 105, 116, 136, 143, 147, 148, 149, 151,
    154, 160, 163, 167, 168, 169, 171, 172, 174,
    176, 177, 178, 180, 182, 184, 185, 186, 187,
    189, 190, 192, 194, 195, 196
Gaul, people of, 34, 35, 37, 43, 45, 53, 116, 165,
    167, 177, 194
Geta, Publius Septimius, 156, 157
Glabrio, Manius Acilius, 49
Glaucia, Gaius, 85
Gordian III, 164–165
Goths, 131, 165, 166–167, 172, 180, 182, 185, 186,
    187, 189, 193, 194, 195, 196
Gracchi reform movement, 78–85, 86, 89
Gracchus, Gaius, 81–83, 86, 89
Gracchus, Tiberius Sempronius, 54, 63, 79–81
grammar, 101–102
grammatici, 101
Gratian, 186, 187, 193
Greece, 17, 18, 20, 23, 37–38, 44, 45, 49, 50, 51,
    53, 56, 74, 88, 100, 118, 130, 144, 149, 152,
    161, 162, 166
  culture of, 61–63, 65, 101, 102, 118, 140, 144,
    147, 150, 152, 160, 163, 166, 191
grid plan, 141–142

H

Hadrian (Publius Aelius Hadrianus), 112,
    129–130, 131, 133, 134, 136, 148, 149, 150,
    151, 163, 167
Hadrian's Wall, 129, 154–155
Hamilcar Barca, 42
Hannibal, 42–43, 44, 45, 46, 47, 48, 53, 56, 67, 68
Hasdrubal, 42, 43, 45, 46, 47

Herculaneum, 125
Hieron II, 39, 40, 46
Hieronymus, 46
Honorius, Flavius, 193, 194
Horace, 103, 118
Horatius Cocles, 24
Hortensian law, 32–33, 61
Hortensius, Lucius, 51
hospitium, 76

I

Italy, 17, 18, 19, 20, 28, 32, 35, 36, 39, 42, 43, 44,
    45, 46, 47, 48, 52, 53, 54, 62, 63, 64, 66, 67,
    68, 70, 71, 74–76, 81, 86–87, 88, 90, 91, 94,
    97, 99, 100, 106, 109, 110, 111, 117, 124, 130,
    131, 132, 136–137, 138, 139, 140, 147, 149,
    156, 172, 173, 176, 177, 180, 189, 192, 196

J

Jerome, Saint, 193, 195
Jews, 66, 116, 122, 124, 125, 129, 159, 161, 162,
    163, 167, 174, 192
Judaea, 111, 116, 122, 123, 124, 125, 127, 129, 151
jugatio-capitatio system, 174
Jugurtha, war with, 82, 83
Julian, 182, 183–184
Julio-Claudian emperors, 104–124, 126, 132,
    133, 134
Juvenal, 150, 163

L

late empire of Rome, 153–197
late republic of Rome, 25, 26, 27, 33, 74, 77–103
latifundia, 69, 70
Latinization, 142–143, 150
Latin League, 33, 36
Latin War, 36
Latium, 18, 24, 33, 35, 36, 62, 67
legionaries, 113, 114, 126, 127, 129, 130, 149
Lepidus, Marcus, 89–90, 100, 107

Lex de Imperio Vespasiani, 124, 133
lex provinciae, 57, 58
lex Villia annalis, 59
lex Voconia, 64
Licinio-Sextian Rogations, 31
Licinius, 177, 178, 180
Livius Andronicus, Lucius, 62
Livy, 19–20, 21, 25, 31, 32, 33, 66, 118
Lucius Verus, 130
Lucretia, 24, 30
Lucullus, Lucius, 91, 93

M

Macedonia, 45, 49, 50–51, 52, 77, 78, 85
Macedonian Wars, 45, 49, 50–51, 56, 85
Macrinus, Marcus Opellius, 157–158
manipular battle formation, 36
Marcellus, Marcus Claudius, 44, 46
Marcus Aurelius, 130, 131, 132, 136, 137, 144, 148, 151, 155, 163, 164, 166, 170
Marius, Gaius, 76, 82, 83–85, 86, 87, 92, 94, 132, 134
Masinissa, 46, 47, 55
Maximian, 172, 173, 174, 177, 186
Maximinus, 158, 164, 170
Maximus, 187
Metelli family, 82, 83, 92
Metellus, Quintus, 82, 83, 85, 89, 91
middle republic of Rome, 25, 26, 39–76
military tribunes, 30–31, 35
Mithridates VI, 85–86, 87, 88, 91, 93, 101
mos majorum, 80, 92

N

Naevius, Gnaeus, 62
Nero, Gaius Claudius, 45, 116, 122–124, 132, 134, 135, 148, 162
Nerva, Marcus Cocceius, 127, 128
Nicomedes IV, 91
Niger, Pescennius, 153, 154

Numantia, 55
Numidia, 82, 86, 115, 147, 149

O

obnuntiatio, 61
Octavia, 100
Octavius, Marcus, 79, 88
Odenathus, 168
Odyssey, the, 62
Ogulnian law, 32
Oppian law, 64
Orchian law, 64
Otho, Salvius, 124
Ovid, 118, 150

P

Palatine Hill, 20, 23
Parthia, 86, 93, 96, 98, 100, 116, 123, 127, 129, 131, 154, 155, 158, 162, 167
patria potestas, 73
patricians, 24–25, 26, 27, 31, 122
Pax Romana, 146, 148, 160, 169
Perseus, 51
Pertinax, Helvius, 153
Petronius, Gaius, 115
Philip the Arabian, 165
Philip V, king of Macedon, 45–46, 48, 49, 50, 51, 58, 59
Philopoemen, 50
philosophy, 63–64, 101, 102–103, 144, 151, 160, 162, 163–164, 166, 183, 191, 196
plague, 169
Plautus, Titus Maccius, 62–63
plebeians, 24–25, 26, 27, 28–29, 31, 32, 60–61, 135
plebeian tribunes, 28–30, 31, 60, 61, 79, 80, 82, 83, 84, 106, 108
Pliny the Younger, 128, 139, 151, 163
poetry, 102
Polybius, 33, 41, 48, 50, 51, 52, 55, 56, 57, 58, 65, 74

Pompeii, 125, 136, 140

Pompey (Gnaeus Pompeius), 84, 90–92, 93–94, 95, 96, 97, 98, 101, 120

pontifex maximus, 86, 94, 95, 107, 179

Porticus Aemilia, 71–72

Postumia, Via, 75

Postumus, Marcus Cassianius, 165, 167

praesides, 173

praetor, 27, 31, 34, 51, 52, 54, 57, 59, 60, 66, 76, 78, 83, 85, 89, 90, 94, 95, 108, 111, 122, 124, 125, 130, 133, 134, 153, 173, 180

praetorian cohorts, 113, 155, 158

principate, establishment of the, 105–107, 132–133

principes, 87, 89, 94

Probus, 171–172

prorogation, 78

provinicial administration, 57–58, 78, 89, 93, 106, 110, 111–113, 128, 137–140, 173, 175, 184

publicani, 58, 81, 86, 135

Punic Wars, 57, 68

    First, 39–41, 74

    Second, 19, 26, 39, 42–48, 49, 53, 55, 59, 62, 63, 64, 67, 68, 70, 74, 75, 143

    Third, 55

Pupienus, 164

Pydna, Battle of, 51

Pyrrhic War, 19, 20, 32, 37–38

Pyrrhus, 38

Pythagoras, 63

Q

quaestio repetundarum, 78, 82

quaestor, 28, 31, 57, 59, 60, 79, 83, 108, 111, 122, 134, 180

Quirinal Hill, 23

R

regal period of Rome, 21–23

Regulus, Marcus Atilius, 41

Res Rustica, 102

rhetoric, 101, 102, 144, 162, 163, 164

Rhodes, 50, 52, 163

Roman annalistic tradition, 19–21, 24, 28, 29–30, 31, 32, 33, 62

Roman Forum, 30, 32, 71, 144, 151

Roman state, the,

    citizenry in, organization of, 58–59, 139–152, 188–189

    colonial conquests by, 17, 34–41, 42–57, 75, 85–86, 87–89, 115–117, 122, 129, 174

    culture of, 61–65, 100–103, 118–120, 149–152, 163–164, 191

    early history of, 18–23

    economy of, 66–72, 78, 110, 117, 146–148, 168–169, 171–172, 174–175, 190

    family life in, 73–74

    housing in, 73, 135

    law of, 31–32, 34, 102, 111, 120, 133–134, 138, 174–175

    politics of, 58–61, 78, 92–93, 94–97, 110, 120, 134–135, 168–169, 188

    religion of, 65–66, 111, 112, 137, 144–146, 158, 159–163, 171, 172, 176–177, 178–179, 181–184, 186, 191–193

Romulus and Remus, 20

Rutilius Rufus, Publius, 83, 84, 86

S

Sack of Rome, 35, 36

Sagunto, 42

salutation, 72

Samnite people, 34, 35, 36, 37, 38

Samnite Wars, 32, 35–37

Saturninus, Lucius, 84, 85, 86, 126

Scaevola, Publius Mucius, 24

Scaevola, Quintus Mucius, 86, 102

Scipio, Gnaeus Cornelius, 46

Scipio, Lucius Cornelius, 49–50, 59

Scipio, Publius Cornelius, 46–47

Scipio Aemilianus, Publius Cornelius, 55–56, 60, 61, 63, 79, 81, 83
Scipio Africanus, 50, 60, 62, 67, 79, 82
Second Parthica, 155
Secular Games, 118
Senate, 17, 23, 24, 25, 27, 28–29, 30, 31, 34, 38, 44, 50, 51, 52, 53, 55, 58, 59, 61, 62, 65, 66, 72, 78, 79, 81–82, 83, 84, 86, 87, 89, 91, 92, 93, 94, 96, 97, 98, 99, 101, 102, 103, 105, 106, 107, 108, 109, 110, 111, 112, 114, 120, 122, 124, 125, 127, 128, 129, 130, 131, 132, 133, 134–135, 138, 139, 144, 153, 156, 157, 158, 164, 169, 171, 180, 185
Sertorius, Quintus, 90–91
Severi dynasty, 153–159
Severus Alexander, 158, 159, 160, 164
Severus, Septimius, 136, 153, 153–157, 158, 163, 174
Sextus, Pompeius, 100
slavery, 68, 69, 70, 74, 76, 79, 91–92, 101, 109, 111, 139–140
Social War, the, 84, 87, 88, 90
Spain, 42, 45, 46, 47, 53, 54, 55, 57, 77, 88, 90, 94, 95, 96, 98, 99, 100, 105, 116, 136, 137, 144, 147, 150, 167, 189, 190, 194, 195
Sparta, 50, 53
Spartacus, 91
Stilicho, Flavius, 193–194
Sulla, Lucius, 27, 77, 83, 85, 86, 88–89, 90, 91, 92, 94, 98, 120
Sulpicius, Publius, 88
Syphax, king of Numidia, 47, 55
Syracuse, 39–40, 46
Syria, 105, 116, 127, 131, 142, 143, 147, 148, 153, 155, 162

T

Tacitus, 126, 128, 149, 150, 163, 171
tetrarchy, origin of the, 172
Theodoric, 196

Theodosius I, 186, 187, 190, 191, 193
Tiberius, 116, 121–122, 161
Tiber River, 17, 18, 24, 33, 71, 107, 159, 175
Titus, 125, 134
Traiana, Via, 128
Trajan (Marcus Ulpius Trajanus), 127–129, 133, 137, 148, 149, 163, 164, 184
tribal assembly, 28, 29, 31, 32
tribunicia potestas, 106, 107
Triumvirs, 100, 120
Troy, 20
Twelve Tables, 30, 32, 32

U

Umbria, 37, 74, 87
urban centres in the empire, overview of, 140–142

V

Vaballathus, 168
Valens, 184–185, 186
Valentinian, 184–185, 186, 187
Valerian, 165
Varro, Marcus Terrentius, 101, 102
Veii, 31, 34–35
Verres, Gaius, 92, 93
Verus, Lucius, 130, 131, 132
Vespasian, 124–125, 126, 127, 130, 134, 155, 163
Virgil, 103, 118, 150, 191
Vitellius, 124
Volscians, 33, 34

Y

year of the four emperors, 124

Z

Zama, Battle of, 47, 55
Zenobia, 168